➤ FACING THE MU

D0547517

Facing the Music

Shaping Music Education from a Global Perspective

Huib Schippers

OXFORD
UNIVERSITY PRESS

2010

OXFORD
UNIVERSITY PRESS

Oxford University Press, Inc., publishes works that further
Oxford University's objective of excellence
in research, scholarship, and education.

Oxford   New York
Auckland   Cape Town   Dar es Salaam   Hong Kong   Karachi
Kuala Lumpur   Madrid   Melbourne   Mexico City   Nairobi
New Delhi   Shanghai   Taipei   Toronto

With offices in
Argentina   Austria   Brazil   Chile   Czech Republic   France   Greece
Guatemala   Hungary   Italy   Japan   Poland   Portugal   Singapore
South Korea   Switzerland   Thailand   Turkey   Ukraine   Vietnam

Copyright © 2010 by Oxford University Press, Inc.

Published by Oxford University Press, Inc.
198 Madison Avenue, New York, New York 10016

www.oup.com

Oxford is a registered trademark of Oxford University Press.

All rights reserved. No part of this publication may be reproduced,
stored in a retrieval system, or transmitted, in any form or by any means,
electronic, mechanical, photocopying, recording, or otherwise,
without the prior permission of Oxford University Press.

Library of Congress Cataloging-in-Publication Data
Schippers, Huib, 1959–
Facing the music : shaping music education from a global perspective / Huib Schippers.
p. cm.
Includes bibliographical references and index.
ISBN 978-0-19-537975-4; 978-0-19-537976-1 (pbk.)
1. Music—Instruction and study.   2. Multicultural education.   I. Title.
MT1.S34 2009
780.71—dc22   2009011943

Recorded audio tracks (marked in the text with ◯) are available online at
www.oup.com/us/facingthemusic
Access with username Music5 and password Book1745

Printed in the United States of America
on acid-free paper

Facing the Music investigates practices and ideas that have grown from the rise of "world music," developments in ethnomusicology, and a growing awareness of the need for cultural diversity in music education over the past five decades. Drawing on more than thirty years of hands-on experience at various levels of music education, Huib Schippers provides a rich resource for professionals interested in learning and teaching music in culturally diverse environments, from those working in classrooms and studios to those involved in leadership and policy. Each of the seven chapters approaches the topic from a different angle, as Schippers unfolds the complexities and potential of learning and teaching music "out of context" in an eminently readable and accessible manner and develops a coherent model for approaching musical diversity with sense and sensitivity, providing lucid suggestions for translating the resulting ideas into practice.

✦ FOREWORD ✦

PATRICIA SHEHAN CAMPBELL

Facing the Music is groundbreaking work on cultural diversity in music education. This book comes from the pen of an author who thinks thoroughly through some of the most challenging questions confronting music education today. It is cutting-edge in its study of the ways and means of diversifying music in schools, in higher education, and in community contexts. It fills a long-standing need to know not just the music of the world's cultures but also the ways it is acquired, transmitted, preserved, and developed; processes that help us understand musical meaning at its most deeply human level.

It is well worth noting, as readers delve into this volume, that the author writes from the grounded position of one with a long history in performing, learning, and teaching music. Besides being a scholar, Huib Schippers is a sitarist, teacher, and facilitator of musicians and teachers. As a visionary and grass-roots activist for programmatic change in the music that is taught and learned in conservatories and schools, Schippers is uniquely situated to explore the confluence of ideas surrounding music, education, and culture. And so he does here, as he has done for more than three decades, breathing life and energy into the hard questions of multicultural and intercultural matters of music education, of world music pedagogy, and of the realities of cultural diversity in music education.

Facing the Music encapsulates the decades-long journey of an unusual musician and teacher who thinks globally even as he acts locally for profound systemic change in music education. Through our many meetings across the world—in Amsterdam, Dartington, Durban, Helsinki, Limerick, London, Pretoria, Rotterdam, Sydney, Seattle, and the old Moorish walled town of Serpa, Portugal—the subject of our discussion is invariably refining views of "teaching world music" in all of its Technicolor detail, without fear or prejudice. Schippers imagines—and realizes—projects in world music pedagogy and is consistently engaged in transforming and advancing insights into learning and teaching practice. His efforts stretch far beyond the tokenistic nod and superficial songs of entry-level practice in "teaching music of many lands" and instead features projects with the power to revolutionize music education at every level: classroom projects and world music schools in the Netherlands, an international center for world music and dance, and projects working with communities across the globe to forge their own musical futures.

This volume encapsulates ideas at the seams of music education and ethnomusicology and makes sense of pedagogy and curriculum development so necessary for twenty-first century teachers and their students. Music transmission, teaching, and learning are introduced, explored, and analyzed with careful attention to the often problematized realms of tradition, authenticity, and context. The perspectives on music and education unfold and reveal themselves page by page, and as they are rooted in practice, these views can inform curricular and instructional practice across many levels and settings. Educators, ethnomusicologists, and students of music and education at large will be well served by the accessible and articulate presentation of complex ideas that are illustrated with a broad sampling of artist-teacher cases from across the musical world.

→→ A C K N O W L E D G M E N T S ←←

This book is dedicated to the many musicians and educators with whom I have had the privilege to meet and work all over the world during the past thirty-odd years, as performers, teachers, colleagues, consultants, and sources of inspiration. I worked with many of them closely for years or even decades. Others I visited while they were living and working in circumstances that would have driven many away from a life in music: in run-down houses in India, villages in Vietnam, townships in South Africa. I have been humbled and inspired by the work of these colleagues; in spite of adverse circumstances, they just continue to practice, play, and share their music, with unabated passion for the quality and value of their work.

The musicians I feel most indebted to are my two Indian music gurus: Ustad Jamaluddin Bhartiya and the late Ustad Ali Akbar Khan, who, during more than twenty years, have nurtured my understanding of the beauty and intricacies of North Indian classical music. I particularly remember the many early mornings I spent at the house of Jamaluddin Bhartiya, listening to and taking part in his practice after first prayers and hearing stories of great musicians while having tea afterward. The memory of the hours I spent listening and learning at the feet of Ali Akbar Khan in his school in California still fills me with humility and awe, as do thoughts of the many hours I spent in his music room gathering information for articles and his authorized biography, which is still awaiting completion.

Other musicians also greatly contributed to my understanding of world music and education. Foremost among these are my close colleagues at the Amsterdam

World Music School and at the Rotterdam Conservatory. Then there are those I have met across the world during my extensive travels for fieldwork, collaborations, and conferences. Many have become friends, and I cherish our discussions at conferences, between lessons, after concerts, in bars, planes, and homes, which have greatly broadened and sharpened my thinking on the matters discussed here.

While it is rarely acknowledged as an academic method, I have probably learned more than I could ever get from books or formal presentations through informal discussions: over beers with David Elliott in Pretoria, driving across the Spanish countryside with John Drummond, having tea at the Bombay Cricket Club with Joep Bor, seeing Keith Swanwick over lunch in London, sipping hot chocolate in the Seattle snow with Patricia Campbell, climbing Table Mountain in Cape Town with Einar Solbu, or submersing myself in hot debate about community music with David Price in the Liverpool hotel dining room that was the model for the one that went down with the *Titanic*. It is a little ironic (and a little worrying for music education) that David subsequently played a central role in a large and ambitious project called "Musical Futures." On the more formal side of things, I am greatly indebted to my Ph.D. supervisors, Rokus de Groot and Patricia Campbell, who forced me to turn rhetoric into solid argument and dealt gracefully with my occasional reluctance during that process.

The central ideas for this publication can be traced back to a number of presentations and articles published during a twelve-year period. A sketch of chapter 1 appeared in *International Journal of Community Music* as "Musical Chairs, or the Twelve-Step Disintegration of Preconceptions about Music Making and Learning." Some of the concepts presented in chapter 2 were first explored in "Towards a Model for Cultural Diversity in Music Education" in the *International Journal for Music Education*. Most ideas from chapter 3 were published as "Tradition, Authenticity, and Context" in the *British Journal of Music Education*. Chapter 4 builds on ideas published in *Harde Noten,* and chapter 5 expands on ideas first presented at the International Society for Music Education as "Blame It on the Germans!." I outlined the basic idea of the framework elaborated in chapter 6 in "Taking Distance and Getting Up Close" in *Cultural Diversity in Music Education*. Finally, the basis for the Indian music case study in chapter 7 was laid in a conference presentation, "Goodbye to GSP?" and in the *Asian Music* article "The Guru Recontextualized?" I would like to thank the editors of these publications for providing platforms for developing and sharing these ideas.

My gratitude also goes to Suzanne Ryan and her colleagues at Oxford University Press; to Cathy Grant, Kirsty Guster, and Jocelyn Wolfe at Queensland Conservatorium Research Centre; and to Pam Burnard (Cambridge), Heidi Westerlund (Sibelius), Christine Dettman (Rostock), and the many other colleagues who have volunteered to discuss or read drafts of the various chapters (fully listed below).

A number of organizations have enabled me to complete the research for this publication by making available time, travel, or funds. These include my employers from 1993 to 2008: Amsterdam Music School, VKV Association for Arts Education, LOKV Netherlands Institute for Arts Education, Rotterdam Academy for Music and Dance (now CODArts), and Queensland Conservatorium, Griffith University. The Netherlands Ministry of Education, Culture and Science, HGIS Fonds, Prins Bernhard Fonds, VSB Fonds, the Australian Research Council, and the European Commission have all directly or indirectly provided funds toward the research that has led to completion of this work.

And thank you for your understanding and patience, Kelly and Jiao Yen; the partners and children of authors are undeservedly widowed and orphaned for hundreds of hours and deserve to share in any credit emanating from books built on their tolerance and support. I remember with particular fondness how as a four-year-old—well before she could write—Jiao Yen sat on the floor next to my desk making margin notes on discarded pages while her father endlessly worked on his boring book. Finally, I have to acknowledge the voice of my father, whose unlikely combination of skepticism, irony, and a subtle but profound love of humanity and music has breathed life into these pages and, indeed, into much of my life.

Gratitude

This publication would have been impossible without literally thousands of hours of sharing ideas with colleagues and friends over the past 15 years. These are the hundred that stand out most in my memory as I finish the book: Kofi Agawu, Peter van Amstel, Patricia Ardiles, Levent Aslan, Julie Ballantyne, Brydie-Leigh Bartleet, William Barton, Fouad Bennis, Jamaluddin Bhartiya, Joep Bor, Eltje Bos, Paul van den Bosch, Michelle Boss Barba, Pam Burnard, Melissa Cain, Patricia Shehan Campbell, Hariprasad Chaurasia, Christine Dettman, Paul Draper, John Drummond, Peter Dunbar-Hall, David Elliott, Stephen Emmerson, Shanta Gokhale, Rokus de Groot, Andreas Gutzwiller, Catherine Grant, Bart Gruson, Kirsty Guster, Jan Laurens Hartong, Renée Heijnen, Marion van der Hoeven, Gregg Howard, Keith Howard, Zakir Hussein, Roshan Jamal, Bhimsen Joshi, Ali Akbar Khan, Lateef Ahmed Khan, Mira Kho, Ninja Kors, Darshan Kumari, Helen Lancaster, Don Lebler, Marlene Leroux, Richard Letts, Toss Levy, Stan Lokhin, Håkan Lundström, Deborah Maclean, Alagi Mbye, Wim van der Meer, Ricardo Mendeville, Karen Moynehan, Henry Nagelberg, Caroline van Niekerk, J. H. Kwabena Nketia, Selete Nyomi, Meki Nzewi, Ponda O'Bryan, George Odam, Patricia Opondo, Peter den Ouden, Arvind Parikh, Sarah Patrick, Bergen Peck, Pham Thi Hue, Paco Peña, Svanibor Pettan, Oscar van der Pluijm, David Price, Suvarnalata Rao, Peter Renshaw, Otto Romijn, George Ruckert, Frans de Ruiter,

Eva Saether, Ramon Santos, Laurien Saraber, Ibou Secka, Anthony Seeger, Walter Slosse, Einar Solbu, Keith Swanwick, To Ngoc Tan, Tran Quan Hai, Tran Van Khe, Ceylan Utlu, Kari Veblen, Terese Volk, Dirk de Vreede, Annette de Vries, Jennifer Walden, Heidi Westerlund, Donna Weston, George Whitmore, Trevor Wiggins, Erk Willems, Wang Yu-Yan, and Ken Zuckerman.
Thank you to all.

A NOTE ON TRANSCRIPTION AND TERMINOLOGY

Throughout this publication, I have tried to avoid using jargon, describing key concepts in ways that can be understood across (sub)disciplines. For specific terminology regarding various forms of world music, I have followed the transcriptions from the glossary of *The Garland Encyclopedia of World Music* (edited by Stone, 2002) as a first choice, with *Grove Music Online* (edited by Macy, 2009) and *The New Grove Dictionary of Musical Instruments* (edited by Sadie, 1985) as second and third references. For terms that occur in none of these, I have followed the most common spelling in the literature on the subject. As many world music terms are becoming increasingly common in English usage, I have omitted some diacritics and resisted italicizing names of many instruments and genres. The most relevant terms occurring in the text can be found in this book's glossary.

To refer to the European-style tradition of composed art music from the beginning of the eighteenth to the early decades of the twentieth century, I use "Western classical music." When I wish to include other perspectives, or music from before or after that period, I refer to those specifically.

As the central organ in what has often been called "oral" transmission is the ear (and not the mouth), I consistently refer to "aural transmission" for all communication received by ear (whether produced orally, by instruments, or through recordings), contrasting it with notation-based transmission.

Finally, I refer to "transmission" in the sense described by *Grove Music Online* as "the means by which musical compositions, performing practices and knowledge are passed from musician to musician," distinguishing "at least four dimensions: the technical, the social, the cognitive and the institutional" (Rice, 2008b). For the purposes of this book, this definition is eminently useful in its emphatic inclusion of the organizational/institutional context.

The proceeds of *Facing the Music* will be donated to the project "Musical Futures," which aims to empower communities across the world to forge musical futures on their own terms. For more information about this project, please visit http://www.griffith.edu.au/centre/qcrc.

CONTENTS

Facing the Music

"We have inherited from the past a way of thinking about music that cannot do justice to the diversity of practices and experiences which that small word, 'music,' signifies in today's world," says Nicholas Cook in *Music: A Very Short Introduction,* one of the most insightful and delightful books on music in recent years.[1] This shift of perspective has major implications for the way musical skills and knowledge are perpetuated and for the formal organization of music learning and teaching, much of which was designed for the musical realities of the nineteenth century. Many of the key factors we take for granted in our contemporary musical experience did not emerge until the twentieth century.

It is easy to forget that regular public radio broadcasts only started in 1906. During that era, none but a privileged few listened to the early 78-rpm records, which were capable of rendering a maximum of four to five minutes of music. The advent of the "modern" 33-rpm LP was still forty-five years away, and download-able music files were well beyond anyone's imagination. A seventy-year-old at that time had probably heard less music than a seven-year-old of today. Most countries were inhabited predominantly by people who traced their lineage back to largely shared cultures and places. Steamboats already crossed the oceans, but the first commercial passenger flights did not take off until the late 1920s. Migration between continents was slow and limited, undertaken by thousands, not hundreds of thousands.

What happened since then, and particularly in the past fifty years (say, from Elvis to the present), is likely to go into history as the period of most intense transformation in the global musical landscape to date, brought on by developments in travel and technology, in combination with major social and political changes. These have in turn affected the roles music plays in the everyday lives of individuals and communities across the world—which Christopher Small so aptly describes as "musicking": "to take part, in any capacity, in a musical performance, whether by performing, by listening, by rehearsing or practicing, by providing material for performance (what is called composing), or by dancing."[2]

New realities and insights have affected the way music is experienced in both participation and consumption (live or through technology), concepts of high and low art, globalization and diversity, links to identity, the place of creativity, and, of course, how music learning and teaching music are given shape. Musical diversity does not only contain lessons about "new arrivals" in the musical arena, such as world music, but, when looked at closely, it also inspires reflection on approaches to musical practices that many of us have come to see as a primary frame of reference for thinking on music and music education: Western art, jazz, and popular music.

In most music research, processes of learning and teaching music are surprisingly underestimated, while in fact they do not only help sustain musical repertoire and techniques but also deeply influence values and attitudes toward music and therefore the reception and development of music itself. To a large extent, what we hear, learn, and teach is the product of what we believe about music. This holds true for what we usually refer to as *music education* (with a focus on schools), *community music* (music making and learning outside formal structures), and *professional music training* (for those who make, or aim to make, a livelihood from music).[3]

In ethnomusicology, the term most commonly used is *transmission*, emphasizing the passing on of specific bodies of knowledge that underlie many music cultures. The elusive term *enculturation*, used with different shades of meaning by sociologists and anthropologists, is also used by ethnomusicologists and music educators to describe the process of becoming "literate" in a specific cultural idiom.[4] In addition, *acculturation* is used to refer to becoming literate in a culture *other* than one's own. Although my primary focus is on processes of music transmission, I will mostly refer to "music learning and teaching" in order to emphasize the focal importance of the recipient of the instruction and to remind the reader that there is music teaching without learning, as well as a great deal of learning without formal teaching.

From the time that music education started taking a serious interest in musical genres and practices from a variety of backgrounds and cultures some four decades ago, practices reflecting cultural diversity have emerged around the globe. While McCarthy traces multicultural initiatives back to the 1950s,[5] and Volk digs well into the nineteenth century,[6] I take the influential 1967 Tanglewood Declaration[7] as a convenient formal starting point for contemporary approaches to cultural diversity among music educators. This process accelerated considerably in the

1980s, when government and educational policies started recognizing the importance and realities of cultural diversity more widely. Quite interestingly, while the interest in world music at large was predominantly spurred by developments in technology, travel, and commerce, the surge of attention to cultural diversity in music education appears to have been largely driven by demographical change. Nowadays, learning world music (or at least *about* world music) is available to many aspiring musicians and music lovers in some shape or form in school, community settings, or higher education.

With the growth of these practices, one of the key challenges is developing appropriate strategies for learning and teaching. More often than not, music has been "recontextualized" drastically, and choices had to be made between traditional systems of transmission and Western-style formal music education or fusions between the two. In these changing musical environments, encounters (and sometimes confrontations) of music with various cultural backgrounds have motivated music educators and scholars to readdress preconceptions about music making and learning. New practices invite closer examination of a number of concepts and ideas that have featured prominently, but often uncritically, in discussions on music education during the past twenty years.

In teaching methods, assumed dichotomies between atomistic (or analytical) and holistic approaches, between notation-based and oral learning, and between emphasis on tangible and intangible aspects of music invite reexamination in the context of increasing cultural diversity, rapid technological change, and shifts in educational approaches (such as the transition from positivist to more constructivist approaches to learning and teaching). Related to this, the interactions among musical material and ideas, learner, teacher/facilitator, and learning environment have become more fluid.

In the realm of values and attitudes, concepts such as "tradition," "authenticity," and "context" are often still used with firm conviction in discussions on Western classical, popular, jazz, and world music. On closer examination, however, they are often applied with ambiguous or even contradictory meaning. A cross-cultural exploration of these concepts reveals that they are not nearly as clear, stable, and value-free as they may appear. A more dynamic interpretation of these terms can open the road to greater understanding of contemporary realities in music education at all levels, and enable teachers to apply these concepts more successfully to everyday studio, community, and classroom practices.

The importance of understanding cultural diversity in music education has moved well beyond the obvious challenges of teaching forms of world music outside their cultures of origin. Learning and teaching strategies from other cultures (often with demonstrably successful histories stretching back for centuries) question preconceptions about learning and teaching music in Western mainstream traditions and institutions as well. This is not a threat to the status quo but an inspiration continually to evaluate and improve educational practices. The West now has the opportunity to come full circle in its interaction with other music cultures, from knowing only one culture, to exploration, to domination, to exoticism, to tolerance, to acceptance, to inclusion in a new and diverse reality.

In terms of content and approach, the field is coming of age. Many practices of cultural diversity in music education have shed dogmatic approaches from nineteenth-century music education (with pedagogical models derived almost exclusively from Western art and European folk music) and pre-1980s ethnomusicology (with a predominantly static approach to music traditions). In a number of areas, we can witness a receding emphasis on rigid approaches to teaching methods for learners of all backgrounds and levels. Formal, nonformal, and informal "systems" of learning music are beginning to blend and cross-fertilize, by themselves or in interaction with rapidly developing music technologies. Issues such as context and authenticity are increasingly approached as delightfully confusing contemporary realities. The challenges posed by music traveling through time, place, and different contexts are on their way to being addressed for what they are: fascinating studies in the dynamic life of music, culture, and education.

Fifty years from now, somebody will be writing a book (or whatever format is then current for the exchange of ideas) on learning music with an opening much like this: "At the beginning of the twenty-first century, it would have been inconceivable to predict how we learn, live, and use music now." Social, cultural, and technological settings will continue to disappear, and new ones will emerge. The rapid transformations we have seen over the past fifty or hundred years are probably not an exception; they are what we need to prepare and be prepared for as a reality of existence, for ourselves and for those we educate.

A good example is the recent history of the multinational record labels, which have been taken for granted as major players in disseminating music during the past fifty years. Now these giants are crumbling, being overtaken by the unstoppable free exchange of the Internet, in which they now invest feverishly.[8] As a consequence of this new platform with very different economical models, the promotion of selected stars and their recordings may well be replaced by the rise of highly targeted and vibrant niche markets. Young music lovers increasingly construct and pursue their specific musical tastes on their own terms—and on their own terminals.

For all of this baffling change, we can be confident that music will continue to play a significant role in people's lives. That is quite remarkable: the engagement with music is one of the most universal activities of humans across history and cultures that does not have a direct link to our survival as a species (which explains why we breathe, eat, defend ourselves, and reproduce). Nobody ever died from music depravation, yet people work and worship to music, dance and court to music, make love and relax with music, rejoice and grieve with music. Some of this music will be new, generated alone or with peers, and some will be passed down from earlier generations.

One day, it may be possible to learn music by connecting the brains of a person who has particular skills and knowledge (what we now call a teacher) and one who wants them (a student or learner), simply downloading their musical "hard disk." For now, in all of its human limitations and delights, we mostly learn music through listening to live and recorded music and through interaction with peers, teachers, and other facilitators. This book examines that interaction, not from a naive ideal of "harmony among all people" but accepting that encounters may also contain elements of friction and confusion. There are new musical realities; many of these are exciting, and others may be inconvenient or even threatening. *Facing the Music* aims to explore the new insights and pathways arising from these encounters and confrontations in order to nurture a creative, vibrant, diverse musical life on this planet, now and well into the future.

Seven chapters, which can be read in sequence or independently, form the core of this book. In order to do justice to the complexity of the issues, each chapter sheds light on specific aspects of world music in education from a different perspective and/or with a different methodology. Using this seven-pronged approach (heptangulation if you will), the book opens with an *auto-ethnography,* introducing and illustrating key issues addressed in this volume through a number of important personal experiences across the world of music. These are contextualized in a short conceptual *history* of approaches and terminology, referring to the rise of world music and its reception in ethnomusicology and music education. Next, a *deconstruction* of core concepts such as tradition, authenticity, and context aims to establish to what extent these terms are used in the literature and practice, with awareness of the vast diversity in meaning that each entails. This is followed by an *analysis* of modes and methods of learning and teaching in formal, nonformal, and informal contexts and a *critique* of approaches and practices from the past that may have survived in much formal music education.

The study culminates in a *framework* that makes visible a number of the explicit and implicit choices made in music transmission and learning in multicultural societies, with the aim of creating points of reference for evaluating teaching practices, informing curriculum development, and stimulating further research. A final chapter brings the framework to life in an in-depth *case study* encompassing three recontextualized traditions observed in the Netherlands: African percussion in a community music setting, preparations for teaching Balinese gamelan in the classroom, and professional training in Indian classical music. These feature the voices and views of the musicians themselves, firmly testing and linking the theory to the practice. A short epilogue brings some of the book's key concepts back to practical suggestions for action in music education.

Summarizing a significant body of practice and thought that has been only partly documented, this book aims to complement and refine global thinking on music education (or thinking on global music education) by adding dimensions that take into account some of the choices music educators make, often subconsciously, when dealing with culturally diverse surroundings. Written for music students, educators, curriculum developers, administrators, policy makers, musicians, researchers, and ethnomusicologists with an interest in processes of change and transmission, it presents a framework to describe, analyze, and design music learning and teaching in ways that are in line with contemporary musical realities and with much current thinking on student-centered, competency-based, and "authentic" learning. It aims to contribute to creating stimulating learning environments for people of different backgrounds in the diverse cultural landscape that characterizes so many contexts of learning music at the beginning of the twenty-first century.

Facing the Music

Shaping Music Education from a Global Perspective

Huib Schippers

FACING THE MUSIC

CHAPTER I

Journeys in Music

An Auto-Ethnography

The elementary school music teacher I met at the International School of Kuala Lumpur had a slightly unusual background. Jennifer Walden was the daughter of a jazz musician; she played in pop and brass bands during her school days, studied classical guitar, and then moved into music teaching in the International School circuit. This brought her in contact with cumbia in Colombia, ud in Syria, Chinese opera in Taiwan, and sitar, gamelan, and kompang drumming in Malaysia. She included all of these traditions in teaching music to seven-to-twelve-year-olds in the multinational and privileged environment of an affluent private school. A striking example was a lesson I witnessed in 1995, when Jennifer was teaching gordang sembilan, normally played only on nine large standing drums for special occasions among the Mandailing people from north-central Sumatra.[1] Walden did not have nine large standing drums in her classroom. So she divided the children over a Chinese drum, a conga, a djembe, a darbuka, kompang frame drums, cumbia drums, and the tom-tom of the trap drum set. As I sat at the back of the classroom, the ethnomusicologist in me frowned at this perversion of authentic representations of traditional music in cultural context. But as Walden taught the different parts of the drum piece, the music started coming together in rhythm, sound, and, most importantly, in the awareness of the children. They got it. It came to life as what I would not hesitate to call an "authentic" musical experience.

PHOTO I.I.   Jennifer Walden teaches gamelan at the International School of Kuala
Lumpur, Malaysia, March 1995. Photo: Huib Schippers.

This was one of 12 landmark experiences that untaught me everything I thought
I knew about making, teaching, and learning music. Having grown up in
an environment saturated with Western classical music and the systems of music
education associated with that tradition, I came into the world of music with
clear ideas about a canon of great music and a well-structured path to proficiency
in interpreting it. I assumed that gradual progression from simple to complex,
supported by technical exercises, notated music, and regular individual lessons,
was the way people learned music across the world. More than thirty years of
working with highly proficient musicians from various cultures with very different
stories challenged those preconceptions profoundly and took me on a conceptual
journey that stimulated, confused, educated, and inspired new insights into the
nature of learning and teaching music.

The first experience of the twelve, and undoubtedly the most influential,
stretched over a period of more than twenty years. In 1975, I decided to learn to
play Indian classical music on the sitar, the stringed instrument popularized by its
charismatic ambassador, Ravi Shankar. That step caused a major shock to my
system. I found that all of the cleverness I attributed to myself at the age of sixteen
did little to prepare me for learning a complex, vastly different music tradition
in a social and cultural environment that was far removed from my European

middle-class comfort zone. I met my sitar guru, Jamaluddin Bhartiya, in Amsterdam at a time when the initial mists of incense and hashish had lifted enough to see the beauty of the music beyond the illusions of instant salvation that had clouded it for many who had come just before me.

My guru's simple home was a gateway into another culture: no shoes allowed, pictures of saints and ancestors on the wall, the smell of Indian food, and always the sound of Indian classical music. For the first five years, I felt quite lost in an aural, holistic, and mythological universe and was forced to acquire radically new skills to make sense of this confusion and beauty, in addition to the considerable physical discomfort caused by an awkward sitting position and the agony of hard metal strings cutting into my fingers.

Initially, the way my Indian guru interacted with me did not help my sense of musical direction, either. He had learned music from a very young age within the family tradition, through total immersion. Consequently, he taught without explicit attention to (or even awareness of) most of the structures underlying it. As his father had done with him, he just showered me with—often inaccessible—fragments of beautiful music. Somehow, I had to learn and connect these myself. That led to considerable frustration in me and my fellow students, many of whom gave up in despair. Being too stubborn or ignorant to capitulate, I persisted. Slowly, with a lot of practice, listening, reading, learning, and speaking to peers, senior musicians, and scholars, I began to understand (in the true sense of humility the word implies) how rāgas were developed, how tones were sculpted, how rhythmic cycles supported and offset fixed sections and improvisations.

Just when I felt that I was coming to grips with this ancient and complex tradition, a new bout of confusion arrived when I started to take master classes with Ustad Ali Akbar Khan, perhaps the most acclaimed Indian instrumentalist of the twentieth century. That felt a bit like having keyboard improvisation lessons with Johann Sebastian Bach, being exposed to unsurpassed musical imagination and creativity, which Khansaheb (as he is respectfully called) shared liberally with his students but without much explanation.

I can't say I enjoyed this learning process all the time, but in retrospect, I feel that there was great merit in allowing myself to get confused, and that the solutions I found evolved into solid bases for developing my learning skills and musical knowledge. After ten years or so, this was confirmed by the reactions I received from senior musicians as my skills and insights developed to the point where I could perform in India without embarrassment. I still treasure my first *Times of India* reviews of concerts in Ahmedabad and Mumbai, saying that the recital by the "young sitar player from the land of the windmills" was "marked by . . . vital elements of perceptive musicianship" with "many sequences, phrases and patterns subtly conceived and cleverly projected"[2]—although that was not always how I felt.

Even more gratifying was the experience of sitting in my practice room after about twelve years of study and finding that my anxiety about playing truly in tune (important and difficult on the sitar) had turned into a sense of space in approaching and projecting individual tones. Similarly, in playing with rhythmic accompaniment, I noticed that my nervousness about trying to find the key accents in the rhythmic cycle had transformed into enjoyment of exploring the space in a single rhythmic unit. Nobody had taught me these skills or even consciously pointed toward them, and I still would not know how to teach them explicitly; they came with being immersed in the music and the company of senior musicians for ten to twenty hours a week over many years.

This experience led to some important and humbling realizations about learning music from other cultures. An ability to acquire knowledge in a logical step-by-step manner and a visual/analytical environment does not necessarily arm one to engage successfully with forms of world music that are not based on such thought processes. Learning through absorption of the music as a whole can be a slower but ultimately more effective way of learning certain aspects of music. In this process, developing one's own analytical skills and embracing confusion as a major mechanism for learning can be critical success factors. It forcibly brought home that one's perceptions of "how music works" cannot be seamlessly transplanted from one setting to another. In a delightful publication on his experiences and perceptions of world music, my Swiss colleague Laurent Aubert, who walked part of this path with me many years ago, describes this feeling, echoing Socrates and Einstein: "the more I learned, the more I realised the immensity of my ignorance."[3] That is not an easy truth to swallow for an arrogant young Westerner, but a very valuable learning experience.

As I started performing, I came across many Western musicians who had chosen to immerse themselves in the music of another culture. At Laurent Aubert's "Miroirs d'Orient," a festival in Geneva dedicated to such musicians in 1985, I met Andreas Gutzwiller, the first Western "black belt" shakuhachi player. I was fascinated by his description of how one learns to play this flute in Japan. This is how I remember his account: students come into the room, where their teacher sits in front of a low table with the score of the musical piece. The students kneel down on the other side of the table and pick up their instruments. The teacher starts playing the piece, and the students follow as well as they can. After the piece is finished, the process simply repeats.

The teacher does not explain what the students may have done wrong, as that would be considered an insult to their intelligence; they are expected to realize their own shortcomings. In fact, teachers who interfere too much with the progress of their students are likened to farmers who pull at young rice shoots to make them grow more quickly (and, of course, achieve the reverse effect by uprooting them).[4] Consequently, doing exercises or repeating difficult passages does not play a prominent role in the learning process. As I heard these stories, I knew I had to reconsider my preconceptions about the role of the teacher in what I had considered the logical path to master time-honored classical traditions.

More revelations awaited during a visit to the California Institute for the Arts in Los Angeles in 1992. CalArts has a long-standing program of Indian music, gamelan, and African percussion. Its campus-style setup (and long-term support from the Disney Corporation) made it quite conducive to intensive exposure learning, and I was impressed with the dedication and the level of the students. One of the Ghanaian teachers at CalArts, Alfred Ladzekpo, told me an anecdote about the beginning of his classes in Ewe percussion at Wesleyan University, which illustrates the clash of concepts one encounters in teaching across cultures:

> I had just come from Africa, and I was asked to teach a group of students one of our traditional rhythms. So I just started, showing how the different patterns went and how they interrelated. I thought things were going quite well. But then the students started to ask questions. At one point, I had to run out and ask my brother Kobla, who was more experienced: "What do these students mean? They are asking where the *one* is in this rhythm." This is not a concept in our music: we see the rhythm as a whole. In the end, we just decided the *one* was on a particular beat in the bell pattern, and everybody was happy.

Hearing and seeing the advanced class play and dance was an absolute pleasure, with the shifting patterns in Ewe percussion sounding like fugues in rhythm. To this day, the program is quite successful. This strengthened my belief that music from other cultures can be recontextualized and taught quite successfully in Western institutions, if we find settings and modes of communication that truly connect worlds of sound and perception.

This experience was oddly mirrored during a visit to the University of Cape Coast in Ghana a year later. While the head of the music department entertained my colleague Trevor Wiggins and myself, outside his office a student was playing Bach's *Well-Tempered Clavier* on a piano that was seriously out of tune—a unique, ironic musical experience considering the title and background of this particular piece. Our host assured us that besides his serious classes on Wagner and Bach, he also left some room for African music. Some of the cleaners on the campus were Ewe (the same ethnic group as Ladzekpo), and they occasionally were given an afternoon off to work with the students.

I felt sad to witness how the idea of the superiority of Western classical music appeared to have outlived colonial rule by decades in many parts of the world. Later, we found a refreshingly different approach at Agoro, a community arts center in an old movie theater in the center of Cape Coast. Children and youngsters were involved in all kinds of musical activity: a few were practicing traditional drumming outside; in the studio, a highlife band rehearsed; and onstage, three teenagers were choreographing hip-hop to a Ghanaian rap song. The place was alive with music and dance.

That is more than can be said of the next experience that helped shape me as a music educator. While I was on a trip in north Bali in 1994, a village elder in Singaraja told me about a large funeral ceremony in a village in the hills. A long trip along dark and curvy roads on the back of a motorcycle led to the all-night event. As I arrived, the villagers were enjoying the shadow puppet play on the central square. While I was watching with them, I heard the sounds of gamelan music from another part of the village. I walked over and saw a full Indonesian orchestra playing virtuoso pieces. When the performance ended, there was no applause. The entire audience consisted of urns containing the remains of the deceased, who were being accompanied into the next life with these ceremonies. I immediately thought of the contrast with African musicians with whom I spoke about their dance music, who can tell that they are playing well when the women begin to dance.[5] Compared with this, how do these Balinese musicians evaluate their playing? This brought home the importance of the link many musics have with spiritual and intangible aspects of human experience, which can supersede the need for public acclaim.

Sometimes, vast differences between approaches to learning and teaching can be used explicitly as an educational tool. At a conference in Basel, I met Eva Saether of the Music Academy of Malmö in Sweden. She described a total immersion program her institute was developing. They sent small groups of students to the Gambia to work with traditional musicians (Wolof, Mandinka, and Fula) at a custom-built campus. She waxed lyrical about the results. I was quite skeptical and sought and found the opportunity to visit the project in Lamin, just outside the capital Banjul, in 1995. Over a period of a few days, I witnessed Western music students going though a process of excitement, frustration, and finally insight.

After they arrived in a custom-built African-style village and were visited by a host of musicians during their first night under the palm trees, they were elated. They were looking forward to lessons with these amazing musicians. The next day, the lessons started: complex polyrhythms played at real speed (never slowed down), without singling out parts or any form of notation or explanation. This intense exposure to completely different concepts of music making and teaching brought about great confusion in the students at first, followed by considerable frustration. But after a few days, they realized that they were actually playing the rhythms, often without understanding exactly what they were doing, but that it started to sound good. Learning the movements of the corresponding dances—however awkwardly at first—aided in this process. Toward the end, all of them had experienced and realized ways of transmitting music that they did not know or understand before. No amount of overhead sheets and lectures in classrooms in

Sweden could have achieved quite the same effect. My skepticism about the project turned into conviction of its merits and led to introducing similar experiences into my work in teacher training at the Conservatorium of Amsterdam, and later at Queensland Conservatorium in Australia.

I found it revealing to realize a little later that the "new" ways of learning that these students had experienced did not differ that much from common experiences in community music in Europe, which often feature "holistic" learning in groups, without notation. I found that a key feature of this type of music learning was a reversal of roles: the teacher does not go into the classroom with a plan to transmit the music of Mozart or Mahler but looks at the possibilities and ambitions of a group of people and tries to create a meaningful musical experience from that basis. One of the most striking examples of this work that I witnessed in Europe was the project "More Music in Morecambe," led by Pete Moser. Apart from his status as the fastest one-man band in the world (Peter claimed he was featured in the *Guinness Book of Records* as doing 100 meters in twelve seconds with 100 instruments attached to his body), he musically revitalized this dismal beach town in the north of England by organizing a samba band that marched by the beach every Saturday throughout the summer, one-man-band festivals, and songwriting projects about people's everyday experiences ranging from their old stoves to the rubbish bins in the alley. It was wonderful to see such musical revitalization of people's lives in a rather gray environment. Similarly, in a socially disadvantaged village in Devon, I witnessed vibrant steelpan playing by an all-girl band called Real Steel. Their enthusiasm infected their parents, who gathered as the wonderfully self-deprecating Metal Fatigue. Later, I found these qualities of passion and humor in community music activities in more challenging environments, such as the townships of South Africa.

I learned a great deal about the need to listen to those for whom we aim to create an attractive learning environment while setting up the World Music School in Amsterdam in 1990, which brought together twenty-three teachers from twelve different cultures to teach world music to more than four hundred (mostly young) learners as an integrated part of the municipal music school. Among its very diverse population (more than half of the school-age children in major cities are non-Dutch), Amsterdam has a large population from Surinam. A popular form of Surinami music is kawina, songs with polyrhythmic accompaniment on drums of African descent, generally played in garages, without any teachers. Participants brought musical ideas and information to the rehearsals, which were pieced together into more or less coherent wholes.

After spending a night in the culturally diverse suburb Amsterdam South-East seeing many vibrant but often technically limited groups playing this music, I naively decided that it was a good idea to "improve" this practice. I hired a great expert in the field, advertised for students, and found that no students came. The idea of striving for *my* concept of quality through introducing formal

teaching—by locating kawina teaching in an institution—which seemed eminently logical to me based on my Western and Indian music backgrounds, did not
match the aims and values of these musicians. They already had meetings that were
musical, creative, and enjoyable (as well as a major factor in attracting girls); there
was no perceived need for a formal music education. Although it was painful to
have organized a course without students, I am grateful for the intuitive insight
these youngsters showed by not coming to the classes. Later, I became a strong
advocate against the introduction of formal criteria and certificates for facilitators
of village brass bands, an attempt to formalize this vibrant Dutch "world music"
tradition. We have to acknowledge that some musics do quite well without
interference by "experts."

Other musics do have a long tradition of organized transmission. While I was
setting up the World Music School, my colleague Joep Bor was asked to develop
a department of world music at the Rotterdam Conservatory, building on the
degree courses in flamenco and Latin jazz. Joep introduced North Indian classical
music, then tango, and later Turkish music. While he strategically designed
curricula that closely resembled standard conservatory curricula, the dedicated
subjects and critical mass opened the way for other learning styles. Indian music
remained an aural tradition and was supported by classes in Indian music history,
rāga analysis, and Hindi.

With more than a hundred students taking these specialized degree courses,
the department became a pillar of the World Music and Dance Centre that opened
in 2006, joining the community- and school-focused world music activities of the
municipal school for arts education. In combination with a high-quality but easily
accessible performance venue at the center of the building, this created the basis for
synergy among community, school, vocational, and scholarly training, breaking
down the often artificial divisions among various modes and levels of engagement
with music. Discussions continue on finding the most effective way to approach
and teach music traditions far away from their context, but the new center—with
an architectural design conducive to both social and musical interaction within
and between world music cultures—has considerable promise. Returning to this
vibrant place, which represents in glass and stone many of my dreams and ideas
of the past fifteen years, is a powerful and moving experience, with different music
onstage and in the practice rooms every day.

Introducing traditions with a long history of aural transmission into conservatory environments is not without challenges in the countries of origin, either.
In 2006 and 2007, I visited the Hanoi Conservatory (now Hanoi National
Academy of Music), which has been teaching traditional instrumental music of
the Viet majority in Vietnam for several decades. While this does not address the
plight of the fifty-three ethnic minorities which all have distinct musics, many of
which are in danger, it does create a positive starting point compared with the
situation in many other countries. The government is dedicated to preserving and

developing traditional music. Moreover, many students enter the conservatory as early as age eight and graduate when they are twenty-three. This allows for a fifteen-year learning process under the supervision of highly skilled specialists, in contrast to the three-to-six-year length of most degree courses, which tends to be an obstacle to mastering complex aural traditions.

Still, after this long and luxurious learning experience, some of the students and teachers feel the need to go back to the villages and learn from old masters to get the "real music," including abilities to improvise and compose. With Russian-style conservatories as its primary point of reference, the Vietnamese conservatory setting risks turning living traditions into unchanging canons rather than helping to sustain an ecology for the dynamics of music to flourish. This "one-size-fits-all" approach is applied to a number of traditions across the world.

For all of the professionalism and dedication of the teachers and students, I did understand the desire to learn in the traditional way with old masters when Hue, one of the teachers at the Hanoi Conservatory, brought me to a village fifteen kilometers away from Hanoi, where she sat on the veranda of a little village house learning the intricacies of ca trù, an old style of sung poetry, from her seventy-year-old teacher, sipping tea and leisurely discussing text, rhythm, and ornamentation in great detail. In a benign way, modern times had entered this

PHOTO I.2.   Pham Thi Huè learning ca trù from Nguyễn Thị Chúc in Ngãi Cầu Village, Vietnam, January 2007. Photo: Huib Schippers.

idyllic setting. Hue did use written notes to remember the words while she was learning, and her mini-disk recorder was on the tea cozy so she could play back the song repeatedly while she was taking care of her daughter or cleaning back home.

Even more worrisome than the future of many "classical" traditions—which tend to draw at least some support from music lovers in the country itself and from the West—is the plight of many indigenous musics. Although I had been aware of this for some time, my first extensive and direct contact with such music came with my move to Australia in 2003. Respect, knowledge, and settings for Aboriginal and Torres Strait Islander music are disappearing rapidly, while the white population still seems to be struggling to find an appropriate stance toward the original inhabitants of the country after a 220-year history of displacement, ill treatment, and genocide. The transmission of much of this music, which is closely related to ritual, values, and place, depends on communities functioning healthily. As I saw and heard from heartrending stories, especially while conducting fieldwork in the remote town of Borroloola in the Northern Territory, this is often not the case. While the culture passed down among the women in that community seemed quite strong and largely intact, the traditional songs and rituals of the men were fading fast, as their lives have been affected more dramatically over the past century. This phenomenon is widespread, and consequently, the musical diversity of Indigenous Australia is fading rapidly.[6]

Some musicians who have still learned well in this environment are now venturing out to new musical horizons. In 2004 and 2005, I worked with young didgeridoo master William Barton in the preparation of "Encounters," a festival tracing two hundred years of (harmonious and dissonant) musical interaction between the indigenous population and newcomers on Australian soil. Barton had learned in the traditional way from his uncle Arthur Peterson in the Mount Isa region, and he has experimented successfully with didgeridoo and Western art music. He teaches young Indigenous (and white) Australians through school and community projects but acknowledges that it is problematic to conceive of structured curricula in formal education given the nature and sensitivities of the music, where issues of community ownership play a major role.

Even Barton himself was not immune to this, as Aboriginal people may even object to another Indigenous person using the didgeridoo in a way they consider inappropriate. In 2007, he had to cancel a concert in West Australia because the local elders disapproved of his use of the instrument with classical Western instruments. This opened my eyes to the complexities of appropriation: many Indigenous people do not appreciate the didgeridoo being learned or used by those outside the community or for other purposes. This sense of appropriation is not strongly felt in all musics, however. We most frequently hear of appropriation linked to a long history of suppression of ethnic minorities, such as Amazonian Indians or ethnic minorities in Asia. During my decades of involvement with classical music from India, I have never heard a master object to the sometimes very dubious use of rāgas by good—but more often mediocre—jazz, pop, or digital artists as appropriation; they just shrug it off as poorly informed (and often poor-sounding) music. Ironically, the music of preference of many older Aboriginal people is country,[7] which was "appropriated" from the United States; I have never heard anybody question that. Still, awareness of and respect for cultural ownership are important when using music out of its "home" contexts, whether for education or for research.

The twelve experiences I have just described represent a wide sampling of issues that have emerged with globalization and the rise of cultural diversity. They are not all necessarily examples of best practice. It should be clear from the outset that I am not idealizing other music cultures and their practices. Nor do I want to downplay the achievements of Western music education. I continue to be impressed by the degree of organization this music tradition has achieved in education and training. Just consider the enormous amount of musical training that is needed to put on a Wagner opera: a highly skilled orchestra, a conductor, a chorus, top vocalists, and so on. Taking into account the number of high-level performers of Western classical music across the world, it is obvious that we must be doing something right. At the same time, my experiences with different forms of world music have raised questions about many ideas that seem to be taken for granted and might be ready for reevaluation if we accept the relevance of musics and styles of learning that make up our present-day societies.

The discussion has become much more interesting as music from other cultures has moved into settings previously exclusively populated by music from Europe and the United States. Gamelan music and African percussion are not found only in Indonesian courts and African villages but also in schools in the United Kingdom and colleges in the United States. My experiences in setting up the Amsterdam World Music School, one of the first large-scale extracurricular initiatives for children to learn world music seriously, was a major mind opener. I was quite unprepared for the large number of choices and solutions we had to make—many of which were admittedly born out of panic rather than wisdom—and delighted to learn how some of them later made positive experiences replicable in other settings (or at least helped others avoid the same mistakes).

That is the background of this book, the outcome of a passionate journey of some thirty years through a wide variety of sounds, approaches, and concepts, as an illustration of a process of growing awareness of (as well as a growing confusion with) diversity in approaches to music making and learning. I cannot think of a way to represent more eloquently and more truthfully the rationale for this book: to address the challenges to preconceptions of music making and learning that arise from culturally diverse practices and highlight their potential to inform vibrant musical environments for teaching, learning, and experiencing music.

Such experiences raise questions about key issues in cultural diversity in music education, many of which I believe are key issues in music education across the board.

How do we deal with cultural diversity? What does world music really mean? How do we deal with the confusing issues of tradition, authenticity, and context? What do the ways we teach and learn say about what we believe about music? What does this mean for the relationships between musical material, student, teacher, and learning environment? How does that translate into formal educational environments? Is it possible to map these factors in a coherent framework? And could such a framework be applied to understanding and perhaps even designing music education in schools, conservatories, and the communities themselves? These are the broad and profound questions I address in the following chapters. It can be a challenging journey for those of us who look for clear-cut and convenient answers. Exploring the complexities of cultural diversity in music education often raises more questions than it answers. But the questions get better; and in fields such as this, good questions may be preferable to poor answers.

Finally, it is important to emphasize that this diversity is relatively easy to access. My experiences are by no means unique. While not every musician, scholar, or educator has been in the privileged position to travel and study as widely as I have described, almost everyone with sufficient curiosity and an entrepreneurial spirit can access a wealth of practices of making and learning music. They can take us through a fascinating multiplicity of roles: learner, educator, performer, creator, thinker, and researcher. Over the past four decades, many musicians and educators have documented similar musical journeys (e.g., Aubert, Bailey, Campbell, Dunbar-Hall, Howard, Neuman, Rice, Seeger, Wiggins, Wong). This is not the domain of old-school positivist researchers, looking from the outside in, claiming or pretending to be objective. Truly engaging with these practices means accepting different roles and getting one's hands dirty. We are unashamedly actors in the experiences we have, and the lessons we learn are the results of the interaction with the musics we deal with: mental, physical, social, emotional, and sometimes even spiritual. This is becoming an increasingly comfortable position in both music education and ethnomusicology.[8] It is probably also the logical starting position for anyone involved in teaching world music at any level. Although I realize that I have been exceptionally privileged in being able to travel to many parts of the world in the past three decades, seeking out extraordinary settings for learning and teaching music, many similar experiences are now available in almost any culturally diverse city in the world for the price of a bus ticket. All we need to do is jump on.

CHAPTER 2

Positioning "World Music" in Education

A Conceptual History

In the early 1930s, Martin and Osa Johnson, a couple from Kansas, traveled to central Africa to document the lives of the pygmies in the Ituri forest. Perhaps the greatest value of this expedition to posterity lies in the fact that they filmed their endeavors, in the first movie with sound ever recorded in Africa. They playfully named it Congorilla. *In addition to animal footage, there is much focus on "the little savages" who are being measured, prodded, and exposed to other well-intended but toe-curling experiments. One of the highlights is a scene in which they decide to "give the boys and girls some modern jazz." As a probably unintended but hardly subtle symbol of colonial superiority, the phonograph is installed on top of a traditional drum. Osa Johnson, in full tropical gear, shows the natives how to clap their hands and bob up and down to the music, displaying great enthusiasm but limited sense of fluid movement. The pygmies comply politely. Martin Johnson observes: "It was remarkable the way they quickly caught the rhythm of our modern music; sometimes they got out of time, but they quickly came back to it again."* [1]

Apart from some documentation on the early dissemination of European music, this is likely to be one of the earliest filmed examples of music instruction that transcends cultural boundaries. It also offers an unintended ironic picture of "pioneers" in the field of cultural diversity in music education. The Johnsons are effectively "bringing back" Afro-American music ("our modern music") to black Africans and teaching them to move to it in the rather stiff manner one tends to associate with people from colder climates. If we take this scene as a starting

PHOTO 2.1.
Dancing with pygmees.
Osa Johnson teaches jazz
moves to "little savages."
Still from the movie
Congorilla (Johnson, 1932).

point, it antedates the conceived beginnings of music education across cultures by several decades.[2] With this odd experiment in cross-cultural arts education, the effort to find appropriate terminology, approaches, and content for cultural diversity in music education can be traced back more than seventy-five years.

A number of musical and extramusical factors have influenced what is now widely referred to as *world music* and its role in music learning and teaching. These factors extend over a number of interrelated fields: sociology, anthropology, ethnomusicology, and music education. They span the decline of colonialism and the rise of globalization against a background of decades of unequaled developments in technology, travel, and migration.[3] The discourse on cultural diversity from these multiple perspectives has generated terminology that is often undefined or used loosely in a remarkably wide range of meanings: the terms *multicultural, intercultural, cross-cultural,* and *transcultural* are applied in conjunction with references to ethnic, world, migrant, or minority arts, often without defining specific meanings or relations (real or assumed).

This should come as no surprise: position, context, worldview, and political correctness have influenced the words used to refer to cultural diversity in its many manifestations. There is little hope of arriving at uncontested definitions in such a diffuse field. However, from a historical and conceptual overview of terms used, it is possible to deduce a number of working definitions. Even if this cannot eliminate ambiguity altogether, at least it can explicitly try to embrace it and assist in understanding the phenomenon of cultural diversity in music education as an important influence on the musical realities of the twenty-first century.

The Term World Music

The recent history of the term *world music* is well documented. For its origins, many authors refer to a famous 1987 meeting on the floor above a London pub.[4] Representatives from a number of small independent U.K. record labels had gathered to promote recently "discovered" music from Africa and Asia, which they considered exciting and new, mostly mixing Western pop with indigenous sounds or instruments. They felt that their cause was not served by a shared place in either the "International" bin with the dulcet tones of George Zamphir and Nana Mouskouri or under "Ethnic," which they associated with obscure tribal musics of primarily scholarly interest. They decided to develop a marketing strategy featuring display material for record shops in the United Kingdom, which in the course of a few years led to a "World Music" section in thousands of record shops all over the world—although the terms *international* and *ethnic* remained, as did references to specific genres, styles, regions, countries, and continents.

Through this campaign, the term *world music* took a giant leap in public awareness, in many countries and with slight variations across various languages, as *musiques du monde, wereldmuziek,* or *Weltmusik.* In a recent analysis of this phenomenon, Taylor emphasizes the commercial aspect of the term and its link to globalization, commodification, and consumerism,[5] but it is important to remember that it was also strongly driven by the sheer love of discovering new and exciting music. In fact, very few world music artists and recordings have been major cash cows for record companies; in most cases, they have just kept independent labels sufficiently afloat to enable them to embark on their next recording project.

The practical application of the term *world music* may well predate the London pub meeting by more than twenty years, however. It is, in fact, closely linked to music education and ethnomusicology. Robert E. Brown claimed to have first used the term in the 1960s to describe a hands-on approach to ethnomusicology at Wesleyan University in Connecticut.[6] In introducing practical music making into degree programs, Brown built on a format pioneered by Ki Mantle Hood in the 1950s.[7] Hood introduced playing the gamelan as part of the training of ethnomusicology students at UCLA, in a discipline where (the illusion of) objective distance from the objects of study had previously been paramount. This sentiment was so strong that Hood told me that his teacher Jaap Kunst, the founder of ethnomusicology, probably never actually touched a gamelan during his many years of fieldwork in Indonesia. Indeed, in his own work, Kunst only mentions "listening, collecting and reflecting" as his sources.[8]

Initially, the unconventional engagement with world music practice earned Hood the reputation of the "mad professor who sits students on the floor and has them beating pots and pans in the name of music."[9] However, his initiative was gradually followed by many others. Taking the idea to the next stage, Brown stated that his world music programs constituted "a conscientious attempt to restore the cart behind the horse, with living music as sound in a primary position and ethnomusicology as its subsidiary in a position of support."[10] With it, he tried to reverse the approach of earlier ethnomusicology programs that were "trying desperately to minimise the element of cultural interaction."[11] Musical practices and master musicians from other cultures became a substantial part of the program. The development initiated by Hood has now become a key feature of most leading U.S. ethnomusicology programs and a fertile platform for thinking on learning and teaching world music, as evidenced by the numerous views in a recent volume of essays dedicated to this practice, *Performing Ethnomusicology*.[12]

Much has been said and written on the shortcomings of the term *world music* and its relation to the various words and expressions that were used to refer to music from different parts of the world over the past century. The tension probably cannot be completely resolved: the variety of geographical positions, cultural backgrounds, working environments, and personal histories creates a vast diversity of perspectives. However, the discussion can be made more meaningful than a mere battle of terms if we consider how they reflect the worldviews that informed them. It is worthwhile to examine the terminology used in order to provide a clearer insight into the various approaches to the genres and styles of music under discussion.

I will try to create such a perspective on the meanings of specific types of terminology by grouping terms according to underlying approach or sentiment. In this way, in addition to the more chronologically oriented histories published previously[13] and those emphasizing world music as a commercial label,[14] it may be possible to construct a "conceptual history" of approaches to world music, distinguishing eight significant angles: wonder, prejudice, sense of place, sense of time, perceived use or status, nonmusical qualities, music as a meeting ground, and music as a universal language.

Wonder, as in "Exotic Music," "Music of the Other"

Music that causes a sense of unfamiliarity, fascination, and wonder is what much of the contemporary literature has come to identify as "the music of the Other." In the more innocent sense of the expression, this refers to the sincere surprise (and often delight) at encountering a music that sounds different, is presented differently, and comes across differently. It has also been a driving force behind the academic discipline of ethnomusicology, which Nettl, borrowing from Wachsmann, describes as "the study of music other than one's own."[15] This sense of discovery can be a powerful mechanism when introducing music lovers of all ages to new music.

The BBC used "Strange Music" as the title for a series of programs that ran from January to March 1933.[16] *Exotic* sounds a little more alluring and has all of the implications that we commonly find in dictionaries: "having the attraction of the strange and foreign, glamorous," but also "outlandish, barbarous, strange and uncouth."[17] The term may also be defined in relation to the position of the user. In the 1944 edition of the *Harvard Dictionary of Music*, Willi Apel defined *exotic music* as "the music cultures outside the European tradition." Almost sixty years later, Bohlman describes *exotica*, a Web-based genre reviving some of the ideas above at the turn of the century.[18] "Tropical music" and "Oriental music" have similar implications, although the latter comes with more sinister undertones, as we will see below. Commercially, the exotic or mysterious has been an effective marketing tool, from Tropical Music as a record label to The Mystery of Bulgarian Voices as a title referring to a powerful but at the same time very regimented form of state-sponsored choral music from the Balkans.[19]

Prejudice, as in "Primitive," "Preliterate" Music

The 1941 standard guide *Introduction to Musicology* states: "As applied to musical systems, the term 'primitive' is used in two senses; it may refer either to ancient or prehistoric music, or to music of a low cultural level. It is in the latter sense that primitive music is chiefly studied in comparative musicology."[20] The music of American Indians and "African Negroes" are quoted as examples. The influential *New Oxford History of Music* also retained the terminology and the idea that while the West was innovative and modern, the rest of the world stood still: "primitive music scholars had to turn first to the primitive tribes still living in the Stone Age."[21] Dictionaries such as the *OED* provide similar shades of meaning for *primitive*: "having the quality or style of that which is early or ancient. Also, simple, rude or rough like that of early times." In addition, the *OED* offers (quite dubiously from the point of view of contemporary anthropological insights): "that relates to a group . . . whose culture, through isolation, has remained at a simple level of social and economic organisation."[22] However, it is important to note that *primitive* can also be used in a more idealized sense of "uncontaminated," as in the music of the "noble savage," or *primitivism* with its connotations of simplicity and directness in the visual arts.

The term *preliterate* reveals a more subtle form of prejudice. It assumes that musics that do not use notation are not sufficiently evolved to do so. In fact, there are many forms of music of great refinement that do not need notation or that even actively reject it, such as African percussion and Indian rāgas. Notation simply does not serve much purpose in their practices of creation, transmission, and performance, which have a successful history going back many centuries. Some of these

Kanyok and Luba

southern Belgian Congo

CONGO

1952 & 1957

Kanyok, Luba-Kasai, Luluwa, Songye, Luba-Katanga, Hemba

ORIENTAL MUSIC

KELETI TÁNCZENE

PHOTOS 2.2A, 2.2B, 2.2C, AND 2.2D. CD covers representing typical ethnomusicological recordings, Orientalism/exoticism, world music as a commercial label, and the celebration of recontextualized world music. Photos: Huib Schippers.

do use notation in specific stages of the learning process, which could be referred to as "preaural" by traditions that hold the belief that fine musicianship ultimately depends on a well-developed ear, with notation as an aide-mémoire for students only.[23]

Sense of Place: Indian Music, Oriental Music, Non-Western Music

Least confusing in this category are specific indications of place, such as gamelan music from the court of Jogyakarta or vocal polyphony from the island of Krk off the coast of Croatia. Indian music is already a great deal more ambiguous as a denominator: it usually refers to the North Indian classical tradition, while there is a distinct South Indian classical tradition, plus a wealth of folk and religious music and countless popular songs from Bollywood movies, the music most people in India actually listen to. Most of my African colleagues disapprovingly shake their heads when people speak of "African music": although scholars from the region such as Andrew Tracey and Meki Nzewi have identified commonalities, they see and hear little in common between South African isicathemia, Moroccan nuba'at, and Gambian kora music.[24]

The charm of a generic indication such as "African music" seems to be akin to that of "Oriental music" in its appeal to the imagination. The latter was used extensively to refer to music from Arab and Asian countries in a way that acknowledged the "greatness of Oriental civilizations" but at the same time held suggestions of exoticism and a range of implicit prejudices that Edward Said exposed so eloquently thirty years ago: "the Oriental is irrational, depraved (fallen), childlike, 'different'; thus the European is rational, virtuous, mature, 'normal.'"[25] This is the darker side of the "music of the Other" and a factor that still influences the presentation of world music in many settings, including education.

Finally in this category, there is relative position. It seems odd now that one would refer to music by a noncharacteristic, but references to "non-Western" music and "extra-European" music have been quite persistent, remnants of the times when Western music was regarded as the principal frame of reference. In reaction, I have heard an Indian colleague ironically refer to the music of Mozart as "non-Indian" music. The generic term *international music* is still often used to indicate music from across a country's borders as well. Even the rise of the term *world music* has not eradicated the role of geographical position as a determining factor: in FNAC, one of the largest record shops in Paris, South African music is categorized as world music, while in the record shops in Pretoria, French chansons can be found in the world music bins.

Sense of Time: Ancient, Traditional, Classical, Contemporary, Roots Music

"Ancient" music mostly refers to music that can be regarded as a precursor of the Western classical tradition, such as Greek music.[26] "Traditional" music is used loosely for a wide range of art and religious music, as well as folk music from the entire globe. It refers to more or less clearly traceable origins. But the meaning of *traditional* also oscillates between "how the old people used to do it" and "how the community thinks it should be today,"[27] which may be quite distinct. "Classical" is problematic because it rarely represents the same connotations in other contexts as it does in the West; it is, however, widely used for art musics from the world of Islam and all over Asia. While "contemporary" music might be deemed to be music that is not traditional or classical, some classical and traditional music is simultaneously contemporary, as is the case with Indian classical music and other living traditions.

To complicate things further, Indian hit songs from movies of the 1950s and 1960s are now called "classical" in India. With "contemporary," much depends on the culture's sense of time and on whether the focus lies on composers, creators, or performers; it tends to be used primarily for popular music. "Roots" music, mostly used in concert promotion, trade, and journalism, can also be placed in this category, implying that a music has its origins far back in time, most likely in some "exotic" place. Examples of this usage are the names of the U.K. magazine *Folk Roots* and the annual World Roots Festival in Amsterdam. In this context, "roots" reflects some of the meaning of the more neutral "traditional."

Perceived Use or Status: Court, Art, Popular, Folklore

"Court" music has been a common and fairly useful indication of use and background. It is clear in terms of provenance and also serves marketing purposes. "Spiritual" and "religious" music have a more limited appeal in this way (it can safely be assumed that the success of Nusrat Fateh Ali Khan transcended his role as a Sufi praise singer). However, the many musics that thrived in houses of ill repute, such as Argentinean tango, Algerian rai, flamenco from Andalusia, Vietnamese ca trù, and Indian thumri, are rarely marketed on that basis. "Art" music is much vaguer but fits well into a Western preconception: the message is that this can be listened to as music for music's sake. "Popular" music has the double meaning of "of the people" and "the music that people buy"; it mostly refers to the latter. The former tends to be covered by "folk music." "Folk" has been particularly overused with reference to music from non-Western cultures, even if it was obviously considered "religious" or "classical" within the culture itself. This is likely to be a remnant of the assumption that all music that was not Western classical music was folk (and therefore probably primitive). This association was strengthened by the name of the first major "world music" label, Folkways, and the fact that the International Council for Traditional Music (ICTM) was called the International Folk Music Council until 1981. Speaking from the perspective of the geographical areas in which most scholars in this field were based, Slobin characterizes the use of "folk music" during the first seven decades of the twentieth century as referring to "the internal primitives of Euro-America."[28]

"Folklore" has acquired a remarkable stigma, as Aubert observes, and this is possibly a result of associations with "romantic idealisation of music genres with a bucolic character" and tourist promoters and politicians "manipulating folk heritage . . . for deflected ends."[29] As a result, few anthropologists and ethnomusicologists would present themselves as folklorists, while their field of study largely coincides in many cases. Another victim of stigma is "country music,"[30] even though it is the music of choice of many of the people ethnomusicologists study and respect, such as Australian indigenous people.[31]

Nonmusical Qualities of Makers or Owners: Ethnic, Migrant, Black Music

"Ethnic music," strongly anchored in some thinking on music research, as we can see from the very name of the discipline *ethno*musicology, suggests a direct link between ethnicity and particular musics. This may have been a path of some merit until fifty years ago, but as music educators are noticing, the relationship between ethnicity and musical preferences and activities is in fact increasingly fluid. Hindustani hip-hop artist Apache Indian (three widely divergent cultures in six words) raps about arranged marriages, Chinese and Vietnamese pianists are storming the international stages, and Caucasians play jazz (and occasionally even the sitar). "Migrant music" acknowledged the fact that music traveled with people after the major migration from the 1960s. While "migrant music" usually referred to the culture of origin of the musicians, it can be seen as a step in acknowledging the complex dynamics of music traveling.

"Black music" was initially the music of the black population of the United States and associated with the rise of black pride. The term came to be applied surprisingly widely. In the United Kingdom, "black music" even included music from South Asian immigrants in the 1980s, undoubtedly much to the horror of many Indians who pride themselves on having as fair a skin color as possible. In the end, such terminology sends out skewed messages about why listeners should engage with particular sounds. How well would the music of Bach do if it was marketed as "Traditional Caucasian Eighteenth-Century Lutheran Music"?

Music as a Meeting Ground: Crossover, Fusion, World Mix, World Beat

Generally "crossover," "fusion," "world mix," and "world beat" refer to popular music from the Caribbean, Latin America, and especially Africa (e.g., Fela Kuti, Papa Wemba) or to conscious efforts by musicians to transcend cultural boundaries from the 1960s to the present (e.g., Shakti with John McLaughlin, Indian rapper Apache Indian, Paul Simon's album *Graceland*). From a historical perspective, many of the world's established traditions could in fact be placed in this category: few musics evolved without extensive external influences. Bohlman sees the concept of "encounters" as a key aspect of the world music phenomenon at the beginning of the twenty-first century, arguing that these no longer merely represent looking at—or listening to—the "other" but also indicate a more profound interaction.[32] Taylor describes a number of these collaborations and argues that the "hybrid" music forms resulting from them in fact come to be regarded as a new kind of "authentic" music to Western listeners, in addition to the "pure traditional" musics. He also acknowledges that musics mix and have always mixed, so that it is difficult to identify either "pure" or "hybrid" as distinguishing features.[33]

Music as a Universal Language: Weltmusik, One-World Music

The German use of the term *Weltmusik* presents an interesting case. Karlheinz Stockhausen speaks of "the blending and integrating process of all the music cultures of the world" and ultimately a "sort of artificial new folklore," which serves "as a contribution to the concert—the coming together—of all cultural groups."[34] Ernst Joachim Berendt, an influential New Age music publicist, further popularized this vision in the German-speaking countries, linking jazz and Indian music with zen and physics.[35] The 22nd World Conference of the International Society for Music Education in Amsterdam, in 1996, had as its slogan "Music— The Universal Language." However, this motto—devised by an advertising agency—was not well received by the community of music educators. There were many comments about the "flawed proposition" of the nature of music and music education this constituted, both during the conference and afterward in the *International Journal for Music Education*.[36]

The concept of world harmony through music arose quite early, along with the new emphasis in education on "international relations" in the years immediately following World War I. Volk quotes a remarkably naive statement by Frances Elliott Clark from this period:

When that great convention can sit together—Chinese, Hindu, Japanese, Celt, German, Czech, Italian, Hawaiian, Scandinavian, and Pole— all singing the national songs of each land, the home songs of each people, and listen as one mind and heart to great world music [*sic*] common to all and loved by all, then shall real world goodwill be felt and realized.[37]

In addition to the eight angles discussed above, there is the continuing debate regarding singular versus plural: some authors prefer the term *world musics* to indicate that it refers to a many forms of musical expression. Others argue that this is superfluous: "it strikes me as overkill to stress the obvious fact there are innumerable varieties of world music. . . . If we can speak of world theatre or world literature, why should we have to speak of world musics?"[38] There is an argument for the view that if Shakespeare, the author of the Mahabharata, Gabriel García Márquez, and Homer share a singular reference, so can Indian rāgas, salsa, Tuvan overtone singing, and South African isicathamiya. But the discussion hinges around whether we treat *world music* as an analogy of the two OED meanings for *world literature*: "a body of work drawn from many nations and recognised as literature throughout the world" or "(the sum of) the literature of the world." Alternatively, we can consider the two entries for *world language*: "a language universally read and spoken by educated people" or "a language for international use."[39] In the case of music, none of these four is a perfect match. The first meaning of *world literature*, with its implications of excellence, is rarely or never used for *world music*. The second one, which would naturally include Western literature, is not common, either, with reference to music, as *world music* is commonly used to distinguish certain musics from Western music. Of the meanings for *world language*, both would point to a hegemony of a single (probably Western) tradition or a naive "music as a universal language" approach as discussed above.

Two other variants of *world music* commonly encountered are "musics of the world" and "musics of the world's cultures." The latter, somewhat labored denomination was promoted by a special panel created in 1992 by the International Society for Music Education (ISME), which preferred this to all other names then in vogue, including "international music." Although there may be no real objections to using such terminology, there are few strong arguments in favor of it: "of the world's cultures" hardly serves as a distinguishing feature among the many different forms of music we know. But it does express a sense of growing respect and relevance. In a different way, this can also be gleaned from the 1987 launch of the term *world music*, the success of which may be partly attributed to its being introduced at a time when the idea that the West could learn from other cultures started to become more widely accepted.

This entire discussion illustrates that many of the terms used reveal positionality and often an underlying system of beliefs. With the wealth of approaches and terminology explored above, two major fields of influence can be distinguished: the values and attitudes toward (the music of) other cultures and what Bohlman calls "one of the most persistent dilemmas plaguing ethnomusicologists and historians of music: the juncture—or disjuncture—between time and place, between music as a temporal and music as a geographical and cultural phenomenon."[40] From this, five essentially different uses of the term *world music* can be distilled:

1. *World music as a product of a particular people, society, geography, and time.* This recognizes all musics of the world as discrete forms of cultural expression and uses the term *world music* merely as shorthand to refer to this variety, without any judgment.
2. *World music as the "music of the Other" (wonder, prejudice, etc.).* This incorporates both positive and negative aspects of "otherness": the delight in discovering new musics and the possible prejudices attached to those, consciously or subconsciously.
3. *World music as a result of musical interaction between cultures.* This can feature as crossover or fusion, either organic (e.g., salsa or Afro pop) or more conscious (e.g., the mixing of Indian bhangra and Brazilian samba to form sambhanghra).
4. *World music as a marketing tool.* This sees the musics of the world as a product or instrument of globalization, commodification, and consumerism.
5. *World music as a philosophical concept (universal language).* This ranges from strongly idealistic concepts of "one music" for the entire world to more pluralist ideas that emphasize "the unity of the pursuit of music as a universal human endeavour."[41]

Of course, world music can legitimately be considered as the total sum of musical forms that exist on earth (including Western music), which is ultimately inclusive to the point of being meaningless. In order to avoid this type of nondefinition, it makes sense to link closely the concept of world music as it is used today to the dynamics of music, to its ability to develop, mix, and spread across the world. Joep Bor has suggested to me that "world music is non-Western traditional and popular music that has successfully adapted itself to its new, Western environment." Although this seems to do justice to the dynamics of the phenomenon, I would argue for a slightly broader definition: world music is the phenomenon of musical concepts, repertoires, genres, styles, and instruments traveling, establishing themselves, or mixing in new cultural environments.

The rationale for using this definition is that the very concept of world music is primarily based on music traveling and interacting with new contexts. It also dampens Eurocentrism, as it recognizes traffic in all directions: *The Magic Flute* in the Hanoi Opera House is world music from this perspective, as is Tuvan overtone singing in Central Park in New York. For music education, a definition based on dynamics is also particularly useful, as it highlights a crucial aspect of the phenomenon: the fact that music from all over the world exists—and is taught—*outside* its original context. It is primarily this characteristic that creates new challenges in terms of students' familiarity with the sounds, aptitude to learn, openness to traditional teaching techniques, social possibilities to effectuate them, and new opportunities to be explored with the aim of stimulating learning processes and environments.

Cultural Diversity and Multiculturalism

If the term *world music* refers to the journey of a musical style or genre, it has not yet defined its reception in the place where it lands. This can range from total embrace to overt hostility, depending on the sentiments in the community or society where the music or the musicians land. Nowadays, these rarely have a single frame of cultural reference. The term that has been used most over the past twenty-five years when referring to a community or society consisting of more than one culture is *multicultural,* and it has been at the center of numerous governmental and educational policies. It lost some of its appeal with efforts to discredit "multiculturalism," predominantly in the United States since the mid-1990s and more globally since September 11, 2001. Criticism of specific policies *dealing with* multicultural issues turned into rumors of the failing of multicultural societies as a whole and a peculiar nostalgia for a monocultural past. This represents a fascinating confusion between new cultural realities and politicians' responses to these realities. It is unlikely that cultures will ever be "unmixed" (and it is highly undesirable, as ethnic cleansing would be its prime instrument). Although policies may change, the cohabitation of people from different cultural backgrounds simply needs to be addressed. The term currently favored for this reality is *cultural diversity.* I will use this latter term to refer to any situation where more than one culture is represented in a particular environment, and I will use it as a neutral term, without implications regarding how cultural diversity is addressed.

As Taylor points out, cultural pluralism was already recognized in the 1930s by anthropologists Franz Boas and Ruth Benedict. They "rejected the earlier notion of racial and cultural difference as being evolutionary and instead argued for cultural relativism: cultures were merely different from one another, neither superior nor inferior, existing in a pluralist world."[42] However, it took many decades to catch on, in cultural policy, in people's perception, and in education. To this day, one encounters the full gamut of approaches: believing in a single cultural identity for a country (whether out of a sense of superiority or out of a fear of impurity), tolerance for diversity, and conviction that all cultures must mix. These can coexist in a single country, city, community, or institution. This is worth investigating in relation to music education, as it informs what is taught and how.

It is important to realize that cultural diversity is a matter of degree. As John Blacking pointed out decades ago when speaking about the United Kingdom:

> before Caribbean and Asian immigrants formed a substantial part of its population, it was in fact multicultural: differences between the lifestyles of people in the north and the south of the country, between classes and between rich and poor, were as great as between societies that anthropologists would describe as having different cultures.[43]

Although the development of culturally diverse societies has brought cultural differences previously unimaginable within the boundaries of a single nation, the point that cultural diversity is relative is of considerable importance in musical diversity as well.

From the perspective of each individual music learner, one could in fact construct an "unfamiliarity index" (see figure 2.1), which could inform approaches most likely to succeed in engaging with particular musics. For most young music learners, the hit songs of the day would have a low unfamiliarity index, while Japanese Buddhist shomyo chanting would probably score quite high. Within this index, world music is not necessarily always on the unfamiliar end of the scale. In the perception of most young Americans, Jamaican reggae would sound much more familiar than the music of Scriabin or even Terry Riley. On the other hand, Western classical music would sound more familiar to many Japanese than their own traditional music, which exists in the margins of musical life in Japan. In this way, a continuum from very familiar to very unfamiliar can be a useful tool in designing music programs and in evaluating change in learners.

While this index is highly individual, the familiarity of various musics is also strongly determined by the cultural diversity of the environment. It is possible to distinguish cultures with a single national origin where differences are defined by social status or position, education, gender, or age (as described by Blacking

very familiar ⟵——————————————⟶ very unfamiliar

FIGURE 2.1.   The unfamiliarity index

above); a single national origin where differences are defined by ethnic or cultural background (as in the former Soviet Union or Yugoslavia); several national origins with similar cultures (as in many European trading nations in the first half of the twentieth century); and several national origins with widely different cultures. The last is the contemporary reality of most countries in the Western world, where people from European, African, Latin American, and Asia-Pacific backgrounds live together.

Even in these cultures, however, the cultural divides may not be as simple as they seem. Increasingly, representatives from different cultures nowadays do not necessarily identify (only) with the ethnic background of their own culture. A Korean violinist and a Dutch djembe player are more likely to feel that as musicians, they represent European or African culture rather than the culture of their country of birth. I have already observed that in generations that have grown up in culturally diverse environments, the direct link between ethnic background and musical preferences is rapidly weakening. This poses a major challenge for music education based on representation of cultures: the frequently encountered format of "a song from each country represented in the classroom."[44] The concept of large homogeneous groups with single identities is weakening rapidly. Many societies appear to be moving from socially constructed to more individually constructed identities. Musical identities can play a significant role in that process.[45]

When trying to understand which processes lie at the basis of culturally diverse music programs, one of the key factors is to gauge the approach of the society, the institute, or the individual toward cultural diversity in general. Although the terminology differs in various disciplines, I have found it very useful to distinguish among four basic approaches toward cultural diversity: monocultural, multicultural, intercultural, and transcultural. I will use this division, derived from a system employed at Dutch teacher-training colleges,[46] because it provides a framework that clarifies approaches to culturally diverse societies and translates to music education very well.

- *Monocultural.* The dominant culture (in most cases Western classical music) is the only frame of reference. Other musics and approaches to music are marginalized. This may seem outdated but in essence it still appears to be the underlying philosophy of most institutes, programs, and methods throughout the Western world in terms of content and approach.
- *Multicultural.* Different peoples and musics lead largely separate lives. Mostly, this translates into music education targeted at "roots" of learners. Blacks are taught African music, Moroccans learn Arab songs, and whites study Mozart, irrespective of the rapidly changing and blending cultural reality of musical tastes in our societies as outlined above.

FIGURE 2.2. Approaches to cultural diversity

- *Intercultural.* This represents loose contacts and exchange between cultures and includes simple forms of fusion. It has been very popular in northwestern Europe and in some parts of the United States, particularly for music in schools. This approach can be steered largely by feelings of political correctness but also by profound musical interest and awareness.
- *Transcultural.* This refers to an in-depth exchange of approaches and ideas. It suggests programs in which many different musics and musical approaches are featured on an equal footing, not in the margins but throughout general introductory courses, history, theory, methodology, and discussions on the role of music for the community, beauty, or ceremony.

It should be clear that these are not four clear-cut categories, but they tend to blend into one another. Therefore, it is probably more appropriate to present them in the form of a continuum, as in figure 2.2.

It is important to note that there are no implicit value judgments in this continuum. Nor is it necessarily an evolutionary model, although, obviously, many countries have moved from monocultural to multicultural, intercultural, or transcultural—from a single reference to treating diversity as separate entities, facilitating casual contact, or merging in depth. This process can come full circle: the once very terse mix of Spanish and African culture that simmered on an island in the Caribbean for a few hundred years is now seen as a single Cuban culture, with son and salsa as key outcomes. And even if we only go back a few decades, the advent of Latinos in the United States, Italians in the Netherlands, or Greeks in Australia was seen as an insurmountable clash of cultures. Now, these groups are generally regarded as part of mainstream culture, as concern turns to newcomers from other cultures—often with strikingly similar prejudice.

The positions on the continuum also have a relationship to some of the world-music terminology discussed earlier and to the approaches of their users. We can class so-called primitive music as a notion within a monocultural perspective (single frame of reference, also in relation to others); ethnic, exotic, non-Western, and Oriental music as a multicultural perspective (musics exist as separate from one another); crossover and fusion (and maybe even migrant music) would represent an intercultural approach (meeting between cultures); and the concept of *Weltmusik* is an example of a transcultural approach (fusing of deeper values).

At an advanced level, transculturality relates to Homi Bhabha's concept of "a third space" emanating from cultural encounters or hybridity: "Hybridity to me is the third space that enables other positions to merge. This third space displaces the histories that constitute it. . . . The process of hybridity gives rise to something different, something new and unrecognisable, a new area of meaning and representation."[47]

However, it is important to note that even if there were societies in which a transcultural approach to music education prevailed, strands of monocultural practice would remain within those societies. Ironically, as music students develop toward being professionals, they are likely to focus on a single culture. A brilliant violinist is not commonly a master of Western classical music, South Indian rāgas, and Irish jigs and reels. In fact, he or she is more likely to become known for interpreting works from a particular stylistic period or even a particular composer. That being said, eminent musicians from Yehudi Menuhin and Yo-Yo Ma to Paul Simon and Peter Gabriel have argued (and demonstrated) that practical contact with other musical approaches and cultures deepens one's own understanding of music. On the cover of a 1960 recording of South Indian classical music, Yehudi Menuhin wrote:

> It is a sign of the times that along with the beautiful art books which reveal to our regimented urban dweller the dreams and achievements of civilisations far distant in time and space, it is also possible to count on an eager and enlightened public in the world of music. . . . I for one feel that by refining our ear and our sense of perception, by listening to music so utterly strange, as the music on this record, we return to the works we know and love belonging to our own traditions with a refreshed interest and a capacity to react more sensitively and more intensely.[48]

Across the board, there are indications of an evolution from regarding other cultures as inferior or exotic to seeing them as enriching our own perceptions and experience.

Cultural Diversity in Music Education

During the past two decades, a number of major figures in music education have explored cultural diversity. Prominent international thinkers on music education such as Keith Swanwick, Bennett Reimer, and David Elliott have contributed to discussion on the subject, as have John Paynter, Christopher Small, Barbara Lundquist, Kathy Marsh, Marie McCarthy, Patricia Shehan Campbell, Teresa Volk, Peter Dunbar-Hall, Heidi Westerlund and many others. Here, I will focus on the first three, exploring how they fit cultural diversity into their philosophies of music education.

Swanwick was one of the first to break a number of preconceptions about music education in culturally diverse settings in his significant 1998 publication *Music, Mind and Education.* He reacted against the strong contextual bias in most practices of culturally diverse music education:

> One way of dealing with prejudicial value systems—which can set like concrete around potential musical responses—is to avoid labelling altogether until the music has really been experienced. Music educators do well to . . . focus first on the ways sounds behave and the necessary mastery of controlling them, along with encouraging the perception and articulation of expressive character and structural relationships; for it is on these elements of musical experience that real valuing is built.[49]

At the same time, Swanwick seems to be caught in remnants of exoticism. He cites the introduction to the 1979 edition of *The New Oxford History of Music* by Wellesz for a description of the "immersion in music" of Oriental musicians, which he calls "certainly authentic and valid":[50]

> The Eastern musician likes to improvise on given patterns, he favours repetition, his music does not develop, does not aim at producing climaxes, but it flows; and the listener becomes entranced by the voice of the singers, by the sound of the instruments, and by the drumming rhythms.[51]

In fact, what Wellesz describes here is not the way an "Eastern musician" (if there is such a creature) approaches music but how a Westerner may (mis)interpret music from other cultures. To take one example, a professional Indian musician will not recognize his own music making in the description we read above. Indian rāgas are not given patterns but highly abstract melodic organizing principles; improvisation is not a choice but the core of the performance practice; the Indian musician favors not repetition but subtle variation that cannot easily be discerned by untrained ears; and a rāga performance develops according to a well-defined pattern, including fairly spectacular climaxes, most of which should be hard to miss even by lay listeners. And the knowledgeable listener—Indian classical music is most certainly a *musique savante*—actually responds not to the pleasant humming of the instruments but to the dexterity the musician displays in producing new and unexpected variations within the constraints of the chosen rāga and tala, the melodic and rhythmic organizing principles in this music. A similar point could easily be made from the perspective of Javanese, Thai, Viet, or Chinese music.

Besides Swanwick, two other major influences on the philosophy of music education in the past decades have undoubtedly been Reimer and Elliott. Reimer's *A Philosophy of Music Education* has now seen three editions in more than three decades (1970, 1989, and 2003). In the latest edition of this key work, he defends himself against criticism of overemphasizing music education as aesthetic education from a Western "art for art's sake" perspective and addresses cultural diversity extensively. But he expresses himself carefully:

> Are we not being hopelessly idealistic to think that we can be multicultural at will but also disrespectful to each culture's music outside our own, treating it as so much "material" to be homogenized, or cloned, into a resemblance of familiarity so we can treat it as a tamed, comfortable variation of what we already know?[52]

Although he does not answer this question (rich in implicit political correctness) in a straightforward manner, it would seem from his treatment of the issue that he does not see cultural diversity as a reality on the *inside* of music education but rather as a foreign presence on the *outside*, something to be dealt with from an established frame of reference. He does not question the basic parameters of an essentially Western philosophy of music education, taking as a starting point the need for people to be rooted in understanding one (Western classical music?) culture. Reimer comes to the conclusion that people can only "genuinely experience" music from other cultures "to some extent," regarding cultural diversity as an inevitable but rather inconvenient reality.[53]

Even as the editor of a volume of essays on cultural diversity in music education, Reimer remains quite conservative. Describing his topic as "musics from around the world in addition to the music of America's Western heritage," he acknowledges that "previously foreign musics have become increasingly indigenous and therefore harder to ignore," notes that the profession acted with great energy "as the idea of musical multiculturalism took hold, supported by politically favourable attitudes," but expresses grave doubts about whether "the obligations of developing solid world music offerings can be fulfilled despite a weak infrastructure of support" and ultimately asks, "Is what we are doing defensible?"[54]

Elliott, whose *Music Matters* has become an important influence on the thinking of many music educators since its publication in 1995, challenges the parameters of Reimer's philosophy by what he terms a "praxial" approach, placing the "praxis" of music making itself at the center of his philosophy. He sees cultural diversity as an organic part of music education: "If MUSIC consists in a diversity of music cultures, then MUSIC is inherently multicultural. And if MUSIC is inherently multicultural, then music education ought to be multicultural in essence."[55] Simplistic as this reasoning may seem, it does express awareness that for a full understanding of music, it is necessary to address cultural diversity in depth. Elliott argues that it should be the basis of music education rather than being treated as an inconvenient intrusion.

He continues to link culturally diverse approaches to music with the central concepts in his book:

If it is accurate to say that music education functions as culture as much as it functions in relation to culture, then induction into unfamiliar musical cultures offers something few other forms of education can provide. A truly multicultural MUSIC curriculum connects the individual self with the personhood of other musicers and audiences in other times and places. And the effectiveness of music in this regard resides in its essential nature as praxis: as thinking-in-action. A MUSIC curriculum centered on the praxial teaching and learning of a reasonable range of music cultures (over a span of months and years) offers students the opportunity to achieve a central goal of humanistic education: self-understanding through "other-understanding."[56]

It is interesting to note that Elliott does not see the cultural gap that Reimer identifies as an obstacle for active engagement with world music, but equally interesting is that his aim seems to be humanistic rather than musical praxis. As Volk points out, Elliott's early analyses of concepts of multicultural music education appear to be based on Pratte. Elliott favours "dynamic multicultural- ism," in which "musical concepts original to the culture replace a strictly Western aesthetic perspective."[57] This addresses one of the challenges Reimer leaves unan- swered but does not fully take into account the dynamics of contemporary culturally diverse societies, in which the musical concepts original to individual cultures are increasingly difficult to identify or have even become irrelevant. It remains one step short of transcultural.

While Reimer seems to take the hegemony of Western classical music as a starting point, Elliott challenges the core of the organization of Western music education, claiming that it creates a modernist learning environment in a postmodern reality. Elliott criticizes Western education as "based on modernity's scientific-industrial concepts, including standardized curricula, standardized achievement tests, teacher-centred methods, restricted instructional time, and age segregated and ability segregated classes."[58] This calls to mind the work of Bourdieu, with his stern criticism of a culture that creates inequity, supported by "an educational system offering (very unequally) the possibility of learning by institutionalised stages in accordance with standardized levels and syllabuses."[59] This can indeed create major obstacles for learners from different cultural back- grounds. Many who have seen talented emerging musicians from other cultures fail in Western educational institutions can attest to this.

There can be little doubt that monoculturality, with Western (art) music at its center, still pervades much of the thinking on music and music education in the Western world and most of its practice. In criticizing the treatment of world music in standard reference works on music as side excursions (often with implications of primitiveness), Cook writes:

It is hardly possible to miss the implicit associations in such a scheme of non-Western cultures with beginnings and of Western culture with progress. That such thinking was commonplace at the turn of the twentieth century, the time when the sun never set on the British Empire, is only to be expected. That it is still to be encountered at the turn of the twenty-first is astounding, for it offers an entirely inadequate basis for understanding music in today's pluralistic society. It is hard to think of another field in which quite such uncritically ethnocentric and elitist conceptions have held such sway until so recently.[60]

What Cook says here of books on music may well hold true for music education as a whole. There appears to be a substantial dichotomy between intention and practice in music education. The reasons for this may well lie deeper than terminology or policies. The drastic changes needed to accommodate the realities of cultural diversity require a reappraisal of implicit values and belief systems, as well as different approaches to the formal organization of music education.

Ethnomusicology

An obvious source of inspiration for reexamining constructs in music education is ethnomusicology, which, since its beginning—at least one of its beginnings—as comparative musicology in the 1880s, has shifted from a primary interest in product to a focus on process, from hard facts about music (instruments, structures, scales, and rhythms) to examining music in its cultural contexts (place in society, role of musicians, and later musical change). Important contributions to thinking on teaching world music have been made by a number of key players in ethnomusicology who have taken keen interest in music education, including John Blacking, Ki Mantle Hood, Bruno Nettl, Timothy Rice, Charles and Anthony Seeger, Jonathan Stock, Ramon Santos, Ricardo Trimillos, and Deborah Wong, to name but a few.

It can be argued that Hood first advocated hands-on learning as research when he introduced playing gamelan into the training of ethnomusicologists.[61] Merriam brought greater awareness of cultural context by making the case for an anthropology of music.[62] Blacking challenged Western preconceptions about making and learning music by comparing his experiences to those of the Venda in South Africa.[63] However, the shifts in ethnomusicology as a discipline from the 1980s probably paved the way for these views to be embraced more widely. Nettl's statement that "a musical system, its style, its main characteristics, its structure, are all very closely related with the particular way in which it is taught, as a whole and in its individual components,"[64] can easily be read as an invitation to look at these in reverse order as well: investigating or experiencing transmission

in order to understand systems and structures. Many who have immersed themselves in either short or prolonged learning processes have found this to be
eminently fruitful.

In the early 1990s, Nettl, who chronicled ethnomusicology throughout much
of the second half of the twentieth century, signaled transmission as a strongly
emerging focus within the discipline: "one way ethnomusicology has changed since
the 1950s involves the vastly increased importance of learning and teaching."[65]
However, the evidence of this was still very much in the process of emerging. The
487-page handbook *Ethnomusicology: An Introduction* from which this quote is
taken devotes a little more than one page to learning and teaching. It does identify
learning music as a key strategy for ethnomusicological fieldwork, although
this immersion may go well beyond the implications of superficiality in the
ethnomusicological adage that "learning to sing, dance, play in the field is good
fun and good method."[66]

The joys and complications of engaging with hands-on music making in
ethnomusicology have been explored much more profoundly in the more recent
volume *Performing Ethnomusicology*.[67] In the context of "ethnomusicology ensembles" at U.S. universities, Trimillos mentions a host of concerns that resonate
throughout this book, which are all relevant to the discussions on music education
at other levels as well: the institutional environment, the multiple role of the
teacher, pedagogical approaches, cultural context, teacher identity, archetypes
of instruction, and various perceptions of authenticity, including staged authenticity and idealized representation.[68]

In a 2002 overview of ethnomusicological work on music transmission in
The New Handbook of Research in Music Teaching and Learning, Szego asserts:

> the ethnographic study of music transmission and learning in ethnomu-
> sicology predates that of music education. Still, ethnomusicologists and
> folklorists have spent relatively little time studying these processes or
> the ways they are shaped by culture. Because of the holistic nature of
> ethnography, ethnomusicological accounts do frequently contain refer-
> ence to music transmission and learning; but these references, embedded
> in larger discussions of socio-musicological phenomena, often are very
> brief or very general.[69]

This is corroborated by Rice, who finds

> few ethnomusicologists have examined the process of learning music in
> the many aural traditions they study. Though they routinely point out
> that children in many traditions learn by imitation, often without the aid
> of lessons and through a process of trial and error, there are only a few
> studies that document the learning process in any detail.[70]

In a 2003 article, Rice identifies only four narrative contexts in which learning and teaching tend to be emphasized:

> (1) when it is the central theoretical point of the work; (2) when it is one of many topics in the survey of a music culture; (3) when authors report reflexively on their own attempts to learn to sing, play or dance; and (4) when biographies of individuals figure prominently in the narrative.[71]

Szego[72] qualifies this (and his own) perception somewhat by mentioning a few significant contributions, such as Booth, who compared the Indian rhythmic system of qaidas to the Western pianistic tradition,[73] and, in an earlier article, Trimillos, who examined the relative importance of musical and extramusical properties in ancient Hawaiian chant, South Indian drumming, Philippine vocal, and Japanese court music.[74] In fact, the list now expands into the dozens, including in-depth monographs such as Neuman on Indian music,[75] Berliner on Zimbabwean mbira,[76] Hopkins on Norwegian hardingfele,[77] Rice on Bulgarian instrumental music,[78] Brinner on Javanese gamelan,[79] McCarthy on Irish music,[80] Wong on Thai Buddhist music,[81] Dunbar-Hall on Balinese music,[82] and Howard on Korean music.[83] Proceedings and journals from organizations such as SEM and ICTM (ethnomusicology) and ISME and MENC (music education), as well as a number of dedicated publications, such as those that have emanated from the Cultural Diversity in Music Education network,[84] have added to the body of literature on learning and teaching world music.

While it can still be argued that the ethnomusicological literature on transmission remains a relatively modest body of works among the multitude of pages devoted to organology, musical structure, history, performance practice, and music in culture, publications during the past decade do suggest a growing and more focused interest in this topic. It is striking, however, that the observations on practices of learning and teaching are often quite impressionistic. There is little structure in the wide array of reflections on topics such as master-disciple relationships, technical aspects, aurality, and aspects of tradition and change. The bridges are being built, however. While perhaps taking little note of some excellent work done in this field by music educators, an increasing number of ethnomusicologists seem more seriously interested in what is now usually referred to as "transmission" in that discipline. And from the other side, a number of senior voices in music education have worked with ideas from ethnomusicology, such as Campbell, Dunbar-Hall, Floyd, Marsh, and Volk.

The voices of these ethnomusicologists and music educators will return frequently in the discussions that follow.

Conclusion

The field of cultural diversity in music education is challenging in its ambiguous terminology, but there are some tools that are helpful in creating pathways to shared understanding. Examining the variety in terminology can make explicit some of the underlying value systems, in many cases revealing preconceptions and prejudice. At present, the term *world music* (and, incidentally, its plural, *world musics*) is perhaps the least objectionable term to refer collectively to music from various cultures, with an emphasis on the fact that music travels and establishes itself away from its place and culture of origin. When observing societies and their approaches to cultural diversity in music education, the terms *monoculturalism, multiculturalism, interculturalism,* and *transculturalism* are useful instruments to indicate positions on a continuum with increasing room and tolerance for other cultures.

Both music education and ethnomusicology engage increasingly with how music is learned and taught across cultures and settings. Although we can trace serious interest in these processes back for more than forty years, it is still a relatively young area of study, with perhaps too modest a presence in academic discourse (in ethnomusicology) and in music education in schools. For the latter, the flow from advanced philosophical and policy frameworks into the practical realms of teacher training and finally into the classroom may be the greatest challenge.[85] This will undoubtedly take time, given the complexity of the subject matter and the dynamics of most processes of change in institutional environments: by the very nature of its organization and training, the translation of educational thought into widespread practice tends to have a delay of several decades, especially when the situation is complex and the stakes are high.

CHAPTER 3

The Myth of Authentic
Traditions in Context

A Deconstruction

In 1993, I visited British world-music educator and scholar Trevor Wiggins in Accra, after he had been conducting some fieldwork into the balaphone music of North Ghana. While we were discussing the nature and state of traditional music in the region, the told me about his interaction with one of his consultants. After recording this musician, Wiggins asked whether the song he had just heard performed was traditional. The answer was an unequivocal yes. This greatly excited the ethnomusicologist in Wiggins, and he proceeded to ask whether the musician was perhaps aware of the creator of this particular song or an approximate period of creation. Without batting an eyelid, the musician disclosed truthfully that he had composed it himself, just a few days earlier.

Tradition and the related concepts of authenticity and context have been sources of both inspiration and confusion for discussions on cultural diversity in music education and for how world music is being presented across educational settings. It has been an inspiration in nurturing awareness of ancient roots, complex systems of musical values, and intricate relationships of various musics with their environment. It has caused confusion by the sheer ambiguity of the concepts involved and by the (often self-imposed) impossible demands of attempting to realize "authentic traditions in context" within educational settings. For music educators, the challenge is to develop an understanding that is sensitive to culturally diverse realities but workable within specific educational environments. This requires a close examination of the various meanings and applications of tradition, authenticity, and context.

PHOTO 3.I.   Starting young at learning to play the balaphone in
Ghana. Accra, May 1995. Photo: Huib Schippers.

Tradition

In much writing about music, *tradition* is defined fairly statically and mostly in
terms of aural transmission: "The act of handing down . . . from one to another, or
from generation to generation . . . esp. by word of mouth or by practice without
writing."[1] The sociologist Hobsbawm distinguishes custom from tradition. He
argues that the former "in traditional societies has the double function of motor
and fly-wheel"; it does allow innovation and change up to a point, although this is
limited because "it must appear compatible or even identical with precedent," to

give desired change the "sanction of precedent." About tradition, however, he states that its "object and characteristic...is invariance," which represents an unequivocally static interpretation of the concept.[2]

In contrast, in his dictionary of philosophy, Willemsen includes in the concept of tradition "everything that has been man-made and—from one generation to the next—has been passed from the past to the present, irrespective of its reception being appreciated or not. In this interpretation, tradition is an essentially dynamic reality." He also refers to a "more trivial" meaning of tradition as "the stagnation of morals, customs or habits, to which people resort who do not wish to accept progress." He dismisses this widespread meaning of the word as "inauthentic."[3]

This tension between static and dynamic perceptions of tradition merits further investigation. It is eminently relevant to music education, which for the past three decades has oscillated between emphasis on perpetuating a body of masterpieces on the one hand and nurturing creative musicianship on the other. Cook considers the *canon* a major obstacle for looking at music from a wider perspective. He argues that from the time of Beethoven, the "musical museum" came into existence, which, in the case of Western art music, "provided the conceptual framework within which music took its place in the cultural heritage,"[4] the repertory or canon:

> The term "classical music" came into common currency. Borrowed from the "classical" art of Greece and Rome, which was seen as the expression of universal standards of beauty, this term implied that similar standards had now been set in music, against which the production of all other times and places must be measured.[5]

Similar static canons exist in a number of musics across Asia, such as the gagaku repertoire of Japan, a court music that has been officially regulated by a government bureau since the early eighth century.[6] Other traditions are also deeply rooted but are more fluid, such as maqam from Iraq, dastgah from Iran, or raga from India. In the sense of model and standard, the latter is not dissimilar to the Western tradition. While it is not written down, it nevertheless consists of a strict and complex set of rules governing the reproduction, restructuring, and generation of melodic and rhythmic patterns. A rāga can be seen as an abstract "Gestalt" or "idea," which is translated into audible sound every time it is played. While none has succeeded in defining the exact rules for any rāga in detail, most senior musicians will largely agree on what is acceptable in each rāga.[7] Widely respected recordings of particular rāgas by celebrated musicians exist, but these would never be considered the central body of works, and writing them out would be seen as futile. There is a clearly identifiable "classical" tradition in North India, but it is defined in quite different terms from Western classical music.

The traditions of Iraqi, Iranian, and Indian classical music are perhaps best understood as a set of rules governing musical practice. In some ways, this compares well to Western classical music up to the end of the nineteenth century. Morgan speaks of "an essence, dictated by a transcendent power and preserved by an equally transcendent tradition." But he continues:

> Within the dynamic context of Western cultural history, this preservation has had to be tempered by some latitude for change, at times quite extensive. Yet these changes have tended to be defended either as superficial adjustments, beneath which the essential principles persisted, or as necessary corrections of previous digressions that had diverted music from its true course, distorting its essential nature.[8]

This is much like an Indian perspective, where even radical change tends to be presented as a logical continuation of ancient wisdom. Up to the beginning of the twentieth century, it was possible in the West to maintain this canonic "belief in a communal musical language, prevailing underneath a wealth of superficial, time-bound stylistic transformations."[9] However, it is naive to assume that such rules will ever represent the full picture. As Brinner states, working primarily from the perspective of Javanese gamelan: "It has not been demonstrated that the complexities of an entire musical system can be successfully encompassed in a rigorous set of rules."[10]

The deconstruction of the canon in Western music opened the way to traditions that were more performance-oriented than text-based,[11] as in works by Cage. From a global perspective, this shift created room to accommodate aural traditions from other cultures, which were often defined more by performance than by preexisting repertoire or rigid rules. Many of these have an explicit or implicit theory at their base, but the exact organization of tones is not predetermined. In that way, each individual performance becomes the moment of truth: it is then and only then that expressions of traditional concepts or new ideas are accepted or rejected by listeners on the basis of a wide set of criteria. These can range from practical matters, such as inspiring people to dance, to considerations of whether it fits in a specific tradition[12] and even metaphysical factors, such as effectiveness in bringing forth trance or calling up spirits of forefathers.[13]

Tradition approached as "music in culture" (or even "music as culture") has come to favor in Western thinking about music traditions beyond Western classical music, pop, and jazz, particularly since Merriam argued that "there is little validity for treating it as though it were divorced from social and cultural considerations, for . . . music is inevitably produced by humans for other humans within a social and a cultural context."[14] There is much to be said for this view; music is often an inextricable part of a larger event, whether it is a wedding in an

American church or a circumcision ceremony in Guinea. However, considering context as a static phenomenon may lead to musical misunderstanding as well as dubious educational principles, as will be discussed in the section on context later in this chapter.

The idea of tradition as a mechanism addresses one of the crucial concepts causing confusion, particularly with reference to cultures other than our own. Many scholars have been predominantly interested in traditions as relatively static phenomena in the sense of Hobsbawm (and of Willemsen's "inauthentic" meaning), handed down with little change.[15] However, traditions that keep changing with the demands of the times, in an organic way, or in a conscious effort to retain relevance to their audiences are probably rule rather than exception.

The mechanism underlying this process, which may be made up of the judgment of communities (of insiders and/or outsiders), systems of transmission, available technology and infrastructure, and a number of other musical and extramusical factors,[16] accounts for the occurrence of what is generally referred to as "living traditions." Change within certain boundaries not only is allowed but is also in fact part of the essence of these traditions: "the nature of tradition—musical in this case—is not to preserve intact a heritage from the past, but to enrich it according to present circumstances and transmit the result to future generations."[17]

Many traditions have tendencies to attribute or suggest more ancient beginnings to pieces of music, performance styles, instruments, or lineages than can be justified. Observing these suggestions of antiquity that cannot be supported historically, Hobsbawm speaks of "invented traditions," defining them as "a set of practices, normally governed by overtly or tacitly accepted rules and of a ritual or symbolic nature, which seek to inculcate certain values and norms of behaviour by repetition, which automatically implies continuity with the past."[18] In Western classical music, the nineteenth-century dress code that performers tend to follow when playing Bach or Mozart is a good example: it suggests a time-honored practice, which in fact did not exist at the time of either of these great composers.[19] In the same manner, most Indian musicians will attribute the origins of the sitar to the thirteenth-century courtier-historian-poet-musician Amir Khusrau, rather than the much less conspicuous but more likely eighteenth-century inventor of the instrument, Khusrau Khan.[20] Ancient beginnings often lend prestige in music traditions.

This overview suggests five distinct approaches to tradition, with varying degrees of dynamism: tradition as a canon or body of works, a standard with an explicit or implicit set of rules, a performance practice, music in culture, and a mechanism of handing down music. It is possible to identify a number of indicators for predominantly static or predominantly dynamic approaches to tradition.

static tradition ←————————————————————————→ constant flux

FIGURE 3.1.   Approaches to tradition as a continuum

The predominantly static approach would be characterized by a body of work that has been in existence for a considerable amount of time, with no new additions, in a closed system, where the tradition is a sign of distinction for an established class, whether social or religious, with sometimes less emphasis on artistic value than on function in society (as in much ritual music). The dynamic approach would typically show music styles deriving their existence from a continuous process of change and innovation, with the music being continually exposed to new influences. As any examination of different music traditions will illustrate, virtually no music tradition would qualify as *all* static or *all* flexible. A continuum from static tradition to tradition in "constant flux" is more appropriate to represent the diversity and nuances of contemporary musical realities (see figure 3.1).

Tradition and Music Education

Methods of transmission should be anything but an afterthought in the study of music traditions across the globe; they are crucial elements in their survival. Especially in the case of unwritten traditions, this is where the music of the recent past is handed on and preserved. This is mostly achieved through well-developed protocols and processes, including a formalized relationship with a senior bearer of the tradition, a long apprenticeship, and mechanisms such as rote learning, imitation, and modeling.

But the process involves more than the music material itself. In both written and unwritten traditions, a complex combination of thoughts and approaches to music are handed down from teacher to student. In forms of music that do not have a written tradition to refer to, teachers often express a conservative approach to the music they are handing down. Almost without exception, they will praise the past and express concern about the future, criticizing young musicians for a lack of knowledge or respect for the tradition. In India, there are reports of old masters literally climbing onto the stage mid-concert to give an erring young musician a public thrashing with their walking sticks.

This perception of decline seems to exist in all times and may well be a characteristic of traditions. Bor traces references to the perceived decay of North Indian classical music from the late eighteenth through the twentieth century: Indian music has declined "since the Mohammedan conquest" (1792); "most native performers of this noble science are the most immoral set of men on earth" (1834); "the art had fallen from favour and only the commonplace aspects were in vogue" (1850s); and "the science and art of music have fallen into a decadent condition" (1916).[21]

If such views were correct, most aural traditions would have been deteriorating for centuries, which is unlikely given the artistic level of contemporary performers of Indian rāgas, Balinese gamelan, and mbira music from Zimbabwe. It is more likely that old masters regret next generations abandoning some aspects they held dear, while perhaps not fully appreciating new ideas and techniques developed by the next generation. However, conservatism forms an important mechanism that is in the interest of living tradition: it stops or slows down random or "faddish" change, which may increase the risk of throwing out the baby with the bathwater.[22]

When examining music education in the classroom, it is possible to distinguish between various approaches to tradition. There is a strong tendency to present world music traditions as frozen in time. Bohlman traces this back to the nineteenth- and early twentieth-century conception that the Western world is modern and dynamic and that other cultures stagnated in their development at various stages, from the "primitive" cultures of Africa and Oceania to the (relatively) "high cultures" of Asia and the world of Islam.[23] Approaches emphasizing the dynamics of music across the world require more diverse musical examples, complex insights, and innovative methodologies. There is an emerging body of literature recognizing these dynamics, but it would be optimistic to say that this awareness has pervaded classroom practices across the world. Much remains to be done.

Authenticity

Authenticity is another concept frequently discussed in the context of culturally diverse music education, particularly in writings emanating from the United States. Mautner's *A Dictionary of Philosophy* defines *authenticity* as "the quality of being genuine, being true to oneself," and traces its use from Socrates, who referred to the "authenticity of the self" as the genuineness of thought and actions, on to Saint Augustine, who emphasized the spiritual nature of the true self as opposed to the inauthentic demands of desire and the body. Next, Rousseau contrasted the true, authentic, natural self with the corruption imposed by society, while Kierkegaard insisted similarly that the authentic self was the personally chosen self, as opposed to one's public or herd identity.[24]

In music, "authentic" has been strongly associated with "historically correct" from the early-music revival movement that emerged in the 1950s and 1960s and with "in original context" by ethnomusicologists, especially from the mid-1960s to the mid-1980s. However, it is difficult to maintain that any art form exists merely to be reproduced in a historically correct manner or in original context. Others argue that the key to authenticity lies in creativity, aesthetics, spirituality, or emotional effect. The discussion revolves around whether the essence lies in the notes, the instruments used, the setting, the context, the sound, the attitude or frame of mind of musicians or audience, or other intangible aspects of the total musical experience.

What should be considered an authentic performance of a work by Mozart is less obvious than it seems. Is it one where the performer follows the improvised cadenzas in a piano concerto as written by the composer (or a later one) or where the performer follows the tradition of improvising that particular section? In this and almost all considerations of authenticity, the reference (e.g., the written work, the performance practice) and the criteria (e.g., historical accuracy, aesthetic effect) have to be defined and prioritized, as they may conflict. Cook emphasizes the challenges of arriving at "authentic" scores even for established classical composers, commenting on the phenomenon of authentic performance, now usually referred to with the less pretentious epithet "historically informed":

> As a slogan, "authenticity" neatly combined two things. On the one hand, the claim was that performance on the appropriate period instruments, based on the performance practices codified, was "authentic" in the sense of historically correct. On the other, the term "authenticity" brought into play all those positive connotations I talked about [in an earlier chapter], the idea of being sincere, genuine, true to yourself. In this way, if you played Bach on the piano—if your performance wasn't authentic—then you weren't simply wrong in the scholarly sense: you were wrong in the moral sense too.[25]

Grove Music Online provides a more accommodating and perhaps more satisfying description of historically informed performance, touching on many of the areas discussed before:

> "Authentic" performance may refer to one or any combination of the following approaches: use of instruments from the composer's own era; use of performing techniques documented in the composer's era; performance based on the implications of the original sources for a particular work; fidelity to the composer's intentions for performance or to the type of performance a composer desired or achieved; an attempt to re-create the context of the original performance; and an attempt to re-create the musical experience of the original audience.[26]

In approaches to world music with a focus on tradition, "authentic" is often used to refer to "coming from the right country," being "unaffected by outside influences," and "exactly as it is in the original social context," in addition to "historically correct." In the "authentic" world music movement, this has sometimes led to shunning new developments, particularly those that attract large audiences in their culture of origin ("If it's popular it can't be authentic"), and "bastardizations" that involve modern instruments and amplification. This approach is difficult to maintain in the modern realities of performance and education, as it bypasses considerations of power of expression and ability to communicate to audiences, including young learners.

Senior musicians in almost any tradition have clear thoughts about what constitutes the core of their music, ranging from tangible elements such as instruments, ensembles, and repertoire to more intangible aspects. In that context, concepts such as rasa (India), duende (Andalusia), saudade (Brazil), and tarab (world of Islam) come to the fore, all used to indicate "the real feeling" or "essence" of specific musical styles and genres. Consequently, this is an area of crucial importance in defining authenticity from the perspective of culture bearers or opinion leaders in specific traditions, who constitute an invaluable source for music educators.

In his study on "global pop," Taylor approaches the subject as follows:

> I have already touched upon the authenticity with which most regular listeners to music are familiar: authenticity as historical accuracy (in "art" music) or cultural/ethnographic authenticity in world musics. Increasingly, there is confusion over these authenticities and an authenticity that refers to a person's positionality as racialized, ethnicized, and premodern.[27]

Taylor distinguishes a third authenticity as "a sincerity or fidelity to a true self."[28] This definition echoes the philosophical approaches and appears to work well in the context of popular music. It is supported by the entry under "authenticity" in the digital version of the *Encyclopaedia Britannica*: "The defining term in rock ideology is authenticity. Rock is distinguished from pop as the authentic expression of a performer's or composer's feelings and the authentic representation of a social situation. Rock is at once the mainstream of commercial music and a romantic art form, a voice from the social margins."

Cook also contrasts the alleged inauthenticity of pop stars with the authenticity of rock musicians:

> Expressed a bit crudely (but then it *is* a bit crude), the thinking goes like this. Rock musicians perform live, create their own music, and forge their own identities; in short they control their own destinies. Pop musicians, by contrast, are the puppets of the music business, cynically or naively pandering to popular tastes, and performing music composed by others; they lack authenticity, and as such they come at the bottom of the hierarchy of musicianship.[29]

Although the dichotomy that Cook creates is more likely to survive scrutiny when presented as extremes of a continuum ranging from purely commercial/inauthentic in intent to pure expression of the self/authentic, he does create a clear and useful framework for considering authenticity in popular music.

In relation to world pop, the debate gains another dimension. Taylor points out the confusion and ethnocentricity that surround the concept of authenticity in pop and rock music: while Western pop and rock musicians are appreciated for breaking cultural barriers, non-Western pop stars are often condemned for not being "authentic." He introduces "strategic inauthenticity," a quality that he ascribes to strong, independent world musicians such as Youssou N'Dour and Cheb Khaled, who refuse to be pigeonholed and choose to move freely between their musical heritage and new influences.[30] Taylor designates the concern with being true to one's tradition (in the sense of music fixed in culture) as premodern, while he calls the more eclectic approach an expression of postmodernism.[31] This provides an intelligent and realistic perspective, in which pop music provides a refreshing new basis for thinking on authenticity.

These reflections reveal five ways of looking at authenticity: following ancient scores or the canon; using period instruments and ensembles; re-creating the original setting or context; obedience to rules and the approach to playing defined by the tradition; or aiming at sincerity of expression, meaning, the essence of a musical style.

Authenticity and Music Education

Issues of authenticity play a major role in two arenas of learning and teaching world music: the demand for "pure tradition" in instrument-specific teaching and the much-expressed desire for authenticity in the area of music in schools. The latter, as Johnson points out, often focuses on hierarchical, static interpretations of authenticity, rather than fluidity.[32] In her eminently sensible book *Music in the School*, Mills warns against such approaches and argues that "no music stands still in time, even without the involvement of schools. It would be unauthentic to view any music as a museum piece and to try to perform it only as it is thought to have been performed 'originally'."[33]

In instrument-specific teaching, the quest for authenticity is probably fueled by the values and attitudes of some of the world musicians involved in such settings. Being physically removed from the center of a living tradition and its organic processes of change, both the teachers and the students tend to be conservative. I have noticed that even accomplished masters often "freeze the tradition in time" when abroad; their aesthetic frame of reference seems to remain at the time of their departure.

This is often reinforced by Western students: coming from outside the culture, they also seem to be more interested in what is "ancient and original" in the culture they are learning. Consequently, developments in a tradition that have taken place after a teacher left his or her country are often discarded as superficial, newfangled fads. Students may develop an approach to music that is a full generation behind the country of origin. Being aware and part of this process myself, I occasionally catch myself snubbing the way 50-year-old sitar players living and working in India "cheapen" the tradition, having inherited my musical sensibilities from masters who are now more than 80 years old and have been abroad for 35 to 45 years. In expatriate "living traditions," strong tendencies can emerge toward historical authenticity, going back to the last extensive contact with the culture of origin.

In music education in the classroom, two approaches to authenticity are common. One is to take songs or instrumental pieces from staff notation and interpret them as if they were Western music. The apparent reasoning behind this is simple: if the transcription is correct, the notes are authentic, and, consequently, so is the music. In fact, this suggests aspects of "universality" in music: once notated, we are dealing with music that can be interpreted by anyone. In practice, however, subtleties may be taken away from the music, and if nothing is substituted, there is a risk of having traditions stripped bare. All aspects of the music that cannot be written down may be ignored or replaced by Western interpretations. The music may well lose the other important aspect of authenticity: power of expression. Teachers increasingly use authoritative recordings with the purpose of at least approximating authenticity of sound. Another approach is to achieve authenticity by re-creating as much context as possible. Here, the choice of *relevant* context is of crucial importance in order to support a viable claim for "authentic" world-music education. This will be discussed in detail in the following section.

Lundquist cites a number of divergent views on authenticity: Pembrook asserts that "using authentic instruments may be the most effective way of introducing music from another culture," while Campbell endorses the capability of representatives of a culture ("culture bearers") to determine what is authentic musical and cultural representation. Lundquist proceeds to Klinger's more complex and realistic position that "two individuals from the same ethnic group may interpret the same piece of music quite differently," and "multiple 'authenticities,' equally legitimate, yet different from each other, can and do exist." The key challenge is perhaps best stated by Santos, who argues that "while authenticity is indeed a legitimate concern in the context of preserving tradition, its very concept is founded on the idea of cultural stasis, a belief that has been refuted by modern scholarship and the very dynamic nature of living traditions." Lundquist's summary is short and to the point: "Authenticity is a complicated issue."[34] The desire for a static and clearly defined authenticity simply does not correspond to the musical realities, in which various approaches to authenticity overlap and interact.

In research on the subject across music education and ethnomusicology, Campbell found that "interestingly, authenticity was deemed by some of the ethnomusicologists interviewed as having minimal importance." She heard Yung explain: "I almost never use 'authentic' to discuss the music of China, because it implies absolute values" that are nonexistent within so historically long and varied a nation. This leads Campbell to wonder, "Where is one to draw the cut-off line between the authentic and pure music and the music that has been borrowed, adapted, and accepted as their own by the people of a designated culture?"[35]

Meanwhile, some educators continue to argue that authenticity can best be defined narrowly. Campbell reports Loza as saying, "Once you take the music out of its cultural context, it's no longer authentic."[36] An interesting example of an effort to emulate this type of authenticity is the project "Culture Bearers in the Classroom," which was carried out by a number of schools in the Seattle area along with the University of Washington. In this project, rather than using approaches deemed less opportune, such as singing songs from transcriptions, experimenting on indigenous instruments, or merely listening to music, people who could be considered carriers of the tradition were asked to work with children in primary schools.[37] Although this does resolve the limitations of some other approaches, it does not address the problem raised by Klinger relating to multiple authenticities. Its main vulnerability, however, probably lies in pedagogical challenges that many culture bearers face when they have little or no training or experience in working with children in American, Australian, or European schools. "Authentic" or not, there is no learning when there is a failure to connect.

An unorthodox approach may sometimes be more successful. I have already described a Canadian music teacher at the International School in Kuala Lumpur successfully teaching an indigenous Sumatran drumming tradition to a mixed student population, using an eclectic mix of drums from six different cultures: a Chinese drum, an African djembe, cumbia drums from Colombia, Malaysian kompang frame drums, bongos, and the tom-tom of the trap drum. I have also seen Turkish darbuka players convincingly teaching their art to children beating the back of plastic buckets in a classroom. In the light of the preceding discussion, we can argue that these experiences can be authentic in the true-to-self sense. The focus was on creating a vibrant musical experience for the children rather than on replicating a musical practice in another culture.

In a way, the task of the educator is one of making choices of "strategic inauthenticity," where the relationship between the original and the new reality in each of the areas we have mentioned can be represented by two circles (as in figure 3.2) that may overlap (I) completely (the educational experience is identical

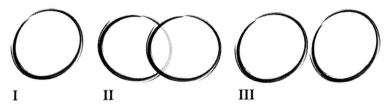

I   II   III

FIGURE 3.2.   Relationship between original musical event and new reality

'reconstructed' ←——————————————————————→ 'new identity'
authenticity   authenticity

FIGURE 3.3.   Approaches to authenticity as a continuum

to the source or model—which is rare), (II) partly (certain aspects correspond to
the source or model—which is most common), or (III) not at all (the new
experience has a completely new identity—which defeats the purpose of most
world-music programs). This overlap can be viewed from each perspective of
authenticity discussed above: following scores, instruments, ensembles, setting or
context, rules and approach to playing, or sincerity of expression.

To sum up, in both music performance and music education, authenticity
is an elusive and particularly laden concept. Because of its implied sense
of "goodness," the discussion often becomes muddled. While some schools of
interpretation refer to authenticity as corresponding to original models in historical or geographical terms, it is not necessarily clear which aspects of the music need
to be "correct" in order to be deemed authentic. The discourse on pop and rock
music adds to the confusion by introducing the notion of being true to oneself,
irrespective of models or traditions. In world music, we encounter a variety of
interpretations. With the change of musical tastes of second- and third-generation
minorities, eclectic musical mixes, and new musical realities, it is increasingly
difficult to establish what a culture as a whole considers authentic, so authenticity
in the narrow sense is becoming an unsustainable position.

Authenticity undermines its own significance by how it is used in diverse and
even contradictory senses. While the early music practice aimed at faithful reproduction of historical originals, rock musicians (as opposed to commercial pop
musicians) emphatically do not want to *copy* an original but aim to *be* original.
Paradoxically, the aim of both approaches is to create the most "truthful" musical
experience possible. A nonstatic approach to all of the factors discussed and their
interaction is needed for fully understanding music education in culturally diverse
settings. As in the case of tradition, the various approaches to authenticity can
be represented as a continuum, ranging from interpretations tending toward
reproduction to emphasis on originality (see figure 3.3).

Context

While tradition and authenticity are contentious issues in music education, context
is perhaps at the core of the debate. Merriam's 1964 *The Anthropology of Music*
inspired ethnomusicologists to regard music primarily as a product of its culture.
This view prevailed into the final decades of the twentieth century and beyond. In a
1980 article, Nettl states that many anthropologists still "favour a definition of

music in and as culture," while at the other end of the continuum, he places musicologically oriented researchers whose primary concern is the structure of the music itself. Nettl lists five characteristics around which the field revolves, including that "music can be understood only in its cultural context."[38]

More than ten years later, the influential handbook *Ethnomusicology: An Introduction* defines the discipline primarily as "the division of musicology in which special emphasis is given to the study of music in its cultural context—the anthropology of music."[39] Ethnomusicological approaches to world music have had a strong impact on music education. The influential 1996 ISME *Policy on Musics of the World's Cultures* (which Nettl co-formulated) states: "Music can best be comprehended in social and cultural context and as a part of its culture. Properly understanding a culture requires some understanding of its music, and appreciating music requires some knowledge of its associated culture and society."

While appreciating the original context of any form of music may indeed result in a deeper understanding, there are numerous examples of music reaching and touching audiences that have little or no knowledge of these contexts, in both "Western" and "world" musics. If ritual music from West African villages appeals to concert audiences in São Paulo and Paris, if Indian court music finds willing ears from Sydney to Stockholm, and if eighteenth-century Lutheran German music is appreciated in twenty-first-century Tokyo and Toronto, ideas concerning the necessity of original cultural context need to be reexamined. It may be naive to say that music is a universal language that transcends all boundaries, but as I have argued before, it would seem that many musics travel remarkably well.

A key concept in understanding the contemporary dynamics of music is "recontextualization," introduced by Nketia in the 1960s. On closer examination, this shifting of contexts is norm rather than exception. Obviously, all performances of Indian classical music in the West are recontextualized. But so are all performances of Indian music in India to a considerable extent, when a middle-class audience of predominantly Hindus in expensive saris and suits go to a concert hall in Calcutta to listen to a singer who sings through a microphone on a stage, not in a music room at a Moghul court. The same can be said for any contemporary concert-hall performance of Monteverdi's *Maria Vespers*, composed for a Catholic church-going audience in 1610. Some would refer to listening to jazz piped into a shopping mall, salsa on an iPod while flying on a plane, or recordings of live rock concerts on DVD in the home theater as "decontextualization," but I would argue that even the most impersonal (or very personalized) setting creates a new context, which influences how the music is experienced.

Recontextualization can be manipulated, for instance, by evoking a context that suggests a desirable setting but does not necessarily correspond to that in the culture of origin. Urban African musicians, for example, are sometimes asked to perform in sets that resemble the imagined charm of African village life: a return to exoticism. Another powerful example of this phenomenon, used as a marketing tool, is the emphasis Ravi Shankar placed on the spiritual context of Indian classical music when he brought it to the West. Shankar chose to downplay the worldly context of this music (which he knew intimately), because he sensed that young Westerners in the late 1960s were more interested in its spiritual qualities. The 1970 film *Rasa* about the life and work of Shankar, with images and sounds of spiritual life dominating the overall picture, illustrates this creation of new context: "invented contexts" as an echo of Hobsbawm's "invented traditions."

In this light, it is difficult to maintain that works of music can ever be seen as either autonomous works of art or expressions of cultures in the strictest sense. Whenever they are heard, they are heard in a new context. Even the most objectively inclined researcher will make choices dictated by context. The decision to focus on establishing pitch changes in time rather than physical impact on the listener, social effect, or the power of music to call forth spirits of the forefathers constitutes far-reaching choices, ones that will have decisive effects on the outcome of the study or experience of music. While Western thinking on music has now outgrown the misconception that Indian rāgas are primitive because they do not use counterpoint and harmony, it is equally inappropriate to state that rap is unsuccessful as music because it does not explore the full range of melodic possibilities in contemporary music. The fact that it appeals to millions of young people across the world is testimony to its success in its specific context.

As one of the first music educators to embrace the dynamic view of context that arises from this discussion, Swanwick argued:

> musical procedures can be absorbed and re-used over centuries of time, between vastly differing cultures and across miles of geographical space; they are not irrevocably buried in local life-styles, even though they may have their birth there. Musical elements—that is to say, the sensory impact of sound materials, expressive characterisation and structural organisation—share a degree of cultural autonomy which enables them to be taken over and reworked into traditions far removed from their origins.[40]

Although this approach may lean too heavily toward claiming that the essence of a music lies in its formal qualities, it does open the road for a less static view of context.

Looking at the issues from a wider perspective, a range of approaches to temporal, acoustic, ideological, and social context emerge at the crossroads of tradition, authenticity, and context. Insistence on trying to re-create particularly the latter as closely as possible in musical events is common, but increasingly so is acceptance of the dynamics of music moving from one time and place to another or even an emphasis on this dynamism. Because of these inevitable dynamics, truly original context is quite rare. However, an insistence on its importance can be

FIGURE 3.4.   Approaches to context

found in various types of music and settings across the world. We can represent the various approaches discussed as another continuum, from original context to complete recontextualization (see figure 3.4).

Context and Music Education

Context in music education has major implications for two key areas of activity: teaching specific traditions and teaching world music (and about world music) in the classroom. The former is a subject that has received surprisingly little attention in the literature; the latter has been much discussed.

Regarding music education in schools, Campbell reports on a "heated debate amongst teachers," with radically opposed views between the experts she interviewed, ranging from "What's the purpose of playing Thai music on specially tuned xylophones if students don't know where Thailand is or what it is?" (Miller) to Yung's experience in learning Western classical music in China and Hong Kong: "No one gave me information of the cultural background or context of the music, but by listening I developed a sense of what was 'good music.'" Yung proceeded to explain that "verbal knowledge about music is less important than the sound itself" and claimed that "an emphasis on the cultural and social background may even block the students' opportunities to develop a closeness with the music,"[41] echoing the views of Swanwick and supporting my earlier argument for a more dynamic approach to issues of context.

When discussing context in relation to specific traditions, it is important to be clear about focus. Is it on the context of the original musical practice or on the context of the transmission process? This creates four possible situations, all of which occur at some time or other: teaching of traditional material in a traditional manner, traditional material being handed down in a new context, nontraditional material being handed down in a traditional manner, and nontraditional material being handed down in a nontraditional manner. The first is most likely to occur in "home contexts" of music traditions, while the second tends to be the reality in formal education; the final two are outside the direct scope of this discussion.

In practice, the situation is often directed by the possibilities and constraints of the new institutional or social environment. Music teachers will generally adapt their styles of teaching and possibly the material they teach to the new context in which they function. Even when a student goes to India and studies with a "genuine Indian guru," he or she will be creating a new context. There, the music has been a practice linked to its local environment and mostly a strong family tradition with well-defined intergenerational codes of behavior.[42] In such and virtually all other contemporary settings for music learning and teaching, static concepts of context are challenged.

Classroom music teachers are generally aware of the concept of context and its importance in teaching world music. Many introductions to world music— particularly for education—begin with a long introduction to the country. Lessons will very often start by indicating the origin of a particular piece of music on a world map: "This sound comes from the little turquoise country next to the big green one." Even among young teachers who have been taught alternatives, this is a persistent practice. This is something that struck me with the teaching practice of a number of the students at Amsterdam Conservatory, who had recently been to the Gambia to experience other forms of learning. When insecure, beginning teachers seem to reach back to learning experiences from their own childhoods (which may in turn reflect those of their teachers' younger years). This leads to a possible fossilization of educational practice that can last for generations.

But how do those who are more adventurous re-create the appropriate context in African percussion lessons when working on rhythms linked to circumcision? It may not be long before teachers run out of boys if they take faithful representation of the original context too seriously. Or, at a more innocent level, does it really help students understand Javanese gamelan if they know that Indonesia consists of 16,400 islands? In the case of Indonesia, it might help to point out the many differences between Balinese and Javanese gamelan that have developed on two separate islands, with different religions and customs. Similarly, it may help in appreciating Cuban music when the Caribbean is depicted as an area with strong (and dubious) historical links to both Europe and Africa. That type of information can add a layer of understanding in approaching many musical styles. But it is important to remember that not all context is relevant and that random context does not make for a more interesting or convincing music lesson.

From this discussion, five principal approaches to recontextualization emerge:

1. Trying to re-create the original context.
2. Explaining the original context in detail.
3. Using aesthetic references of the learners as a point of entry into any given music.
4. Using musical structure as a point of entry into any given music.
5. Using the actual musical practice as a point of entry into any given music.

The last three correspond closely to the views advocated by Reimer, Swanwick, and Elliott discussed in chapter 2.[43]

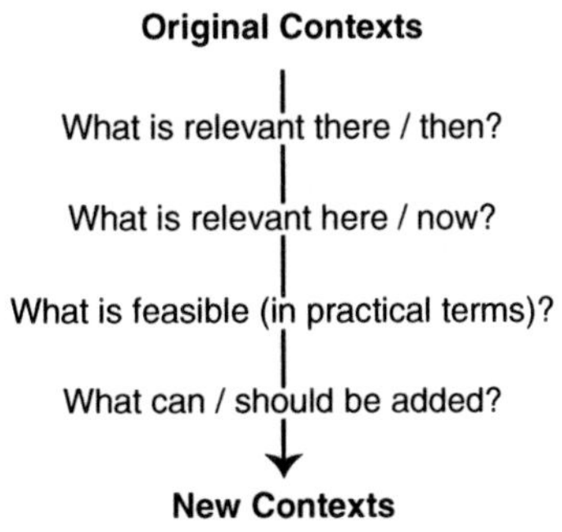

Original Contexts

|

What is relevant there / then?

|

What is relevant here / now?

|

What is feasible (in practical terms)?

|

What can / should be added?

↓

New Contexts

FIGURE 3.5.   Recontextualizing music in education: a dynamic approach

There is no stock answer to the question of what and how much context should be included in teaching world music. Decisions can only be based on intelligently weighing the various arguments for each specific situation and the educational goals. In music education, not only for world music but also for Western music from eras and locations removed from contemporary experience,[44] a five-step procedure can make educators aware of the main points to consider when dealing with recontextualization (see figure 3.5).

This "commonsense view" of context has not pervaded everyday practice yet. Across the music education literature of the past two decades, concerns are expressed about teaching world musics outside their original context, including these in music curricula. For many experienced world musicians and music teachers, however, this is merely a reminder to be aware of choices: there is always a new context.

In her excellent historical survey on approaches to cultural diversity in music education, Volk voices a number of shared concerns relating to tradition, authenticity, and context:

> Although many agree that teaching from a multicultural perspective can enable students to more clearly understand other people through their music, there is the concern that an inauthentic presentation of that music could confirm stereotypical ideas about these people. Indeed the entire issue of authenticity comes into question when considering that the very act of transferring music out of its cultural context and into the classroom destroys its authenticity. Proponents acknowledge this problem and say the simplest ways around it are to use recordings of authentic musics and to invite community culture bearers into the classroom to present their music firsthand.[45]

Although this seems to make excellent sense at first reading, it raises a number of questions. First, it seems to suggest that the purpose of dealing with world music is justified by the extramusical purpose of "understanding other people." Next, it mentions inauthentic presentations as confirming stereotypes. Although it is easy to call to mind situations where this happens (I remember in horror a school project in 1993 in which our efforts had been to focus on the sheer musical experience of African drumming class, while the teacher had added her own choice of context by presenting the children in reed skirts with broom spears, pretending to be cooking a missionary in a large pot onstage), an ill-chosen "authentic" performance is at least as likely to confirm stereotypes.

It is interesting to place Volk's words in the context of Slobin's perceptions on music in the "global flow":

> world music looks like a fluid, interlocking set of styles, repertoires, and practices, that can expand or contract across wide or narrow stretches of the landscape. It no longer appears to be a catalogue of bounded entities of single, solid historical and geographical origins, and the dynamics of visibility are just as shifting as the play of the—scapes [as defined by Appadurai (1996)]. To flesh out the scope of visibility in music-cultural flow, it might just be possible to identify a few common processes. Shifts of profile are very common nowadays; some are self-generated, others just happen. A music can suddenly move beyond all its natural boundaries and take on a new existence, as if it has fallen into the fourth dimension.[46]

Almost all music is transmitted out of context. Our entire formal education system—for music and all other subjects—is a major exercise in recontextualization. With more than thirty years of experience in world music, I could not say what exactly constitutes "recordings of authentic musics" or their application in music education. If they are ethnographic recordings of "pure" traditions, they would be quite likely to meet with little interest from children (in the West and in the countries themselves), who will find it very difficult to link a recording of such "strange" music to their musical awareness. Community culture bearers represent a more fruitful avenue, but there, the risks of music that is considered poor quality by the standards of that culture (which children also do tend to distinguish from good music) and awkward presentation have to be taken into account.

Volk, as quoted above, implicitly—and defendably—cautions against using school editions in which musical styles from other cultures are stripped of all qualities but those that translate into Western concepts such as harmony and notation, which indeed can make for very disappointing musical material. But in the end, a powerful piece of music presented "inauthentically" out of context may engage learners more than an academically approved, representative traditional piece, especially if the connection with the learners is well conceived and carefully presented.

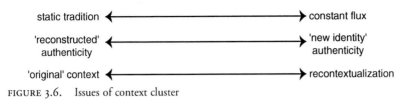

FIGURE 3.6.   Issues of context cluster

This leaves educators with a personal responsibility rather than a set of unambiguous guidelines for engaging with world music: the responsibility to deal intelligently with the dynamics of tradition and authenticity in order to create rewarding learning experiences in contemporary contexts. It also offers a new vocabulary to assess existing or future projects and programs. Has the teaching situation been shaped with a static idea in mind or, rather, a concept of constant flux? Does the situation attempt to re-create an original context for the music, or does it see the music as largely recontextualized? And does the situation reflect a tendency toward reconstructing an authentic (in the sense of culturally and/or historically correct) version of the music, or does it work from the view that the music has a new identity in the new context? This leads to a combination of the three continua discussed in this chapter (see figure 3.6).

This set of continua constitutes a powerful instrument in determining approaches to complex issues when planning strategies for learning and teaching music from various cultures. It invites teachers (or institutions) to be aware of the various factors discussed. At the same time, it allows a facilitator to make choices and justify departures from dominant, static views of tradition, authenticity, and context, in order to create new, meaningful musical experiences for music learners in studio practices, community music settings, or the classroom.

CHAPTER 4

Global Perspectives on Learning and Teaching Music

An Analysis

As part of the intercultural curriculum development of the teacher training degree at the Amsterdam Conservatory, young Balinese gamelan master I Ketut Gede Rudita is offered a residency to work with the students, exposing them to new musical content and ways of learning. The complex interlocking patterns of the gong kebyar style, taught at real—and high—speed from the beginning, proves highly challenging for the students. They try but sit in wonder, with a growing sense of inadequacy and frustration. There seems to be little consideration on the part of the instructor for the fact that this music is new to the students and needs to be learned from scratch.

Situations like this do not necessarily arise from insensitivity or lack of care. In speaking about their musical training with Ketut and project manager Henrice Vonck after the workshops, it became clear that most Balinese musicians would say that they did not have to learn the music, they "just know it."[1] And they have a case: in the communities, children sit on their fathers' laps for hours on end while they are rehearsing and playing deep into the night. By the time the children get their hands on a mallet to strike one of the metallophones, they already know most of the repertoire by heart, including subtleties in timing and dynamics, having absorbed it without the conscious effort of learning. They are also deeply aware of the context of the music, whether it is for entertainment or ritual purposes, having been immersed in its actual practice for many years.

The way music is taught and learned is inextricably linked to the specific music tradition that is being transmitted, its contexts, and the underlying value systems. This has been well recognized by ethnomusicologists. Earlier, I referred to

Nettl, who acknowledges that "a musical system, its style, its main characteristics, its structure, are all very closely related with the particular way in which it is taught, as a whole and in its individual components."[2] That has two major implications, which are closely related: analyzing methods of music transmission can be used as a tool to establish what is considered important in the learning process of any specific tradition by the musicians and communities who shape it, and at the next level, to understand what aspects of any particular music are seen as essential in order to be able to transmit it successfully. Particularly in aural traditions, where virtually all knowledge and skills pass directly from teacher to student, "what you teach is what you get" from the perspective of what aspects are preserved from generation to generation. It is obvious that systems of learning and teaching are crucial to the sustainability of such traditions.

Transmission relates not only to learning musical material but also to the enculturation of approaches to a musical style or genre at large. For those familiar with Western classical music, it is easy to forget how much knowledge and how many underlying concepts about music are picked up by listening to teachers and fellow students, listening to recordings, going to concerts, hearing comments by real and would-be experts, reading books and program notes, witnessing manners among musicians and audiences, observing the spaces deemed fit for classical music, and seeing how it is advertised. Grove Music Online defines *transmission* as "the means by which musical compositions, performing practices and knowledge are passed from musician to musician." It distinguishes "at least four dimensions: the technical, the social, the cognitive and the institutional."[3] In this chapter, aspects of the first three will be examined from the perspective of world-music practices, following on from the discussions in previous chapters. The institutional dimension of music transmission will be scrutinized in depth in the next chapter.

The powerful system of Western classical music training as it has developed at many public and private music schools tends to focus on reading music, (instrumental) skills, repertoire, theory, performance, and interpretation. In more advanced stages, as most conservatory curricula will demonstrate, history and analysis tend to be added, as well as playing in large ensembles. Over the past hundred years, there has been a shift in balance and sequence of these aspects. Many nineteenth-century educators advocated heavy emphasis on theoretical skills in the earlier stages, based on views that musical literacy skills were a prerequisite to the growth of musical understanding.[4]

This practice can still be found in some institutions. In most Western countries, however, it has gradually shifted to musical performance, conceptual learning, and more development of musicianship through performance-based activities, ensemble playing, creative composition, and improvisation, as well as deep listening. These changes were influenced by Jacques-Dalcroze, Orff, Kodály, and the writings of Swanwick, Reimer, Paynter, Small, and Elliott. But an underlying emphasis on theoretical skills has survived, particularly in formal instrumental teaching. In private practices to learn Western art music, the emphasis has gravitated toward playing skills, with theoretical skills being introduced gradually during the process to support the instrumental or vocal development.

In exploring music learning in Western popular music, Lucy Green paints a very different picture. She convincingly sketches pathways toward musicianship that proceed through self-discovery and peer learning: "performance, composition and improvisation abilities are acquired, not only individually, but crucially, as members of a group, through informal peer-directed learning, both conscious and unconscious."[5] For jazz, Paul Berliner describes in great detail the progression toward becoming a soloist in *Thinking in Jazz*, where formal education and theory are considered of marginal importance by many, and the jazz community itself is seen to serve as an educational system in which one learns largely by osmosis.[6]

And then there is the rest of the world. In its *Policy on Musics of World's Cultures*, the International Society for Music Education takes a primarily ethnomusicological stance, listing three aspects: "A music should be studied and may be understood as a system of sound and of audible processes, as a set of behaviour patterns, and as a system of ideas and concepts."[7] This view echoes Merriam's influential ideas from *The Anthropology of Music*, in which he devotes chapters to concepts, physical and verbal behavior, social behavior, and the process of composition. These present interesting alternative or additional foci for music education, instruction, or transmission.

Various other perspectives—similar and dissimilar—on the nature of musical knowledge appear, exploring the cultures beyond the West. Nketia argues that "African music must be viewed at different levels of abstraction: a) the conceptual level or level of theory; b) the processual level or the level of creativity and performance; c) the level of values, including aesthetic and social values; d) the contextual level."[8] Speaking of what he calls "African musical arts" at large, Nzewi observes that "within a musical arts culture, type and/or style, there are then generic, typological and stylistic conventions, procedures of creativity, organisation, presentation and evaluation."[9]

Flolu considers the following characteristic as common to most music learning in Africa: "Listening, observation and participation constitute the reciprocal dimensions in the development of musicianship. Musical memory and aural skills are not tested separately: they are demonstrated in the learner's attitude to music; musical analysis is an integral feature of music composition."[10]

In his delightful public lectures, Andrew Tracey emphasizes that most African music depends on complementarity; others refer to the concept of *ubuntu* to highlight African music as a shared and community experience from the perspectives of both audience and performers.

During the 1996 conference "Indian Music and the West"[11] and its sequel, "Teaching of Indian Music,"[12] a great deal of the discussions revolved around the relationship between guru and śisya, teacher and student, a relationship Neuman describes as "devotion of the disciple to his guru and the love of the guru for his disciple" in its "ideal form and essential nature,"[13] and which Slawek reports to be "of a spiritual nature. The guru is likened to a god, and the disciple must fully submit to him."[14]

This relationship has a strong basis in Indian society at large but can also be regarded as a logical consequence of the nature of musical knowledge in this tradition: learning to work with abstract melodic and rhythmic structures that generate different variations with every performance within a narrowly defined traditional framework. Many will argue that this knowledge is so elusive that it can only be learned through extended live interaction. The guru embodies this abstract knowledge, as well as the system of values and attitudes underlying it. There are no self-taught musicians of significance in North Indian music. This also explains the humility many music students show toward their teacher, not necessarily as a superior human being but as the carrier of a tradition that is greater than themselves.

Shifting cultures once again, we can see that the process of learning Bulgarian instrumental music strongly contrasts with this system. Rice speaks of music "that is learned but not taught" when reporting that in learning to play the gaida, there is no formal system in place to learn basic technique, with older musicians possessing "no way to teach cognitive skills such as the relationship between fingerings and pitches, how tunes were articulated with ornamentation, and how melodic fragments or whole melodies could be remembered." Seasoned musicians are not in the habit of showing core melody and ornamentation separately, so "boys learned to play an instrument by listening to and watching older musicians and then retreating to the outskirts of the village to understand and apply what they had seen and heard."[15]

Working primarily from the perspective of learning Javanese gamelan, Brinner is critical of simplistic "checklists" of musical competence. He digs deep into literature and experience, from which he emerges with four contrasting pairs of concepts relating to musical skills and knowledge: active/passive, intuitive/explicit, conscious/automatic, and procedural/declarative, which he sees as "continuously variable attributes rather than strict oppositions."[16] He defines musical competence as the

> individualized mastery of the array of interrelated skills and knowledge that is *required* of musicians within a particular tradition or musical community and is *acquired* and developed in response to and in accordance with the demands and possibilities of general and specific cultural, social and musical conditions.[17]

From this small sample of perspectives, it is clear that different well-established music traditions have a broad variety of priorities and approaches, sometimes similar but at other times contradictory. The perspectives on foci in music learning and teaching may vary considerably from culture to culture, genre to genre, institution to institution, and individual to individual (within the school where I am writing these words, for example, it is easy to establish that the Russian classical pianists have a remarkably different perspective on what is crucial in playing the piano from that of their colleagues in the jazz department). The interaction with the learning environment varies considerably with different aims and perspectives: a child learning a pop song by listening to a recording has different learning priorities from the classical violinist being prepared for a competition or, for that matter, a Buddhist monk rehearsing chants for an important religious ceremony.

Explicit and Implicit Foci

On the basis of the discussion above and the many examples and experiences behind it, five key domains emerge to describe the subject matter, the "what," in learning music across cultures: (1) technical (instrumental and vocal) skills, (2) repertoire and performance practice, (3) theory (explicit or implicit) (4) creativity and expression, and (5) culture and values.

This subdivision is not an attempt to set an absolute frame of reference; it merely serves as a useful tool for exploring various approaches to music transmission across cultures. I will deal with each separately. In virtually all systems of music transmission, we can distinguish a combination of the domains named here. However, not all domains are equally important in all music traditions. Balance and interaction are determined by internal factors, that is, the form and content of the music tradition itself, but also by the external factors, such as the position of the art in society and the history of its methods of transmission. This implies a cyclical system, where the music tradition partly determines the systems of transmission, but the exact shape of survival and development of the music is determined by where the emphasis lies in handing it down. A closer examination of each of these domains will make clear how they can contribute to a better understanding of music transmission across the world.

Technical (Instrumental and Vocal) Skills

Appropriate control of the instrument or voice is of importance in any musical practice, although what this means may differ significantly between Chinese opera and grunge. The skills that are needed can be self-taught, developed through peer learning, or taught explicitly or implicitly by others. This learning can involve graded exercises, etudes, and gradations in pieces or the introduction of new repertoire and techniques without much or any explanation. Largely, this process is definable and controlled: playing position, breathing, embouchure, and fingering lend themselves to practical explanation.

However, part of what we would consider technique is less easy to define, even by participants in the transmission process. There may be subtle variations and ornamentations that the student can possibly play or sing before he or she is aware of them. I remember the frustration at trying to master subtle ornamentations in Indian classical music, where months of practice would not get me anywhere until, with conscious effort exasperated, some abstract connection was made between sounds heard and fine motor skills, and the imagined sound would emerge. It is not uncommon for instructions in such techniques to be given on a subtle level, often using metaphor. In a Chinese text from the third century, the correct approach to fingering on the q'in is described in poetry:

> The fingers of the musician evoke the movement of waves.
> Lightly, they float over the strings, with elegant and precise strokes.[18]

Other metaphors reported by Goormaghtigh include "how a dragonfly touches the water in his flight," "like a carp beats its supple and heavy tail," and "the dragon grabbing a cloud in his flight."[19]

Ali Akbar Khan told his students to play a certain tone "as if there is a small bird sitting on your finger." It is not difficult to appreciate that this is infinitely

PHOTO 4.1.   Imagery can communicate subtleties: "the dragon grabbing a cloud in his flight." Ceiling painting from the ancient city gate of Daegu, Korea, October 2007. Photo: Huib Schippers.

more effective than instructing a student (with much greater scientific precision) to apply 20 milligram less pressure on the string with the left index finger. This type of language is quite common in master classes in Western classical music as well. During a 2004 piano master class in Carnegie Hall, Leon Fleischer advised a student to "play like a cat, but with sheathed claws," another to "clothe the bass line in summer linen, not wool." He admonished a student by saying, "Your plaintive, yearning creature, your nymph or naiad, is turning into some horrible, saliva-dripping alien."[20] A famous violinist likened the inexpressive playing of a student to "unravelling a complex knitting pattern."[21]

On the other side of the world, the Kaluli of Papua New Guinea may correct an unbalanced phrase with one of the water-based metaphors that pervade their musical language: "The waterfall ledge is too long before the fall."[22] Corrective metaphor is not all flowery poetry, however. Coming back to Ali Akbar Khan when he perceived a lack of crispness and clarity (metaphors in themselves) in the sound production of our advanced class, he likened the sound to what emanates from the backside of a donkey.

While technique may seem at first to be the most tangible aspect of learning music, it appears to be a matter of degree: although the emphasis lies on relatively unambiguous, physical instruction (the clichéd slap of the ruler when playing a wrong chord on the piano), it extends to highly imaginative use of language, evocative of the right attitude needed to play the right technique.

Repertoire and Performance Practice

When speaking of repertoire, the first associations are with classical master works, jazz standards, or pop songs. In a global context, repertoire can refer to such bodies of works but also to remembered and commonly sung (or played) pieces of music, as well as standards and sets of rules governing (partially improvised) performance practices (see chapter 3 above). Moreover, in examining foci in transmission, it is important to remember the distinction between traditions that are relatively static and those that allow significant degrees of creativity on the part of the performer.

The degree to which a musical style or genre remains unchanged correlates strongly with its instruments of transmission. For example, extensive notation exists in a large number of traditions from the Western world and Asia. It is an eminently useful tool for ensuring sustainability for complex musical structures. Notation systems have various states and ambitions of being a complete representation of the musical work. Ellingson distinguishes a number of conceptual contrasts in notation systems, the most important being prescriptive (notation) and descriptive (transcription).[23] In education across many traditions, prescriptive notation is often the primary instrument, supporting the memory at any stage from early learning to actual performance. The next section of this chapter will take a closer look at these systems, how detailed they are, what status they have, and how they are applied in the learning process.

In contrast, there are aural traditions where musical knowledge and repertoire are primarily embodied in living musicians. The "living national treasures" that countries such as Korea and Japan fund and recognize as crucial players in the survival of music traditions are an example of this.[24] Fascinating in this context is the phenomenon of traditions being preserved and handed down with the help of, or even primarily through, recordings. The music of the great Egyptian diva Oum Kolsoum exemplifies this, as does, for that matter, that of the Swedish pop group ABBA, who composed their quite intricate pop songs without using or knowing notation.

It is early to gauge fully the effect of this mechanism of music transmission on formal learning and teaching, but there can be little doubt that it is already highly influential. There is a vast amount of self-directed learning going on from recorded and downloaded music, probably outweighing formal music education in quantity if not quality. Some of this may be highly derivative and "unoriginal," but the Internet has become a major instrument in preserving and transmitting repertoire. Whether notated, digital, or live, repertoire is quite a concrete aspect of music learning. But again, there is variation on the basis of the nature of the material, from the written score of nineteenth-century Western classical music and the rock video clip to the elusive and abstract "Gestalt" of a rāga, swing in jazz, or the "feel" of an Ewe rhythm, which are all much less tangible.

Theory (Explicit or Implicit)

Across the world, we can distinguish between *explicit* theories, which have been formulated as the basis for the rules governing the creation and performance of a particular style of music in a particular period (Western classical harmonic theory is an example of this phenomenon), and *implicit* theories, which have established criteria but have never been formulated. The West African percussion tradition of the Mandinka featuring the djembe, for instance, contains no formal description of what is right or wrong, but a master drummer has a completely clear idea of what is acceptable within the tradition and what is not, which will be shared by most other master drummers and communicated to students. This is related to what is sometimes referred to as *tacit* knowledge, which should not be confused with *passive* knowledge (which is more likely to reside in the listener or a dancer); tacit knowledge informs the act of making music.[25]

Even traditions in which theory is defined may not be as clear as they seem at first sight. In North Indian classical music, music practice and theory have gone separate ways since the late Middle Ages. As a result, there is a highly refined music theory—dividing the octave into as many as 66 steps, of which 22 are actually "used" in music[26]—which is almost completely dissociated from musical practice and awareness of practicing musicians, who do use intentional subtle variations of intonation in specific rāgas but not in a mechanical manner. Some may argue laconically that this is actually a very satisfactory situation: theoreticians are not bothered by the erratic behaviors of musicians that challenge their neat theoretical models, and musicians are not burdened by a theory for which they feel they have no need in order to practice their art at the highest level.

The disjunction between theory and practice in Indian classical music echoes the way some (ethno)musicologists have approached the underlying structures of various musics. Blum describes how the analyst in the tradition of Von Hornbostel (1877–1935) tries to "enumerate the components of a system and to identify their typical functions and relations, distinguishing the more permanent (or 'essential') elements from the more changeable (or 'incidental')." The analysis of musical systems by comparative musicologists and music folklorists may have been influenced by the ideas of Hanslick and the followers of his formalism, which refuted the "unscientific aesthetics"[27] of sentiment and feeling and believed the beauty of music could be explained by its "formal characteristics,"[28] separate from the aesthetics of feelings.

Such a position is difficult to maintain now that insider's voices are increasingly valued. Even Hornbostel himself was aware of the danger that "such theoretical constructs will inevitably exclude features treated as 'essential' by those who perform and best respond to music."[29] This has led to the insight that "musical analysis is the discipline we learn, above all, from musicians,"[30] representing a shift of musical theories superimposed on musics of other cultures to those based on the actual practice and its underlying systems of musical knowledge. The latter are eminently useful in training musicians to be performers, because it is the musical concepts in the practicing musician's mind that need to be transmitted, rather than abstractions made from a scholar's or listener's point of view.[31]

Creativity and Expression

Creativity can function at several levels: it may refer to (1) the creation of new works, either within a particular tradition or as an innovation—sometimes fed by technological progress; (2) improvisation, which is an important feature of many genres of music; and (3) the interpretation of existing works. In many traditions, the role of creator and performer is unified within a single person, but it is also not uncommon to separate these functions, with specialized musicians composing and not necessarily being part of the performance. This is the case in much Western classical, pop, and film music. As a consequence, appropriate competencies for creativity differ widely from tradition to tradition.

In many people's minds, creating new work in Western art music is associated with an inspired individual sitting at the piano in his study or garret (preferably in great internal turmoil), painstakingly working musical ideas into coherent pieces of music, to be played by others at a later date. The resulting compositions may be steered by adherence to a particular format or tradition (whether it is a sonata, a tango, or atonal music) or by a desire to break with a tradition. In jazz and rock, compositional processes often take place while working with colleagues. In contemporary computer and Web-based composition, external performers are sometimes not even needed to realize the music in sound, as when a composer/performer uses multitrack recording and digital support to realize a creative process from initial concept to final product, possibly published online.

The exploratory nature of such efforts makes them akin to improvisation, but then again, so was composition in eighteenth-century organ music. As improvisation plays such a modest role in contemporary approaches to the Western classical traditions, the concept gives rise to much confusion when applied to world musics. Often, improvisation is misconceived as the creation of entirely new music on the spot. Various improvised musics in fact have elaborate systems informing various degrees of improvisation.

In practice, this often translates more into rearranging and/or recombining of musical ideas that have been learned previously or developed in practice. Hood writes: "The crowning achievement in the study of oriental music is fluency in the art of improvisation." The musician aims to be "free to follow the musical inventions of his own imaginations [but] must be guided through the maze of traditional rules that govern improvisation. These can be consciously learned but can be artistically used only when the whole tradition has been assimilated."[32] Performers in many of these traditions might argue that this is a slightly overly romantic view: even the most accomplished jazz musicians, African drummers, and sitar players regularly revert to standard riffs or slight variations of existing material in almost every performance.

Important to this discussion is the fact that the rules are often not verbalized. Improvisation is mostly learned by absorption rather than by explanation (except in formal education). This also requires different learning processes, often using subconscious analytical skills. The system of learning improvisation has parallels with how a child learns a language, without being taught grammar explicitly. In practice, learning improvisation usually proceeds through three stages: (1) exact imitation of examples from recordings, teachers, or other sources; (2) spontaneous creation or simple assignments evaluated by peers or the teacher; and (3) independent improvisation. The skills needed for learning improvisation are generally less tangible than those for learning technique or repertoire. The rules for improvisation are rarely explicit, and the borders between acceptable and unacceptable improvisations are usually learned through a long process of trial and error, guided by peers or an acknowledged master.

Evidently, creativity plays a role in interpreting precomposed works as well. No two interpretations of a Mozart sonata are exactly alike. Within the narrow constraints of a prescribed succession and timing of tones, the master musician painstakingly searches for a way of expressing the work as a dialogue between the composer (often long gone) and the moment of performance, marrying technical, structural, historical, emotional, and sometimes spiritual aspects.[33] In this exercise, some regard the composer's (assumed) vision as the absolute reference; others, such as the idiosyncratic pianist Glenn Gould, believe it is the duty of the performer to take liberties and create something well beyond the faithful realization of a score in performance.[34]

This form of creativity naturally leads the discussion to expression. While lecturing for students at the Amsterdam Conservatory, I have frequently used a video recording of the song *Les Vieux* by the legendary Belgian chansonnier Jacques Brel. It is a slow, sad song about two old people essentially waiting for death to arrive, while an old clock on the mantelpiece marks the time. The song requires no vocal virtuosity, uses a limited melodic range, and is supported by a simple arrangement. Subject matter, language, musical idiom, and technical aspects are not likely to engage a young, early twenty-first-century audience. Yet students hardly ever fail to be moved, as were vast audiences across the French-speaking world while Brel was still alive. In discussions about why this is so, the very general term *expression* arises, but when urged to be more precise, students mention aspects such as intonation, timbre, diction, facial expression, body stance, and movement.

The most directly musical of these aspects is probably expression as a product of controlling the musical sound. Juslin confirms that most musicians and music teachers regard expression as the most important aspect of a performer's skills.[35] But it is also difficult to define and teach. It is linked to expert musicianship. These—and not so much conscious mastery over technique, theory, or repertoire—are the qualities that separate Pablo Casals from a merely technically brilliant cellist, Youssou N'Dour from another competent African popular artist, and Paco Peña from a mediocre flamenco guitarist. They represent essential aspects of musicking that cannot easily be taught as courses with measurable outcomes in conservatories and therefore rarely feature in curricula and course outlines (although they do, of course, emerge in the teaching studio).

Expression is largely taught implicitly and ranges from qualities dictated by the tradition to highly personal expression. Among connoisseurs of Western music, there is a relatively consistent image of the ideal sound quality of the voice of a soprano, which is quite different from the ideal sound for an Azerbaijani mugam singer, with his powerful, piercing use of the head voice. These are difficult to teach: the "sponge method," enculturation by prolonged exposure and absorption through close association with a master, is probably the most effective way of transmitting such intangibles. This is perhaps why so many traditions insist on a long apprenticeship with a master.

With regard to world music, Hood noted as early as 1960 the importance of sound quality for convincing musicianship in other cultures, remarking that what needs to be learned is "not only the melodic line, the style of ornaments, . . . but the very quality of sound itself."[36] This is confirmed by many senior Indonesian musicians I have spoken to, who commend the technical skills of many Western gamelan ensembles but say that they still do not sound right. In the video *One Monkey, No Show*, salsa teacher Doy Salsbach says about his students: "I always tell them that the way you sit or stand determines the sound you produce." He insists that one cannot play the clave correctly unless one sits energetically upright: if you lean back, "it will always sound sleepy."[37] Internal as well as physical factors seem to play a role here.

Master musicians across the world are aware of these aspects and often have found creative ways of communicating to students what they consider important to achieve expression. I have witnessed flamenco virtuoso Paco Peña in his guitar classes at the Rotterdam Conservatory telling an advanced student that a certain passage sounded as if he was marching and that he had to open up the rhythm. The difference when the student played the same passage again was remarkable.

Jamaluddin Bhartiya explained to me how great musicians sometimes deliberately use a phrase that does not seem to fit into the traditional movements of the rāga: "It is like when you see the moon, and a cloud covers it up temporarily. Once the cloud has passed, you see the moon more clearly. This is called *avir bhav, tiru bhav* ('out of mood, into mood')." while metaphor is used to improve technical skills on a regular basis, it pervades the language of music teaching in this area;

PHOTO 4.2.   Paco Peña teaching flamenco at Rotterdam Conservatory, the Netherlands, spring 2002. Photo: Frank Dries.

possibly, it is the most appropriate instrument to transmit the least tangible aspects of learning music.[38]

Values

The final category may be even more evasive, as it is often not directly reflected in the actual musical sound. Mentioned by Nketia, Nettl, and others in the opening of this chapter, it refers to the rules and values among insiders to the music culture, which are often not made explicit. This ranges from abstract moral concepts to clear rules of behavior. The former has played a role of some importance in the selection of musical material for music education from Plato and Aristotle in ancient Greece[39] to Confucius in China, as well as contemporary Western society, where first jazz, then rock, and now gangsta rap raised discussions on appropriateness.

The nineteenth-century American music educator Lowell Mason lectured on the "tendencies . . . to corrupt both musically and morally" of "negro melodies and comic songs."[40] This is much in contrast with the idea of *ubuntu*, the spirit of togetherness that many Africans attribute to music making. Indian classical music has connotations of spirituality that are considered by the participants as part of the essence of the music but are not expressed directly. Much ritual and healing music is based on spiritual or religious values that form an integral part of the music, as with music of the American Indian or Australian Aboriginal people.

Behavior and communication among musicians can provide simple examples of more tangible values. I will never forget the grunt of disapproval that the famous tabla player Alla Rakha treated me to when I was a beginning sitar student during a visit of Ravi Shankar to the school of my music guru, Jamaluddin Bhartiya. Unable to sit cross-legged for a long time, I accidentally turned the bottom of my feet to him while stretching. This is extremely bad manners in India. I have not repeated it since—in more than thirty years. Similar rules of conduct exist throughout Asia, as they do in Europe. Just think of the dress code for opera first nights or, for that matter, for raves, where a three-piece suit and bow tie might raise some (pierced) eyebrows.

Within this category of values lie more music-related concepts, including ideas about musical tradition and innovation that were discussed in chapter 3. For example, when is the musician considered conservative? When innovative? When a rebel? What is the ideal reference for a particular music in terms of attitudes toward music, performance, and audiences? What is expected in personal or more formalized emotional expression? This in turn may depend on the role of the musician in the ensemble or his or her stage of development within the tradition. A second violinist in an orchestra is not expected to express personal feelings too emphatically, but Isolde in her Wagnerian interaction with Tristan would not be expected to be overly restrained.

Values are generally taught partly explicitly, partly implicitly, and often through stories, anecdotes, and legends.[41] A famous story that most students of Indian music encounter during their studies is that of the legendary sixteenth-

century musician Tansen and his patron, the great Moghul emperor Akbar. This is
how my music guru Ali Akbar Khan recounted the story:

> Tansen was a highly respected musician at the court of Emperor Akbar, the
> greatest Moghul ruler, who lived at the close of the sixteenth century. Akbar
> was very proud to have such a prestigious musician at his court. One day,
> after a sublime performance, he told him: "Surely, you must be the greatest
> musician of India." Tansen humbly replied: "No, my patron, it is not I who is
> the greatest musician of India, but my *guru*, Swami Haridas." From that day
> on, Akbar became restless and more and more anxious to hear this singer, that
> would even surpass the greatest master at his court. He told Tansen to invite
> Haridas to his court to sing, but Tansen said: "He will not come; he lives in a
> temple in the woods and does not care for courts and riches." Akbar said:
> "Then take me to him; I must hear him sing." Tansen said: "That would be of
> no avail either; he will not sing for anybody on request."
>
> Finally, they devised a plan. Tansen would go to see his *guru*, and
> Akbar would accompany him, dressed as his servant. When they arrived
> at Haridas's humble place in the woods, Tansen requested his master to
> sing something for him. Haridas declined. Then Tansen started singing,
> and while doing so, he deliberately made small mistakes. Unable to bear
> these faults, Haridas started to correct his disciple, and broke into song
> for hours and hours, mesmerising his two courtly listeners, and leaving
> them in tears. When they had finally regained their composure on their
> journey back to the palace, Akbar asked Tansen: "How is it possible that
> Swami Haridas can sing like this?" Tansen answered: "When I am
> singing, I make music for a worldly ruler, but his patron is in heaven."[42]

Other stories frequently told include calling forth flowers from the ground, enchant-
ing animals, and causing cloudbursts by singing rāgas associated with the wet season.
In China, imperial orchestras were deemed essential to maintaining cosmic harmony.
In West Africa, kora players say they received their instrument from a spirit in a well.
While these legends do not necessarily need to be taken at face value, they do make
learners aware of the value system and respect underlying the tradition.

Both external and internal context play a role in value systems, ranging from
physical surroundings to social role and spiritual meaning. Finally, this category
covers the area of aesthetic meaning attributed to any piece or genre of music and
forms the basis for musical criticism beyond establishing whether performances are
technically correct. All of these are often clear in the original context; but need to be
explained or highlighted in recontextualized learning and teaching, requiring
conscious and intelligent choices in new contexts. While many subtle aspects of
any music may be considered crucial to full understanding and enjoyment, there is a
constant risk of overburdening the musical experience with contextual information.

tangible ⟵————————————————————————⟶ intangible

FIGURE 4.1.   Continuum emphasis from tangible to intangible aspects of learning music

This broad and somewhat random sampling only scratches the surface of the wealth of values and attitudes that various cultures attribute to specific aspects of making and learning music. It serves to demonstrate that in each setting (or even moment) of music transmission, choices are being made in terms of the relative weight of each of the five aspects discussed above. Very often, a balance can be observed toward either more tangible or more intangible aspects of music making and even within each aspect, as we have seen. There are concrete and more elusive aspects in technique. Some repertoire is more clearly defined than others. An explicit theory tends to be more tangible than an implicit one. The criteria for creativity can be well defined or highly elusive. Expression can involve concrete simple physical action (e.g., baroque gesture) or only be suggested by the use of figurative language. And values range from clear rules to abstract spiritual concepts.

In their relationship to learning and teaching, these aspects of music can be seen as five overlapping continua, which roughly gravitate from tangible to intangible in the order in which we have discussed them: technique, repertoire, theory, creativity, and expression. These can be summarized in the graphic representation shown in figure 4.1, onto which the "degree of intangibility" for each moment (or trajectory) of music transmission and learning can be indicated, creating a tool to make explicit an important cluster of choices that has often been ignored in the organization of music learning and teaching across cultures.

Approaches to Learning and Teaching

Within a single tradition, the musical development of an individual musician, or even a single lesson, a wide range of approaches to learning and teaching can be used, depending on foci on various aspects of the particular music. In early writings on teaching world music,[43] there has been a tendency to generalize about non-Western music traditions, stating that they are handed down aurally, as opposed to Western music teaching, which is seen to be predominantly based on notation. Often, these approaches were considered synonymous with holistic and analytic ones. As Van den Bos began to explore in his contribution to the landmark 1993 symposium on "Teaching Musics of the World" in Basel and the successive proceedings, the reality raises more complex tensions, such as "the rationalisation and controlling of the analytical approach with the subsequent loss of musical meaning as opposed to the idea behind the holistic approach that musical meaning has to be understood and can only be found by playing and experiencing the music."[44] This strongly echoes Elliott's "praxial" approach to teaching music, which emerged around the same time and has gained considerably currency since.[45]

Notation and Aurality

There is no such phenomenon as a completely notation-based music tradition. Although as late as 1985, a U.S. *Research Guide to Musicology* still expressed the belief that "music itself, that is the musical score, is the most important primary source material for the musicologist,"[46] most would agree that musical sound is generally the primary reference for music. This section will explore the relationship between Western staff notation as an abstract, symbolic, prescriptive reference to actual musical pitches and duration on the one hand and aural systems of musical perception and transmission on the other.

Cook considers the most obvious function of notation to be conservation. But he argues that if that were the only function, it would have disappeared with the advent of the much more comprehensive medium of sound recording. There are other functions: "For through the process of communicating information from composer to performer, or more generally from one musician to another, notations at the same time do something much more complex: they transmit a whole way of thinking about music. A score sets up a framework that identifies certain attributes of the music as essential."[47]

There are major advantages for some but drawbacks for others when using staff notation for musics for which it is not designed. To the reader with no knowledge of the tradition, most world music will look like poor Western music when represented in staff notation, just as Indian *sargam* notation of Western music will look like confused and incorrect rāga music. The nonwritten aspects, which the Western music learner naturally fills in while reading the score as a result of enculturation, do not complement the notation when reading music of unknown traditions. Hearing a great deal of music plays a role of unsung significance in becoming an appreciative listener, a competent amateur, or a highly skilled professional. The importance of the vast "aural library" of musicians tends to be underestimated, which, in the case of Western classical musicians in their forties, would typically consist of well more than 40,000 hours of listening, playing, reading, and thinking,[48] a resource that influences virtually all decisions in practical music making.[49]

Cook acknowledges that ethnomusicologists who use staff notation for world music are "painfully conscious that in doing this, they are shoehorning Indian or Chinese music, or whatever it might be, into a system that was never designed for it." As an example, Cook relates how staff notation describes music as separate notes, while in some traditions, it is the "notes between the notes, so to speak, that are responsible for the effect of the music." As a consequence, Cook refers to "endless controversies between those ethnomusicologists who see staff notation as a blunt but necessary instrument for conveying something of the music to readers unfamiliar with the notational system (if any) of the musical cultures in question, and those who regard its use as a kind of neo-colonial exercise in which Western notation is set up as a universal standard."[50]

However, Cook continues to argue that notation distorts Western classical music as well and describes how a synthesized performance of a Chopin prelude with every note equally long and equally loud will make any listener realize that a key aspect of our enjoyment of such music lies in the "shaping of time and dynamics that any pianist brings to the music, quite possibly without even thinking of it."[51] There is a major difference, however. Staff notation has been developed for Western classical music and is generally learned in conjunction with its practice. In the case of many world music cultures, staff notation is superimposed on the music, and the stylistic references are lost for the uninitiated reader of the music. At best, this can be slightly misleading. At worst, it can become a blatant lie about what counts in a particular music, which may in fact be not just the "work" but the entire musical event: Small's concept of "musicking."

The notation of Western classical music is among the most precise and prescriptive in the world. But it still needs a musician with a sense of the structure of the music, the instruments, and the sounds to bring it to a meaningful performance. Notation is excellent for preserving musical ideas of the past, although by its very nature it allows atrophy of the musical memory (many a third-year conservatory student will despair when asked to play some music spontaneously: "How can I if I don't have the score?"); it can also be overpowering and exclusive.

There has been a great deal of criticism regarding the hegemony of staff notation in the musical discourse, particularly in relation to world music. In this context, Ellingson refers to notation of world music as generating "misconceptions, violations of musical logic and distortion of objective and acoustic fact."[52] Throughout my many years of working with world musicians, I have witnessed a misplaced sense of inferiority felt by many capable musicians from across the world in not mastering this system, to the point of compromising their musical convictions to conform to what they perceived as the only way to be taken seriously as musicians.

At the other extreme is the purely aural (or oral) tradition. Rice summarizes its key aspects:

> The techniques of oral transmission . . . are memory and performance. Since memory is presumed to be faulty, it is often assumed that compositions cannot be fixed but are subject to constant variations, intended and unintended. In some traditions, like Vedic chant or African drumming, mnemonic devices such as inverting text syllables or the use of drum

syllables help to reinforce memory. In others, such as jazz, Middle Eastern music and Hindustani music, variability is made into a virtue and improvisation (composition at the instance of performance) is favoured over the repetition of fixed compositions.[53]

These "mnemonic devices," short formulas that assist the student in remembering particular aspects of the music, abound in aural traditions of world music. The bols, or syllables, representing the various sounds of the Indian tabla form an often quoted example, where *da, ge, tu na,* and *ti re ki te* imitate the sound of the drum and help students remember complex patterns (in what could be described as onomatopoeic mnemotechnic monosyllables). Japanese court music uses a similar system:

> In learning or recalling an instrumental part, a performer may sing either syllables indicating precise finger positions or drum strokes (as for sha-kuhachi or *sho*), or a set of mnemonics that primarily represent relative pitch rather than specific fingerings or absolute pitches (as for the no flute or *hichiriki*). The most common general term for all such systems in Japan is *shoga* or *kuchi-shoga*.[54]

Similar systems exist for African drums and string instruments.[55]

While such tools exist to develop the memory in many aural traditions, an even more powerful instrument is understanding the structures that underlie performance. The dynamics of many aural traditions do not necessarily serve to compensate for weaknesses of memory, as Rice suggests above, but may be a conscious musical choice. Flolu contends that "essential aspects of Africanness in music making include the oral-aural and practical approaches. Indeed traditional African music has survived not because of the development of written notation but in spite of it."[56] Musicians who seem to improvise effortlessly for hours on end almost invariably work from a very solid conceptual framework that guides both the detail and the larger structure of performance, whether it is the awareness of the different parts that constitute the build-up of a rāga performance[57] or the complex rhythmic structures that underlie an evening of Ewe drumming.

As they are not written down, musics transmitted almost entirely aurally are subject to change and variation over time. If few conservative safeguards have been built in, these musics tend to change considerably. Many music traditions, however, have their own mechanisms for conservation and innovation. For instance, as illustrated in chapter 3, many aural traditions place great value on material handed down from the past and use meticulous imitation as a means of handing down the stable part of the tradition.

In contemporary Western cultures, the word imitation is used almost invariably with negative connotations. The *OED* Online defines *imitation* as something that is not real: "made (of cheaper material) in imitation of a real or genuine article." *Grove Music Online* ignores the concept as an important aspect of tradition: the entry for *imitation* only refers to the word as a Western compositional technique. There is a short entry devoted to the related concept of *mimesis*, which hovers between the abstract and the concrete: "Varying translations of the term illustrate the difficulties of interpretation associated with it. 'Imitation' stresses the concept of copying; the preference for 'representation' emphasizes instead that of creative involvement. Neither translation conveys the full sense of the concept of mimesis."[58]

Grove Music Online also defines *modelling*: "the use of an existing piece of music as a model or pattern for a new work, in whole or in part. Modelling may involve assuming the existing work's structure, incorporating part of its melodic or rhythmic material, imitating its form or procedures, or following its example in some other way."[59] In this interpretation, both mimesis and modeling represent advanced stages of imitation, which usually starts with copying.

In the "tradition" of Western classical music (as well as the other arts), the latter form of imitation was standard practice until the middle of the eighteenth century. Grout attributes the genius of Bach to five factors, one of which is "the laborious but fruitful method of assimilation from all sources by copying scores."[60] However, from the Romantic period onward, personal creative genius has been stressed over imitation and adherence to established rules. Composers from that time to the present tend to be perceived as great innovators rather than followers of a tradition, with Beethoven as possibly their greatest champion.

This concept of the artist as a rebel rather than a follower has only been challenged incidentally in the West. In his essay "Principles and Criteria of Art," the Swiss philosopher Frithjof Schuon, who published extensively on what he considered the essential, primordial, and universal qualities of various religions, takes an extreme position toward imitation and its relation to innovation in "high art," which he calls "sacred art":

> True genius can develop without making innovations: it attains perfection, depth and power of expression almost imperceptibly by means of the imponderables of truth and beauty ripened in that humility without which there can be no true greatness. From the point of view of sacred art or even that of merely traditional art, to know whether the work is an original, or a copy is a matter of no concern: in a series of copies of a single canonical model one of them, which may be less "original" than some other, is a work of genius through a concatenation of precious conditions which have nothing to do with any affectation of originality or other posturing of the ego.[61]

While such barely concealed attacks on the star pretensions of some artists may not resonate strongly with contemporary audiences, it is important to realize that in many traditions across the world, imitation in one or more of the senses described above is a force to be reckoned with and acknowledged as a common and central concept in the learning process. Some music traditions (particularly ones with primarily ritual purposes) seem hardly to value individual expression.

Nonetheless, the concept of imitation in the negative sense does exist as well: Indian classical musicians speak of "carbon copies" to describe young musicians who mimic their guru or another example too closely and without personal expression. Years of imitation in the training of many young musicians in a wide variety of traditions in Latin America, Asia, and Africa ideally lead to confident, independent musicianship, as happens also in jazz and rock music. In this way, imitation is the mechanism for developing a skill base or model for production of new music within the tradition, rather than perpetuating existing repertoire and interpretations. In recent decades, this process has been greatly facilitated by the availability of sound recordings, although the long-term effects of unguided imitation may lead to a loss of depth in some traditions.

In the interaction between musical characteristics and values on the one hand and systems of music transmission on the other, each tradition is likely to develop an approach that is conducive to handing down its most important qualities. Table 4.1 illustrates this by taking a closer look at two of the traditions that have featured in the discussions so far. Although such analyses are inevitably over-generalized, they do present a strong case for the thesis that musical differences are directly linked to modes of transmission.

A new factor of great importance is emerging in this arena. During the past several decades, we have seen the advent of new teaching aids, such as the cassette recorder, the MP3 recorder, video, and the Internet. Campbell reports that "Yung observed that children in China who are motivated to become more musical do so by watching adults perform and then imitating them, [but] many more . . . learn music from television, video, karaoke sets, cassette tapes, and CDs."[62] This has expanded exponentially since the 1990s. Most children are exposed to many hours of music every day, hearing and (partially) learning hundreds of songs a year, consciously or unconsciously. This is a contemporary reality to be reckoned with at

TABLE 4.1. Contrast in focus between notion-based and aural traditions

Notation-based (Western classical music)	Predominantly aural (Indian classical music)
Centrality fixed compositions	Room for improvisation
Pieces of music relatively static	Organic changes, every performance different
Complex relation between melodic lines	Single melodic line central
Regular, linear meter	Cyclical rhythmic structure, sometimes "free rhythm"
Single intonation system for all works	Intonation variable between works (within rules)

See Van den Bos, "Differences between Western and Non-Western Teaching Methods in Music Education," 173.

notation-based ←——————————————————————→ aural

FIGURE 4.2.   Continuum emphasis notated to aural aspects of learning music

all levels of music learning and teaching. The use of video and computers in world music education is still fairly modest (with the most spectacular form of this, distance learning by video, as a fascinating challenge to context).

Overall, however, the use of recording equipment of various kinds is widespread and constitutes a teaching aid that is potentially one of the greatest blessings to teaching aural traditions in settings where limited availability of exposure time to live sources has become an issue. At the same time, it raises questions about how it affects the music transmission process and ultimately the skills of the young musician and the music itself, especially in terms of developing a musical memory and avoiding "carbon copy" interpretations. It is too early to determine the full consequences of learning music through recordings, but it is an issue for all musics increasingly handed down with the help of this medium.

Whatever the exact implications of the choices, the discussion above again leads us away from an either/or perspective when considering notation-based or aural transmission. Musical realities are reflected more accurately when each moment or trajectory of music transmission is placed on the continuum from completely notation-based to utterly aural, forming an important next point of reference for analyzing processes of music transmission and learning (see figure 4.2).

Atomistic and Holistic Approaches

The belief in the effectiveness of an analytical or even "atomistic" approach to teaching lies at the core of most methods for learning music in the West. It goes back to well before the first decades of the nineteenth century, when some of the most influential principles of Western music education were laid down by Swiss educator Johann Pestalozzi (1746–1827), who advised "to teach but one thing at a time—rhythm, melody, and expression, which are to be taught and practiced separately, before the child is called to the difficult task of attending to all at once."[63]

This atomistic approach was strengthened in the late nineteenth century by the rise of the "Herbartian method of scientific, organized lessons with measurable results, translated into note-reading methodology by Holt, as well as the tonic sol-fa system of notation."[64] Consequently, this development was supported by the formalist view that music could be understood through analyzing its structure. This logically connects to an atomistic approach in which music is taught piece by piece. Ideally, the musical challenge is divided into easily digestible partial challenges, which are then reassembled into a coherent piece of music.

In recent years, however, scholars across disciplines have begun to doubt the validity of only using atomistic approaches:

> At one time it was believed that the best way to teach reading was to have students learn all the letters of the alphabet, then words, then phrases, and then sentences. This method, called the "ABC-method," seems logical. However, people do not always operate logically, or what appears to be logically. Research studies uncovered the fact that people actually read by fixing their eyes on groups of words, not letters or individual words. The faster readers have fewer fixations per line than the slower readers. Hence, what had been accepted as the truth about reading was abandoned, and better methods for teaching reading are the result.[65]

Although the battle between proponents of the skills approach and those of the whole-language approach is still raging,[66] it is interesting to note in the global context that children in Java traditionally learn to read on the basis of a text they know well and gradually come to recognize the words and letters that represent this text. And in fact, Pestalozzi himself advised teaching "sounds before signs and to make the child learn to sing before he learns the written notes or their names."[67] Both approaches advocate learning in which the learners are first presented with material and settings that are meaningful to them and only afterward with abstractions.

In many traditions in Africa, both in music and in dance, this pedagogical approach dominates. Berliner describes the system of learning by children in his study of the music of the Shona:

> The music does not slow down for the child's benefit, nor does anyone necessarily explain the steps or provide practice of them out of the context of performance. This same teaching process is part of the experience of mbira players, who, as Luken Pasipamire expressed it, must learn by "pinching" knowledge from more experienced musicians. The teacher does not slow down his playing or separate the piece into its component parts to make learning easier; he simply allows the younger player to watch his fingers move on the keys and to memorise the piece.[68]

In some cases, the learners are even deliberately prevented from seeing the fingers on the mbira in order to sharpen their hearing. Mbira player Chartwell Dutiro, after explaining how his brother and teacher did not break musical pieces down, reports on a conscious withholding of information in teaching an instrument where visual copying can only be gained from looking into the gourd of the instrument from behind the player:

In my learning, sometimes when I walked around behind him to try to see how my brother was playing, he would turn away from me. He didn't want me to see what he was doing with his fingers, but wanted me to get the sound in my head. It's like saying that you've got to have a good ear and a good memory at the same time.[69]

While speaking with traditional Vietnamese musicians, Pham Thi Hue, one of the teachers at the Hanoi National Academy of Music who more recently immersed herself in the threatened ca trù music, described learning music deeply without scores, explanation, or analysis simply and eloquently—"It's how your heart, your mind works,"—and sees this as a basis for educating "good musicians performing not only mechanical[ly], but performing with heart, performing with spirit" (personal communication, January 2007).

These are typical descriptions of what I like to call holistic learning and some others have referred to as osmosis.[70] It occurs in many cultures and allows for intangible aspects to be transmitted as a matter of course. Of her qin teacher, Tsar Teh-yun, Bell Yung writes:

In teaching, she applies the method of playing in unison with her students, and this has proved to be the only way for us to grasp her musicality. The reason is that her rhythmic interpretation of a piece almost never follows a simple metrical pattern; the rhythm appears to be always shifting and to be quite inimitable. Certainly, some aspects of her playing could never be captured in musical notation. Even multiple listenings to a recording do not reveal the secret of particularly elusive passages. But by repeatedly playing with her in unison, patient and perceptive students could eventually capture the rhythmic nuances, without even realizing how they did it.[71]

Van der Meer reports similar experiences with learning North Indian vocal music: "I often tried analytically to understand what happens. The only way, however, appeared to be simply imitating the teacher without thinking. After having learnt this in a practical manner the analysis follows easily."[72]

In a holistic approach to teaching, a piece of music that is considered part of the real repertoire (not exercises or etudes or even simplified renditions of real pieces) is presented to the student as a whole. This creates substantial challenges for the student to understand and master the piece. But it also has advantages. For instance, after having gone through this exercise a number of times, the student is more likely to be able to grasp other pieces by himself or herself. Perhaps counterintuitively, a holistic approach is likely to address the analytical skills of the learner more then an atomistic one.

At first sight, some music traditions may seem to defy analysis, but as Blacking claims: "Insofar as music is a cultural tradition that can be shared and transmitted, it cannot exist unless at least some human beings possess, or have developed, a capacity for structured listening. Musical performance, as distinct from the production of noise, is inconceivable without the perception of order in sound."[73] Structured listening and ordering of sound can be trained but already exist in almost all humans as spontaneous, nonformalized forms of analysis, which help learners of music construct an understanding directly from how they perceive a piece of music.

Successful holistic learning (such as Western children learning songs from the radio or Venda learning fairly complex songs that they know well more easily than simpler ones that are unfamiliar) challenges preconceptions about proceeding from simple to complex. This supports the argument of Blacking that the progression from familiar to unfamiliar may make more sense than that from simple to complex.[74] It stands to reason that it is easier to learn music that one has heard extensively than completely new melodic and rhythmic structures.

This idea has major implications for teaching music out of context. Unfamiliar forms of music may require more effort to teach than familiar ones, as there has been no holistic processing of this music in the mind of the learner (compare the "unfamiliarity index" in chapter 2). This, rather than the still occasionally encountered "it's in their blood" fallacy, may well account for different aptitudes for gaining expertise between learners from inside and outside a specific culture.

Directly related to this is student motivation. Students are more likely to work hard at mastering material they know and love than they are with something unfamiliar. That said, it is possible to make the unfamiliar attractive. In my own sitar-teaching practice, I have observed that students who are particularly eager to learn a particular new technique or piece of music or technique are likely to transcend the boundaries of what they can reasonably be expected to grasp. Mentioning that a particular composition is a rare and secret possession within the tradition is likely to generate high motivation and consequently greater display of concentration, technical skills, and memorization.

In this context, the value of confusion as a powerful instrument in learning music should be addressed. Whereas Western music education seems to attempt to exclude confusion as much as possible from the learning process, as we have seen in the discussion on Pestalozzi, in traditions leaning toward holistic approaches, it often plays an important role. The learner is confronted with techniques or pieces of music that are too difficult, gets no support in breaking these down, but has a strong desire to master them. The process is often triggered subconsciously but may also be applied as a conscious strategy.

This mechanism is recognized in contemporary educational literature as cognitive dissonance, advocated by Neighbour[75] and others. It can lead to a process of highly motivated internal analytical activity, which may make students achieve above their expected level. I have witnessed this extensively in various stages of learning Indian classical music but also in observing (particularly master) classes in other traditions. Confusion is likely to be most effective when applied in good measure, however. If overused, the strategy can lead to shortcircuiting and demotivation.

Holistic learning may well be the most common means of acquiring musical skills. It does not occur only when children learn popular music from the radio or recordings (often including subtle timing and complex ornamentation), but the very sound ideal of Western classical music is learned holistically through listening to peers, teachers, and (recordings of) professional performers. The result of a holistic learning process may be audibly different in the students' performance from an atomistic approach, particularly in aural traditions.

As I have observed from experiments in my own teaching practice in the 1990s, both have advantages and drawbacks: after a holistic learning process, ornamentations and subtle variations in timbre, timing, or intonation may be copied perfectly but without understanding, while an atomistic approach may result in a correct but slightly stiffer rendering of a work, without clear consciousness of the whole.

The pedagogical approaches associated with atomistic and holistic learning have been prominent in debates about education for almost a century now. An atomistic/analytical approach corresponds more closely to an emphasis on monodirectional didactic teaching of a "single truth," while a holistic approach leaves more room for learners to construct their own musical knowing, leading to a more individual approach, even if the body of knowledge (the canon or tradition) is quite closely defined.

TABLE 4.2. Objectivist versus constructivist approaches to learning

Dimension	Characteristics objectivism	Characteristics constructivism
Attention to structure in processes	Structured	Unstructured
Assessment of learning process	Linear and uniform	By networking
Orientation on context	Emphasis on abstraction	Real world
Based on which type of motivation	Extrinsic motivation	Intrinsic motivation
Taking into account individuality	Denial of individual differences	Recognizing and supporting differences
Attention for cooperation in learning	Focus on individual	Focus on learning together
Type of responsibility for instruction	Didactic relation	Mentor-student relation

Valcke, *Onderwijskunde als Ontwerpwetenschap*, 44.

atomistic/analytic ⟵————————————————⟶ holistic

FIGURE 4.3.   Continuum atomistic to holistic approaches to music learning and teaching

Valcke associates the extremes of holistic and atomistic respectively with constructivism, which is associated with postmodern thinking, and with the more modernist objectivism.[76] Even though the formulation of some of the characteristics in table 4.2 raises suspicion of a distinct predilection for constructivism over objectivism, the correspondences are striking.

It is difficult to find examples of either atomistic or holistic learning and teaching in a pure form. But the contours of the extremes are quite clear. In order to capture actual practices, these two concepts are best represented in another continuum, as shown in figure 4.3.

By a relatively simple analysis of pedagogical approaches and material, every moment or trajectory of music transmission can be placed on this continuum. There is some coherence with the one mapping of degrees from notation-based to aural. Often the position on the notation to aural line and the line from atomistic to holistic is roughly the same: Western classical music teaching is generally toward the left (notation/atomistic), while the traditional ways of handing down African percussion are very much to the right of both continua (aural/holistic). Japanese traditional music, however, is taught from notation but entirely holistically, while South Indian classical music tends to be handed down aurally but in a very rigid order and atomistic fashion.

Most music learning in practice involves a wide range of activities in different places on both continua. This is strengthened by contemporary tools for learning, such as the Walkman and the iPod, which bring the aural and the atomistic closer by combining the experience of reproducing the real-time sound and the possibility of endless repetition while practicing (Arvind Parikh speaks of "having a guru in your pocket"). We may also suspect some coherence with the tangible-intangible continuum: notated, atomistic pedagogies are more likely to emphasize tangible aspects of learning music.

Alternating between methods can be an effective tool. Hood describes how in his gamelan lessons in the late 1950s, he first allowed his American students to use notation and then withheld it.[77] Almost forty years later, Elsje Plantema reports on her teaching of Javanese gamelan to Western students in a similar way:

> I'd rather they don't write. But some people are afraid they won't remember next week....The need for this piece of paper is something typical of our [Western] culture. When I see too many papers in class, I walk through the room and turn them all around. The students panic at first, but they just play on. They don't really need it.[78]

This illustrates that successful enculturation into aural traditions is possible for those who are used to (and more comfortable with) notation.

Increasingly, in contemporary educational settings, a shift from atomistic to holistic learning is occurring in the context of competency-based teaching. As competencies commonly refer to a set of skills rather than a single skill, we find that assignments in contemporary curricula begin to cross narrowly defined boundaries of traditional subjects. This is particularly apparent in curricula for Western popular music, which is now broadly recognized to require different formats from Western classical music training. It is not uncommon to find assignments that instruct ensembles or bands (which form the focus of the teaching, rather than individual instruments) to compose a song, notate it, learn to play it, teach fellow band members, perform and record, and register it with the copyright organization.[79] In a single assignment like this, nine separate subjects are combined: technique, repertoire, composition, arranging, theory, teaching skills, recording skills, performance skills, and business skills, thus restoring a holistic approach. In some instances, students are also required to keep a log of the entire process of each assignment, including not only the technical and creative process but also the obstacles encountered in areas such as planning and social interaction among band members. In short, they are stimulated to learn "musicking" rather than merely performing pieces of music.

Conclusion

A brief exploration of processes of music transmission from a cross-cultural perspective reveals that many aspects of learning and teaching contain multiple layers and areas of choice. Different cultures have developed various approaches to technical skills, repertoire and performance practice, explicit or implicit theories, creativity and expression, and underlying values. The balance between tangible and intangible aspects of music varies among music traditions, genres, and settings for transmission. Related to these aspects is the relative importance attached to notation or aural learning and the distinction between holistic and atomistic approaches to learning.

While atomistic instruction appears to be the prime reference for much organized music education, it is striking to note how closely some of the mechanisms of holistic learning resemble the processes deemed desirable in emerging constructivist thinking on education. The concept that a learner constructs knowledge rather than merely receiving it (which corresponds to a modernist, positivist, cognitivist view) potentially elevates holistic learning and teaching from the status of "underdeveloped" to appropriate to education in a postmodern environment. This invites a thorough rethinking of music education in terms of both content and method. The above discussion generates three important continua in

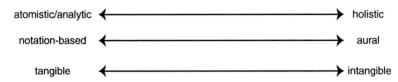

FIGURE 4.4.   Continua cluster approaches to methods of teaching

understanding music transmission from a global perspective, those addressing the actual learning or instruction processes. These can be graphically represented as shown in figure 4.4.

For the music educator, this is not a graph to demonstrate "right" approaches but an instrument to acknowledge, assess, and validate different approaches on the basis of fitness for purpose in specific situations. The next challenge is to consider the roles of learners and teachers/facilitators/examples and the environments in which music learning and teaching takes place, as the institution is one of the key dimensions that define the shape of music transmission across the world.

CHAPTER 5

Communities, Curricula,
and Conservatories
A Critique

In a run-down building in the township of Alexandria in South Africa, a well-polished college jazz ensemble from Florida visits a group of boys learning music from local hero Johnny Mekoa—one of the few constructive things they can do in their disadvantaged community. The two bands play for each other. The ensemble from the United States is well trained: the students play in time and in tune. The African youngsters have obviously had more challenges: they cannot afford their own instruments and have to face daily uncertainties in terms of food, clothes, and basic safety. Their mentor tells us that one of them recently appeared in class with an obvious bullet hole in his T-shirt. Of two brothers, one always has to stay home to guard the gun the family uses for protection. But the playing of the group is passionate, adventurous, and alive; it ultimately impresses those present more than the smoother renditions of their U.S. visitors.

Observing the range of outcomes and "products" emanating from formal music education raises an important question: is a highly structured pathway through music curricula the only or even the best way of ensuring a vibrant musical life for contemporary communities in Africa, Asia, Latin America, and the West? For all of the pride and importance we (often rightly) attribute to well-conceived, well-funded, and well-organized programs of music education at all levels of ambition and competency in our contemporary societies, it is useful (and sobering) to remember that people have always enjoyed, learned, and performed music, even without funding bodies, arts organizations, and formalized music education.

People have a strong and natural urge to engage with music. If tomorrow we were to close down all conservatories and public and private music schools and cancel music lessons in school, certain musical practices would undoubtedly suffer, but music would not stop. It is also a fallacy to think that only simple music will survive: as Blacking and others since have pointed out, the human brain has the capacity of processing very complex music without external formal structures to support it.[1] However, we are fortunate in many countries to have institutions that enable more people to make more music better. As these are largely financed with public funds, this comes with a considerable moral obligation to reflect continually and critically on the rationale, content, relevance, and methods of organizing learning and teaching music. That is the aim of this chapter.

It is useful to consider three major forces that determine cultures of transmission: the form and content of the music itself, the interaction between the learner and the teacher (master, mentor, example, or facilitator), and the learning environment. Within this framework, some traditions tend to focus primarily on what is being transmitted (e.g., technical skills or a canon); others attribute a central role to interaction (e.g., the master-disciple relationship within a conservatory or peer learning in a rock band); and yet others emphasize the setting for transmission (e.g., elite institutions or community projects).

All three strongly influence how music transmission takes place and need to be considered when designing, delivering, or evaluating music education. Their balance and interaction are dependent on aims and contexts for each unique setting. The effectiveness of particular choices will differ vastly between, for instance, a lifetime spent under the guidance of a Thai master with the purpose of becoming a full-fledged performer[2] and weekly one-hour lessons for an amateur in a public music school or community center. There is no value judgment in this distinction: I use the term *amateur* in the best sense and the original sense of "lover of music," rather than "not good enough to be professional." But the difference in ambition translates into different pedagogical models.

Methods of teaching, as well as approaches to concepts such as tradition, context, authenticity, and the position of the music in society, are strongly influenced by the institutional environment. In this chapter, the range of settings for music transmission and learning will be explored: from *informal*, which is characterized by an absence of consciously organized structures for music instruction, to *formal*, referring to programs and structures regulated by governments, in which the institutional environment consequently is a strong influence. In addition, some authors distinguish *nonformal*, where the relationships between teachers and learners are organized by senior musicians or communities themselves. As many practices in this area are quite formalized (such as formal apprenticeships in many forms of world music and private teachers using formalized curricula for teaching Western classical music), I will discuss this as part of the continuum rather than as a separate category.[3]

PHOTO 5.1.   Kora master Alagi Mbye teaching his young son. Lamin, the Gambia, March 1995. Photo: Huib Schippers.

Informal music learning occurs in a manner that could be described as an "organic" process. No teacher or facilitator is assigned to take responsibility for the learning experience. This is a form of learning that is common in music performed in what are now commonly referred to as "community settings" and in much popular music.[4] It also includes the increasingly important mechanism of learning music directly from recordings, radio or the Internet.

Next on the continuum comes learning outside of organized music education where there is deliberate teaching. Private music teachers fall into this category. Control of the learning process is generally in the hands of a single professional musician. The process is not necessarily more random than that of formal teaching, but the social settings and interpersonal relationships can be more complicated: the long association of a young jali with his kora master in West Africa exemplifies such a nonformal setting. This does not mean that there is a lack of structure or direction in the learning process in what Saether calls the "oral university,"[5] but it is controlled by the participants themselves.

Formal systems of music education in many Western and Asian countries takes place at three levels. There is music teaching in schools, where children are introduced to the general principles of music and music making; many countries have public or private music schools for children and adults who want to learn

music without pursuing professional aspirations; and finally, there are conservatories (or schools) of music, where students are trained to become professional
musicians. The institute or public authority, not the individual teacher, largely
determines overall content and quality criteria in these environments.

Informal Music Learning and Teaching

A key setting to consider in understanding music transmission and learning of
world musics is what has become known widely under the 1970s U.K. term
community music. Of course, many forms of world music have been handed
down for centuries in such community settings, ranging from conjunto in Mexico,
bluegrass in the United States, and brass bands in Dutch towns to samba in Brazil,
Irish fiddling, and Javanese village gamelans.

   Various forms of community music have "gone global"; I have already referred
to Sumatran drumming at an international school in Kuala Lumpur, steel-pan
orchestras with "youth at risk" in rural Devon (U.K.), and jazz with children
from townships around Johannesburg. Other commonly found practices include
African percussion ensembles joining black and white disadvantaged communities,
Indian vocal lessons to Hindustani people from Surinam, and popular songs by
choirs of refugee women from the former Yugoslavia.

   While it is relatively easy to compile a long list of community-music activities,
it is much more difficult to arrive at a working definition of what community
music actually *is*. Because community-music activities tend to be flexible and cover
a wide range of styles, formats, and approaches, it is elusive. While there is a wealth
of practices, partially documented in reports and online resources, the phenomenon has largely been ignored by academics. In one of the few doctoral theses on
community music to date, Higgins finds that "scholarly writings dealing specifically with Community Music are rare."[6] Nevertheless, a number of scholars,
including Higgins and Veblen, as well as several community music organizations
and networks, such as Sage Gateshead and Sound Sense, have made inroads in
sketching the outlines of what community music could be.

   An initial obstacle is a definition of *community*. While it is easy to define a
community as "a group of people who have a common interest,"[7] the concept is
prone to vagueness, banality, slipperiness, as well as unreflective and emotive use,
as various scholars have pointed out.[8] Similarly, a survey of definitions of *community music* reveals an oscillation between, on the one hand, meaningless blandness
that fails to distinguish community-music activities from many other musical
activities ("Community music concerns people making music"; "Community
music is active participation in music making") and, on the other hand, sometimes
biased specifics that would not necessarily characterize all or only community-
music activities ("Creating rather than re-creating music"; "Musical activity as a

reaction against formal music education"). While each of these may have merit, they do not create a sufficient basis for shared understanding. This is to be expected: it is difficult to define shared characteristics between an online community of hip-hop artists and a third-age choir singing popular songs from the 1950s in a retirement home.

One of the contributing factors to this confusion is that definitions of *community music* tend to mix descriptions of specific practices with organization, artistic and pedagogical approaches, and sets of beliefs underlying the activities. This is apparent in a fairly typical statement by a well-respected Australian practitioner, who asserts that community music

> brings joy to life; involves lifelong learning; creates pathways for young people; provides work for professional musicians; develops audiences of the future; is an outlet for creativity; celebrates local community life; brings professional musicians into the community; belongs to people of all ages; helps people belong to their community; creates opportunities for all the arts; develops skills of many kinds; develops pride in local cultural identity; celebrates cultural diversity; purchases music commodities; provides entertainment; supports and promotes professional artistic activities; works in partnership with other community groups and organisations.[9]

She uses the definition that "community music comprises music activities in a community where those activities are controlled by members of that community."[10]

Letts sees community music as made up of "programs that, unconstrained by any educational bureaucracy, have found solutions that fit the needs of particular communities."[11] Higgins even describes it as "an active resistance towards institutionalized structures" and traces this back to a reaction against "the emphasis of performance and virtuosity over teaching within university departments, the focus of school music towards the autonomous nature of the musical work, and the prominence of competitive 'talent' shows epitomized on TV with programs such as *Pop Idol* and *Fame Academy*."[12]

Often, community-music activities are defined in terms of what they are not: they are *not* organized top down, they are *not* based on unidirectional didactic teaching, but they are also *not* "just a group of amateurs having a good time."[13] As for content, the most commonly found musical styles are those local to the community, popular (or rock) music, rap, choral music, world music (particularly percussion traditions such as West African djembe and Brazilian samba batucada), but the scope is theoretically infinite: "the music may reflect the cultural life of a geographical community, re-created community, or imagined community," including the "proliferation of communities in cyberspace,"[14] although the latter is rarely considered in a field where direct human interaction is highly valued.

When speaking about artistic and pedagogical approaches, the fact that community music involves active participation tends to emphasized above all, probably as a reaction to the (perceived) dichotomy between listener and performer in much Western music, as well as (facilitated) self-directed learning. The former appears to be true in almost all instances identified as community music. The latter is only partially so: the very presence of a facilitator strongly steers any learning process, as can be deducted from the remarkably similar outcomes particular community music *animateurs* achieve from projects in very diverse settings. Leading practitioner Higgins courageously questions "how often facilitators ... fool themselves and/or fool the participants that they are working in open creative structures" rather than knowing "full well what the artistic outcome will be?"[15]

By far the most extensive list is that of beliefs, from philosophical stances to political convictions, which may or may not be shared by all participants. As Higgins points out, these are often informed by political activism of the 1970s,[16] but they can be traced back much further to Erb, who stated more than eighty years ago that "the aim of a community-music campaign should, in brief, be to create so widespread an interest in such a diversity of musical activities that *every individual* in the community may find an outlet and may be stimulated into musical expression."[17] Veblen traces back the positioning of community music to the binary between *Gemeinschaft* (community) and *Gesellschaft* (society) as made by the German thinker Ferdinand Tönnies in the 1880s. In the former, "personal, deep interactions, enduring social relationships, and clear understanding of individual's play, rooted, and assigned roles" are central:

> In Gemeinschaft, relationships are homogeneous and small scale; church and family are potent factors. In other words, this view of community is pictured as pastoral, rural and idyllic where everyone knew their neighbors, were interdependent etc. By contrast, Gesellschaft or society indicates the presence of these factors: Rational and calculative interactions, fleeting relationships, social and geographic mobility and fluid roles. In Gesellschaft, Tönnies theorized, what you are and achievement are most important. Society is large scale, heterogeneous; the state, business, education and media are powerful.[18]

Undoubtedly the distance from and even mistrust of formal structures has caused community music to remain much in the shadow in statistics, research, and discussions on music education at national levels. Perhaps the most important international platform for exchange of practices and views to date has been the Commission for Community Music Activities of the International Society for Music Education. In a series of sessions on the nature of community music from 1996 to 2002, this group has attempted to define key characteristics, which can be summarized in five points, many of which continue to be topics of discussion:

- Community Music Activities stimulate development of *active musical knowing* (including verbal musical knowledge where appropriate) through multiple learner/teacher relationships and processes, and *flexible teaching, learning and facilitation modes* (aural, notational, holistic, experiential, atomistic);
- Community Music Activities put emphasis on a variety and diversity of musics that reflect and enrich the cultural life of the community and of the participants, with emphasis on active *participation* in music-making of all kinds (performing, improvising, and creating);
- Community Music Activities strive for excellence and quality in both the *processes* and *products* of music-making relative to group and individual goals of the participants;
- Community Music Activities can come into existence *organically* (e.g. Javanese village gamelans), or can be active *interventions* in the musical and social landscape by community music *animateurs* to "restore" music to the community;
- Community Music Activities demonstrate respect for the *cultural property* of a given community and acknowledgment of both individual and group ownership of musics, honouring of origins and intents of specific musical practices, including links to ritual, churches, mosques and temples, but also contemporary rites of passage.[19]

From this list, which again reads as much like a policy statement as like an analysis of community music activities as a whole, we can deduce a number of key characteristics. What is usually called community music is almost invariably an active intervention, which implies a challenge to tradition, authenticity of time and place, and original context. At the same time, it professes to honor cultural ownership. Community music embraces cultural diversity. While there are examples of intercultural or maybe even transcultural practices, the practical choices in this area will often dictate the choice for a single tradition, which mostly translates in a multicultural or even a monocultural approach.

Community music takes actual music making as a starting point, which implies a praxial and often holistic approach, which is reinforced by the absence of a formal teacher who steers the process and the use of a variety of learning strategies. As participants are active in the creative process, they can be seen to construct their own musicality. In actual practice, this is often qualified by the *animateur* taking a dominant role in coaching the ensemble and bringing the music together toward a performance or event.

In a recent policy statement, the ISME Commission for Community Music Activities pulls together a number of strands and places them in a wider context:

Community Music is a vital and dynamic force that provides opportunities for participation and education in a wide range of musics and musical experiences. Community Music activities are based on the premise that everyone has the right and ability to make and create musics. Accordingly, such programs can act as a counterbalance and/or complement to formal music institutions and commercial music concerns. In addition to involving participants in the enjoyment of active music-making and creativity, Community Music provides opportunities to construct personal and communal expressions of artistic, social, political, and cultural concerns. Also Community Music encourages and empowers participants to become agents for extending and developing music in the community. In the pursuit of musical excellence and innovation, Community Music activities also contribute to the development of economic regeneration, create job opportunities in the cultural sectors, and enhance the quality of life for communities. In all these ways Community Music activities can complement, interface with, and extend formal music education structures.[20]

The search for definitions remains elusive: "Just as 'music' and 'community' are situated, contested, contingent, and hard to pin down, so too are concepts of community music as practice and as scholarship. In short, community music is a complex, multidimensional, and continuously evolving human endeavour."[21]

For music education, these characteristics, which do not necessarily apply to every single community-music activity, imply a flexible approach to most of the issues discussed in this publication: cultural diversity, choice of repertoire, tradition, authenticity and context, tangible and intangible aspects of learning, holistic and atomistic, notation-based and aural approaches. In this way, practical examples and experiments in community-music activities can serve research into alternative models of music learning and teaching, in order to widen the framework dictated by the history and structure of formal music education in terms of content, methodology, and practice.

As understanding of community music and its potential for reintroducing organic processes into formal music education advances, it is quite possible that one day, as Veblen claims, it will "constitute a paradigm shift in music education."[22] At the same time, it needs to be acknowledged that many community music activities are still far from ideal for lack of resources, pedagogical insight, musical knowledge, or true engagement with the community, defects that are rarely addressed because of the loose organizational structure behind most projects.

With the growth in academic interest, a number of university degree programs in community music have now been established, notably in the United Kingdom, Ireland, and South Africa, while many multipurpose colleges and universities in the United States have active community-outreach programs. Meanwhile, organization, settings, and practices also mature rapidly outside academia. Music Centre The Sage Gateshead, in the northeast of England, is

> pioneering an approach to music education that aims to bring together the key features of highest-quality community music, music education, conservatory practice, and an international performance center and creative laboratory. The vision is of a center for musical discovery, which acts as a source of energy for the whole northern region of England, recognizing no hierarchy of musical forms or genres but rather seeking to encourage and support all citizens to embrace music as an active cultural tool, choosing musical languages according to their fitness for purpose.[23]

This brief excursion, like the quest for definitions for world music earlier in this book, shows a wealth of divergent and even conflicting approaches to community music: stressing geographical closeness or shared ambitions in cyberspace, rejecting formal organization or striving for centers of excellence, including or excluding music in churches or mosques (or, for that matter, local Rotary Clubs and Wagner Societies). This diversity is not necessarily a sign of weakness or lack of focus but may well reflect the vibrancy and flexibility of the phenomenon. In fact, in an extensive recent study of six vibrant settings for community music across Australia, the research team came to the conclusion that rather than forcing divergent practices into restrictive definitions, it was more fruitful to consider how each community music activity responded to nine domains that seemed to define each individual practice: infrastructure, organization, visibility/PR, relationship to place, social engagement, support/networking, dynamic music making, engaging pedagogy/facilitation, and links to school.[24]

For music education, the lessons lie in responsiveness to five key themes of community practice as formulated by Higgins: "identity, context, community, participation and pedagogy."[25] If community music builds on structures and enculturation processes that are naturally supported in the community (as opposed to superimposed), formal music education may well increase its effectiveness by observing, emulating, and collaborating with community music's most successful incarnations.

Private Teachers

The realm of the private music teacher is probably still the most common single source worldwide for gaining skills and knowledge in art music traditions; in many popular musics, private teaching is superseded by self-directed and peer learning.

In Western classical music, privately organized apprenticeships, with contracts between the teacher and the parents of the student, lasted up to the first decades of the twentieth century.

This structure of transmission, which strongly resembles ones that can still be found in many other parts of the world,

> began as early as the age of eight, whether or not the child was being tutored by a parent. Lasting anywhere from three to 12 years, this agreement between the teacher and the child's family involved either payment during that period or a percentage of the apprentice's income in his early career. The teacher served as a mentor, indeed as an agent for the young musician.[26]

Even within the formal environment of conservatories, much of the master-apprentice relationship has been maintained with one-on-one teaching at the core of most curricula, although there are indications that the singular focus on performance skills may be shifting somewhat,[27] along with the perception of the teacher as the omniscient source of all musical insight. In both environments, the student is increasingly recognized and empowered as the key player in the learning process.[28]

Private teachers are at some disadvantage in relation to institutionalized teaching in the sense that they do not have the support of a team of specialists on various subjects of the profession. They may also not have the knowledge or resources to develop a well-balanced curriculum. Further, there is rarely any public funding for this teaching. On the other hand, private music teachers are not weighed down by government regulations and output requirements. They can concentrate on what they consider to be truly useful for each individual student. However, as most musical practices are surrounded by specific codes of behavior, the freedom of movement of a teacher in a specific tradition may be limited by social forces. Private music teachers do not have to conform to rules and regulations of institutionalized teaching, but they generally lose clientele quickly if they do not answer community expectations in terms of content or methodology.

The social context of music and the educational process defines position and attitude of both learners and teachers to a large extent. In a strongly hierarchical society with high regard for a particular music and music education, the teacher can become like a god, as is the case in India. By contrast, the former president of the International Association of Jazz Educators (now defunct) described the role of the jazz teacher: "The teacher in jazz is not the all-knowing carrier of the art, like in classical music. A jazz teacher serves as an example to his students. The teacher of jazz does not show the only possible way but only a possible way."[29] Although the actual practice of jazz teaching displays a wide variety of approaches, from highly directional to stimulating self-exploration, as a philosophy of jazz education, such a position may well be maintained.[30] This resonates with many world-music traditions where improvisation plays a central role. As discussed before, in popular music, with its absence of a canon, it is often difficult or even undesirable to define a teacher; this applies equally to hip-hop, highlife, and musica popular brasileira. Many practices across the world echo the mitigated master-disciple model of Western classical music, the more egalitarian relationships in jazz, or the peer-learning experiences common in popular music.

These dynamic interactions constitute a complex and fascinating area, as underlying values are rarely made explicit. When the actors in this relationship come from different cultures, the complications multiply, as the conventions may not be understood readily by all involved. Work on intercultural communication from sociology provides an interesting framework for coming to grips with these issues. In a famous study of constructs in corporate headquarters across nations, Hofstede identified five dimensions that strongly influence interaction between people:

a. small versus large power distance;
b. individualism versus collectivism;
c. long term versus short term orientation;
d. masculinity versus femininity;
e. avoiding versus tolerating uncertainty.[31]

It is clear that all of these dimensions are eminently relevant to music transmission across cultures, especially if, for the purpose of relevance to music education, item d is modified into "strongly gendered versus gender-neutral." This set of dimensions can elucidate (a) the egalitarian samba band versus the power of the guru in Indian classical music; (b) the isolation of the Chinese qin player versus the community spirit of the Javanese village gamelan; (c) the difference between a long apprenticeships with an African kora master versus community-music projects oriented toward a performance the next week; (d) rigidly defined gender roles in Aboriginal music versus mixed choirs in the United States; and (e) the problems many Asian students experience when they are faced with postmodern acceptance of uncertainties when learning music in the West (having come from a culture where authorities are attributed absolute insights) versus the inquisitive and challenging minds of young people from America and Europe.

In the light of Hofstede's framework and some of the other factors discussed, three basically different responses by music teachers to the challenges of new environments can be identified:

1. THE TEACHER MAINTAINS THE WAY OF TEACHING THAT HE OR SHE HAS PERSONALLY EXPERIENCED, OFTEN IN THE CONTEXT OR THE CULTURE OF ORIGIN.   This is an attitude that can be fed by allegiance to and respect for the tradition, conviction, arrogance, insecurity, ignorance, or an intelligent appraisal of the market. The first three of these qualities are quite obvious. An excellent example of "playing the market" is the emphasis Indian music teachers in the late 1960s placed on their position as gurus. This answered the expectations that a generation of searching Westerners had of all things Indian. This approach has a substantial risk of failure by not acknowledging contemporary realities that surround the musical practice. While key qualities in the music may be retained, the frustration level among students from another culture causes a significant drop-out rate. I remember that after about five years of study with my sitar teacher, I found myself to be the only survivor of a group of some fifty students that started around 1975. In some instances, this may be an intended mechanism for natural selection; in others, it may be an undesired effect.

2. THE TEACHER COMPLETELY ASSUMES THE STYLE OF TEACHING OF THE HOST ENVIRONMENT.   This generally occurs when musicians strive to be accepted into an established institutional environment, seeking validation for themselves and their music. It is sometimes difficult for musicians who feel truly foreign in these institutions to resist being intimidated and adapting to the dominant culture. For instance, they may resort to notation out of insecurity rather than conviction. When I started working for the Amsterdam Music School in 1990, I was struck by the insistence on extensive use of notation by the Turkish saz teacher, while he performed music that had been played and handed down without notation for generations, although this has changed in Turkey as well (see the section on conservatories later in this chapter).

3. THE TEACHER ADOPTS A MIX OF THE TWO TRADITIONS OF TEACHING, AND POSSIBLY ADDS NEW ELEMENTS INSPIRED BY OTHERS.   In practice, this is the approach most commonly encountered, sometimes inspired by necessity but mostly by choice. The intelligent music teacher assesses the profile of his or her students, weighs the alternatives in relation to the students' ambitions and possibilities, and proceeds accordingly. When applied consciously, creatively, and conscientiously, this can be a highly effective way of adapting teaching strategies, even at a superficial level. When applied haphazardly, it can be no more than a halfhearted attempt to marry the irreconcilable and fail to retain students or develop their skills.

In some communities and a number of private settings, there are indigenous systems of recognition and accreditation. When I was working with young Gambian kora master Alagi Mbye in the 1990s, he proudly told me that the old masters had given him a stick, which signified that he had been accepted into the centuries-old lineage of professional historians and storytellers (*griots* or *jaliyas*) in West Africa.

In India, there is an important ceremony to celebrate acceptance by a guru into a gharana (a style school). Among Hindus, this is performed by a Brahmin priest. A thread (*ganda*) is tied around the right wrists of the student and the teacher, signifying a bond and mutual responsibility for life. The next stages in the process (which may well be ten years later) are performing with the teacher onstage and, finally, getting permission to perform solo. In Hindustani music, the first solo performance is not necessarily marked as a major event, but in South Indian dance this artistic coming of age, known as *arangetram*, is very much a rite of passage.

Aboriginal songmen do not see performance as a rite of passage but simply will not pass on restricted traditional knowledge if they are not convinced that a young man is ready to receive it. This highlights the coexistence of two systems: one where the crucial criterion is whether the student is ready to receive the knowledge and the other to test the skills and knowledge at the end of the process. This is comparable to (but not quite the same as) auditions and final exams in much Western music training. Similar systems exist in other cultures, such as the *iemoto* and *halau* systems of Japan and Hawaii.[32] Western degrees and diplomas may well be regarded as formalized versions of these ancient systems.

Formal Music Education

In the area of formal music education, the aforementioned three major institutional structures dedicated to practical music training constitute the ecosystem: music in schools for general education, which in most countries have programs to introduce children to music; public and private music schools, which are dedicated to extracurricular music education for children, young adults, and amateurs; and conservatories (and the related *académies de musique, Musikhochschulen,* music departments, or schools of music, whether within or outside of university environments). These are at once the flagships of global music education and the settings that need to be scrutinized most critically in the light of cultural diversity.

In her insightful book on Irish traditional music, McCarthy presents musical and educational institutions as "centres of cultural power and reproduction." She argues that "a group's values, its priorities, and its relationship with ancestral culture are visible in such institutions. They are resonant of music traditions of the past; they energise the present by reinventing and reincorporating tradition and in the process shape the future of individual lives, communities, and the cultural life of the nation and its image abroad."[33] This is an attractive scenario.

Others observe that formal structures of music education may be significant obstacles to realizing culturally diverse practices. As Blacking puts it, "Strictly speaking, 'multicultural education' means separate education, because different systems of education cannot be combined; that is, the educational distinctiveness of each cultural system is automatically eliminated as soon as they are presented within a single education system."[34]

At the basis of most formal music education lies a defined curriculum. "Curriculum is grounded on philosophical assumptions about the purposes and methods of education," Jorgensen writes, "as a practical entity, it expresses the philosophical assumptions of its maker(s) much as an art work expresses the ideas and feelings of its creator(s) and performer(s) . . . embodying the assumptions that comprise it, practically speaking, one cannot separate the curriculum from the assumptions that ground it."[35] In that sense, "curriculum is simply the outworking in practice of thoughts, desires, and beliefs about what ought to take place in education."[36]

If curriculum and its translation into practice constitute a crystallization of educational philosophies, it can reflect the present, herald the future, or continue to represent views of past decades or even centuries. As such, the organization of music transmission can be a progressive, stabilizing, or conservative mechanism of considerable influence. This is of the greatest importance for the present discussion.

The following is derived from a paper I wrote and presented in 2004 called "Blame it on the Germans!"—among whom I must admit I conveniently included one Swiss and two Austrians. The first of these is the educationalist Pestalozzi, who, as mentioned earlier, propagated a number of principles that are largely still—or again—current today. During and after his lifetime (1746–1827), these spread across the Western world. This is how the eminent music educator Lowell Mason presented them during his successful campaign to gain a better position for music education in the United States in the 1830s:

1. To teach sounds before signs and to make the child learn to sing before he learns the written notes or their names;
2. To lead him to observe by hearing and imitating sounds, their resemblances and differences, their agreeable and disagreeable effect, instead of explaining these things to him—in a word, to make active instead of passive in learning;
3. To teach but one thing at a time—rhythm, melody, and expression, which are to be taught and practiced separately, before the child is called to the difficult task of attending to all at once;
4. To make him practice each step of these divisions, until he is master of it, before passing to the next;
5. To give the principles and theory after the practice, and as induction from it;

6. To analyze and practice the elements of articulate sound in order to apply them to music; and

7. To have the names of the notes correspond to those used in instrumental music.[37]

Most of these ideas come across as surprisingly contemporary and form the basis of present-day conceptions of organizing music education, with musical sound at the center. However, items 3, 4, and 6 invite critical reflection. In the decades that followed, these were partially challenged but largely reinforced by a number of Pestalozzi's successors. Johann Friedrich Herbart (1776–1841), who was heavily influenced by Pestalozzi, went on to develop a system of scientific, organized lessons with measurable results. To him, "access to the power of an artwork could only be guaranteed through analysis." He even went to the point of claiming that the actual sound of a score was an inessential property.[38]

This emphasis on analysis translated into the note-reading methodology by Holt, as well as the widespread tonic sol-fa system of notation advocated by John Curwen. As Volk states, these were in fact "in conflict with the more Pestalozzian 'rote first' approach and the controversy continued until the turn of the century, though both 'rote' and 'note' methods were accepted in music education."[39] We find examples of both approaches to this day.

Herbart's views on aesthetics came to full fruition in the key work of Eduard Hanslick, 1854's *The Beautiful in Music*. The formalistic approach to music in this treatise, which promoted that the aesthetic effect of music could best be understood by its structure, came to greater prominence in the decades to follow, with substantial impact on music curricula across the world. It peaked in the work of Heinrich Schenker in Vienna, who developed a system of graphic analyses showing the fundamental line (*Urlinie*) of any musical piece (from the Western classical canon), ultimately carrying the reduction of any piece to bare harmonic essentials, the *Ursatz*.[40]

Critics have raised that this system, for all its analytic brilliance, does not necessarily reflect the thinking and experience of the composer, the performer, or the listener. Nevertheless, these influences may explain why so many music curricula seem to have theory and analysis as core subjects but few include aesthetics. Of over fifty conservatories I have queried about his, only two had dedicated courses on music and beauty. That is quite striking considering that they are in the business of training students whose primary aim it is to become practicing musicians and delight audiences.

Other influences of considerable importance were the formal beginnings of musicology and comparative musicology, which are usually traced back to Adler's *"Umfang, Methode und Ziel der Musikwissenschaft"* ("Scope, Method, and Aims of Musicology") of 1885. Although this excellent and forward-looking essay emphatically included the study of musics from other parts of the world, it did so from the viewpoint of the Western researcher, making full use of analysis, partly through the recent inventions for pitch measurement and sound recording. As the beliefs of the time were based on an evolutionary hierarchy leading to Western art music as the top of the pyramid, principles that could be applied to Western classical music were raised to universal applicability.

These developments in turn interacted with positivist, modernist approaches to education, which suggested that there was a structural, linear way in which knowledge could be transferred from a more or less absolute source of knowledge to a recipient of this knowledge. And although most educators nowadays seem to adhere more to the idea that learners "construct" their (inevitably subjective) body of knowledge, much of our higher education and curricular structure still seems to be based on a modernist concept of "one curriculum fits all."

Most formal music education can be described as representing a view of music that is predominantly atomistic, notation-based, and relatively static in its approach to tradition, authenticity, and context. It can be regarded as still following nineteenth-century German ideas and values. It is worth examining to what extent this is true for music in schools, public music schools, and conservatories and how it interacts with the rise of musical diversity.

Music in Schools

In her analysis of historical developments in relation to cultural diversity in music education, Volk concludes that "at the end of the nineteenth century, music education [in the United States], like education in general, reflected a European viewpoint, heavily influenced by advances in German educational methodology, especially that of Pestalozzi, Froebel, and Herbart."[41] At this time, the songs used commonly hailed from a number of European sources, but their background and context was generally ignored. As an illustration, Volk refers to the selection in songbooks by the influential educator Mason, where texts and melodies were recombined at random, which "apparently did not concern Mason."[42]

Even though Volk acknowledges substantial differences in approaches to music education over the next hundred years through the influence of Kodály, Orff, and the development of technology, she maintains that "the methodologies and materials of the music curriculum of the late 1890s are the foundation of music education as we know it today."[43] While this position is difficult to maintain with respect to much musical material, considering the wide range of pop, jazz, and even world music that is used in present-day classrooms, it is relevant to consider in this light choices of musical foci and methodologies for cultural diversity, developed at a time when there was no awareness of world music as it is now perceived.

Music in schools has always been one of the most challenging areas of teaching world music, as it needs to address the question what part world music can play in introducing children to the diversity and musical practices and ideas in contemporary societies. If we take the purpose of contemporary music education in schools to be preparing children to "construct" themselves as "musical citizens," rather than molding them into competent consumers and representatives of a specific idiom, what forms of music education are appropriate for children in a multicultural society?

The answer to that question partly depends on the vision of society in both the near and distant future. Approaches to music education focusing exclusively on Western classical music seem to be losing ground. The argument that everybody in a multicultural society should learn its dominant language is widely accepted, as language is an important tool in the organization of a society. But that does not hold true for music in the same way, particularly if we consider the repertoire children are exposed to? Western classical music is certainly a great music tradition, but it is hardly the most striking feature in the world of sound surrounding children, which includes major input from hearing music in association with other experiences, such as movies, TV, games, and video. That has led to discrepancies with prevailing ideas about linking music education to children's actual musical experience, particularly in the case of children from other cultures. By 1990, multicultural awareness had grown sufficiently in both Europe and the United States to place cultural diversity firmly on the agenda, although implementation often remained problematic.[44]

This is mirrored by challenges in Postcolonial Africa. Flolu writes about the situation in Ghana: "The crucial question is, can music teaching in Ghana not be based on African resources without necessarily continuing to be Western oriented and still share uniformity with the education systems of other countries?"[45] Later, he continues to describe the challenge: "Real music making occurs outside the classroom and the school, but inside the community . . . class music cannot be organised in exactly the same manner as people are seen to be involved with music in the community. Schools are artificial institutions designed by society to explore, analyse and criticise our culture in a special way."[46] He concludes that "the task before us is to define an educational agenda which will synthesise indigenous culture and traditional aurality with the literary and scientific resources of modern formal education."[47] Similar concerns are voiced by others about a variety of cultures.

Intercultural societies, in which many cultures exist more or less independently but interact with each other continually, face a challenge in translating this reality into programs for schools. Schools wishing to prepare children for a society that offers a great variety of music cultures are most likely to achieve that aim by providing them with a structure to order that diversity. Otherwise, the richness of different music cultures can become chaotic to them. This entails the risk of being uninteresting to the children or, some may argue, even threatening and giving rise to hostile reactions.

A transcultural approach could be viable in these situations, introducing children to a wide variety of musical concepts and values from different cultures through a well-devised program, which allows them to choose their own paths of further musical development. However, as most educators will realize, effectuating such an approach requires a great deal of work, a great deal of thinking, a great deal of discussing with musicians and music teachers from other cultures, and a great deal of listening to students.[48] These are substantial challenges, which can only be met if schools and curriculum designers manage to build on developing models for designing new teaching material, and perhaps most importantly, teacher training curricula: the skills and attitude of the teacher are central to the success of cultural diversity in music education. The developing link between ethnomusicology and music education may prove to be crucial in this area.

In many countries, *intercultural* education has been an issue since the 1980s. The activities have been threefold: classroom teachers introduced world music in the classroom by gathering material themselves; new, more inclusive methodologies have been published; and cooperation was realized with "culture bearers"— world musicians who were invited into the schools. All three approaches have led to successes and to disappointments. The value and quality of the material gathered depended heavily on the knowledge and sense of the teacher. The translation of songs from other cultures into staff notation and the ensuing reinterpretation proved particularly challenging in terms of creating an "authentic" experience for children.

New methodologies partially address this problem by offering sound recordings and contextual information (but rarely pedagogical suggestions or insights). Culture bearers come into the classroom with very good intentions but often without sufficient musical and/or pedagogical experience. This can lead to very disappointing results as well, which may include negative stereotyping, the exact opposite of what most educators try to achieve.

A survey of methodologies incorporating world music[49] (subsequently assessed by teacher training students at the Amsterdam Conservatory (classroom observations, November 1998) found some to be factually accurate and sensitive in approach while presenting other cultures. Others still stereotype more than would be expected from Westerners with access to newspapers, televisions, and the Internet. A method for primary schools published in the 1990s stated that people in Africa communicate with drums, slightly dubious in an age when almost the entire continent already kept in contact by e-mail and mobile phones.

Projects with skilled representatives of other music cultures were probably on the increase during the 1990s and constitute a promising format, especially if the experience is overseen by someone who possesses some understanding of both Western educational practice and world music.[50] One of the pioneers in that area, Ki Mantle Hood, was quite severe in his vision of required skills for contemporary music teachers:

Late in the twentieth century, no serious musician of whatever professional commitment can any longer afford to remain ignorant of the
music, for example, of China . . . or of Korea and Japan, which it strongly
influenced. As we near the 21st century, an admission of ignorance of the
primary cultural features (and music is one of them) of India, Southeast
Asia, the North and South American continents is an embarrassing
confession for anyone claiming to be educated.[51]

It is not the music teachers of the world who are to blame; the main weaknesses
lie in teacher training. The new music teachers need to have not only a firm grasp
of the various types of music they teach but also a real understanding of teaching
methods across the world and of themselves as actors in the musical learning
process. They must not become the stereotypical "professional educator who
confuses method with music" of which Hood warned almost fifty years ago.[52] In
any teaching situation, they are required to take position consciously with regard to
the cultural setting they are in, sensitive to the choices open to them with regard
to tradition, context, and authenticity, and choose their approach to teaching
accordingly.

Based on my experience in leading a four-year curriculum innovation at the
music teacher training course at the Amsterdam Conservatory (1996–2000), there
is no evidence that such a skill package is easy to master for large contingents of
emerging music teachers, but it is possible to provide students with tools for
working effectively in classrooms with a limited number of specific world-music
traditions.[53] This addresses at least one of the great challenges: the tension between
knowing a little a bit about many musics and having a solid grasp of a few.

In considering music education in schools during the past two decades, the
general picture that emerges from the professional literature, examining material
and methodologies, and observations of practices is that world music in schools has
generally been intercultural in intention; influenced by government policies,
schools have tried to generate understanding and meetings among cultures.
Much of the content has been multicultural, however, generally focusing on one
tradition at a time and rarely on contemporary music. "Pure" traditions (authentic
in the sense of being practices with a history in their cultures of origin) have been
highlighted over fusion. There has been relatively little concern for authenticity in
the "new identity" sense, with some attempts to explain but few to re-create the
original context.

Much of the practice in schools approaches world music traditions as
objects to be studied and analyzed in much the same way as pieces of classical
music are.[54] As Mills points out, choice of repertoire, appropriate pedagogies,
issues of authenticity, and the dynamics of music, as well as awareness of sensitivities among students (ethnic, religious, or otherwise), require more work than

merely downloading "ethnic songs" from the Internet, but are also more rewarding in potentially delivering students the opportunity to engage with the world of music in all its diversity.[55]

Public and Private Music Schools

Public and private music schools share their early history with conservatories: the famous Paris Conservatoire was as much a finishing school for young ladies as an institute preparing professional singers and instrumentalists. The distinction between the training of professional and amateur musicians was only drawn in the latter half of the nineteenth century.[56] Since that period, amateur music schools have tried to make the heritage of Western classical music accessible to a wider group of learners. At first, the middle-class music lovers who initiated the idea financed this type of music education. As time went by, however, government was conveniently found willing to support public music schools in many countries. In this way, the basis was laid for highly organized systems of music schools, particularly in northern and western Europe.

While these institutions were founded and subsidized to make "quality music" or "high art" (in the terms of the time) accessible to learners from lower socioeconomic backgrounds, they are generally too expensive, even when partially subsidized (with the exception of music schools in some Scandinavian countries, which are free). For example, music schools and municipalities in the Netherlands have found that the student population of music schools hails largely from a fairly affluent cultural elite, where the parents would in fact be able to pay for private tuition (e.g., Profijtonderzoek Gemeente Amsterdam in 1990).

In such settings, reaching out for prospective students across all levels of society has failed at least partially. Music schools have turned out to be a successful community project but mainly for the middle classes. As a consequence, during the 1990s, a number of large municipalities decided to redirect their arts education funding toward programs in schools, in order to reach out to those children who could not find their way to public music schools. In this process, longitudinal, instrument-specific trajectories were sacrificed.

The failure of public music schools to attract a cross-section of society can be blamed on a range of factors. First, formal music education in Western classical music requires more than merely financial accessibility; it needs a supporting context, mostly in the form of a family interested in music or cultural activities at large. Second, the image and prestige of learning music at a music school are only positive in certain circles. It is easy to imagine that in culturally diverse inner-city areas, playing viola da gamba does not generate kudos, while rapping or singing R&B might.

In the 1980s, courses in world music at public music schools were specifically aimed at minority groups. Hundreds of projects were started all over the United States and across Europe, particularly in the United Kingdom, Scandinavia, the Benelux, Germany, and France. Many appeared to be an expression of political correctness rather then driven by artistic motivation, as a questionnaire from the Netherlands Arts Education Association (see below) and subsequent comments from music school directors bore out.[57] The projects could usually be funded externally, so they did not interfere with the "core business" of Western classical music teaching, and a minimum of commitment was required from the institution.

Generally, little effort was made to integrate these lessons, the teachers, the students, and the music into the system of the music schools. The courses were generally isolated from support in terms of content, methodology, organization, and strategic communication. Most were discontinued as a result of problems with teachers, pupils, subsidies, and the culture of teaching, problems that nobody seemed ready to tackle for fear of being politically incorrect. In the sensitive atmosphere around minorities, it was considered inappropriate to ask critical questions.[58]

In 1991, the Netherlands Arts Education Association (Vereniging voor Kunstzinnige Vorming, or VKV) conducted a survey of world-music courses realized and terminated in Dutch public music schools between 1980 and 1990. The responses showed that more than 50 courses had failed, mostly for the reasons mentioned above: students disappearing or teachers leaving, with or without problems. Only in a few major cities, such as Amsterdam and Rotterdam, was there any continuity.

The 1990s brought a shift of approach. In one of a series of PR documents emanating from a project aiming to bring world music to public music schools across the country, I described the new awareness as follows.

"In February 1990, the Amsterdam Music School decided to set up a substantial world music department with a new formula. The programs were emphatically integrated into the regular structures: the same classrooms, the same numbers of students per hour, the same rates, and the same contracts for teachers. Twenty-three specialist musicians were specifically hired to teach music from ten different cultural areas. Some of the musical traditions did have a direct link to minorities; others hardly or not at all. The key criterion was that they were all considered worthwhile from a *musical* point of view.

In that way, the courses in the world music school distanced themselves from serving as a community center but were profiled as an integral part of an institute for arts education, on an equal footing with lessons in classical piano or jazz drumming. The focus was on the art; reaching new groups of pupils was a secondary goal. This world music school model turned out to be quite successful in the Netherlands. By September 1990, just less than 300 students had registered for courses at the Amsterdam World Music School. An informal analysis of names (which provided easy evidence of Moroccan, Turkish, or Asian descent) and visits to classrooms for African- and Latin-inspired music (in order to identify Surinami students, who tend to have Dutch names) indicated that about half of them were of Dutch ancestry, and the other half were people with various non-Dutch ancestries. That provided the institute with the basis for in-depth integration of non-Western music into the school."[59]

Reflecting on these programs from a perspective of being "engulfed in a sea of multiculturalism" and political correctness in the United States at the time, Campbell recalls seeing "teaching world music" as "a concept on the rise in Europe, a movement in the making, and it was the music—the virtuosic, intricate, nuanced, energetic, subtle (and not-so-subtle) music—that was 'driving the bus' and leading the movement." Weighed down by ideology at home, she saw that "young people were learning music from heritage musicians, culture-bearers, traditional artists, and they were motivated by the beauty of the music. How novel, how refreshing, how real, there in Western Europe."[60]

In retrospect, an obvious weakness of these programs was in fact the emphasis on music for music's sake, based on values behind Western art music rather than those of the communities themselves. But it also proved a strength in appealing to the system: directors of other music schools in the Netherlands, who had seen other projects with world music fail in the 1980s, started approaching the Amsterdam Music School in order to find practices suitable for their environment. First the VKV and then the Netherlands Institute for Arts Education (LOKV) took on the responsibility of coordinating the development of world music schools on a national scale.

Within seven years, a dozen major music schools in the Netherlands had a world music department, and several others prepared or expressed interest in starting one. Many of the students were beginning to demonstrate considerable skill in playing their instruments; these were highlighted by annual concerts of world music school students from various parts of the Netherlands. By 1997, more than 1,500 students were taking weekly lessons in one of eight major world music departments at public music schools in the Netherlands.[61]

However, the rise of world music schools (or, more correctly, world music departments within public music schools) did not represent a major shift in musical awareness toward inter- or transcultural models. From an institutional perspective, the picture provided by world music classes in the Netherlands was of a predominantly multicultural approach. There were a few projects that tried to bridge cultures (intercultural), but the largest offer and demand seemed to be tuition in specific traditions. African percussion (djembe) and Turkish folk music (bağlama saz) scored highest, followed by world choirs, Latin, flamenco, and Indian music.

Traditions tended to be approached in a fairly static way, reconstructed authenticity somewhat less so in view of the limited scope of beginning students, and the context of the musics in teaching rooms in a music school tended to be radically different from the original cultural environment. Being in formal education surroundings, teachers had the tendency to lean more toward atomistic, notation-based,

PHOTO 5.2.   Talip Özkan teaching saz at the Rotterdam Conservatory. Rotterdam, the Netherlands, spring 2002. Photo: Frank Dries.

and tangible aspects of teaching. However, strengthened by being surrounded by peers, they also partly retained the methods of learning and teaching that they had experienced themselves, as far as these could be accommodated in the new settings, such as an emphasis on group learning or working without notation. Finally, the term *world music school* was deliberately finite: once the awareness was established that municipal music schools were the place to go for gamelan, saz, or djembe lessons, these were marketed and conducted in the same way as piano or violin.

Conservatories

For all the ammunition they have provided to critics, the words *conservatory* and *conservative* are only very loosely related. *Conservatory* (with its variations *conservatoire* and *conservatorium*) derives from the Italian *conservatorio*, a word initially used to refer to orphanages that safeguarded children and trained them to sing for the church, a practice that started in 1537.[62]

Conservatories as we know them now only came to full bloom several centuries later. In fact, there were no conservatories during the time of Bach and Handel. Distinguishing themselves from earlier music education initiatives that were largely church-based, conservatories started to abound with the widespread closing of monasteries and church music schools in the latter half of the eighteenth century.[63] With the dual purpose of finishing school for young ladies and feeder institution of accomplished musicians to large orchestras, Paris Conservatoire was first, founded in 1784 (just seven years before Mozart's death), followed by Prague (1811), Vienna (1817), the Royal Academy of Music in London (1822), Leipzig (1843), Berlin (1850), and the Royal College of Music in London (1873).[64] During the twentieth century, the model was adopted in most Western and a number of Asian countries. In this way, a powerful and highly successful infrastructure for training musicians in Western classical music was established.

In most countries on the European mainland, there has been a rigid division between vocational and academic training, which means that music was studied either from a performance perspective at a conservatory or from a theoretical perspective at a university. The relationship between the practical study of music on the one hand and musicology on the other is summarized by Cook: "In the first half of the twentieth century music could be studied as a practical skill in conservatories, but only a handful of universities offered it. After the Second World War, however, there was a rapid expansion of the universities on both sides of the Atlantic, and it was in this context that the academic study of music became established as a subject in its own right."[65] In this setting, there were challenges. Cook refers to "a widely shared perception that the interface between musicology and music, between the academic discipline and the human experience, was not everything it could be."[66]

At the government level, most countries have only recently decided to abandon the influential ideas that caused this separation, which can be traced back to the 1820s, when Wilhelm van Humboldt defined the principles on which he based his prestigious and influential university in Berlin.[67] The Bologna Declaration of 1999, in which the European ministers of education expressed their intention to create a single degree system for vocational and academic training, is likely to prove a landmark decision in reversing this separation.

While the focus of conservatories up to World War II had been exclusively on training musicians for opera, symphony orchestras, chamber music, and solo performance in Western classical music, in the second half of the twentieth century, this widened to include church music, contemporary art music, jazz, popular music, and finally also world music. The primary reference to Western classical music persists even more in the United States, where Nettl finds that "the 'music' in schools of music always means, exclusively or overwhelmingly, Western classical music."[68] But in the United States as well, pop, jazz, and world music have entered higher education. World music in the United States is, however, predominantly based in mainstream music departments that form part of the "liberal arts" model of higher education and, in spite of efforts by the National Association of Schools of Music, still has a very modest position in conservatories.[69]

Critiquing the almost exclusive focus on Western art music, Sloboda somewhat unkindly summarizes the characteristics of "classical conservatoire culture" as:

(a) concern with accurate and faithful reproduction of a printed score, rather than with improvisation or composition; (b) the existence of a central repertoire of extreme technical difficulty; (c) definitions of mastery in terms of ability to perform items from a rather small common core set of compositions within a culture; and (d) explicit or implicit competitive events in which performers are compared with one another by expert judges on their ability to perform identical or closely similar pieces.[70]

However harsh this description, the question arises whether conservatory curricula, with their emphasis on skill development and cognitive understanding of music, fully reflect ideas of excellence in music making at the beginning of the twenty-first century.

In addition, it is surprising how often the quality criteria and competencies required from professional musicians are sometimes oddly matched with those stressed in teaching. In many Western conservatories, young musicians who are most likely to play in a classical orchestra are taught with great emphasis on one-on-one settings, with ensemble or orchestra practice often as a side subject or in project form. Ironically, this prepares them quite well for the audition for a classical orchestra, where the applicant is asked to play alone and anonymously behind a screen for the selection committee, but hardly for the complex social context and performance practice of an orchestra. Such apparent disconnections are not exclusive to conservatories. In Indian classical music, improvisation is a key aspect of a performance. Fifty to ninety percent of a performance is improvised, or at least recomposed from existing building blocks and structures. However, most Indian teachers will teach endless short compositions and fixed improvisations, while structures underlying these improvisations are rarely taught explicitly. Yet neither the Western nor the Indian practices described are necessarily examples of unsuccessful music transmission. Although it is rarely made explicit, every system of atomistic instruction builds on assumptions about competencies achieved by the student through holistic learning beyond formal instruction.

Thus, a Western violin student may already have achieved a good sense of timing, tone, and timbre through extensive listening. Complementing these with predominantly tangible skills can make excellent sense. Improvisation does not seem to be a key issue in the instruction of Indian classical musicians, yet most musicians seem to be able to deal with the challenges it poses. If, however, the background of the musician is different, as in the case of non-Indians learning Indian music, he or she might need different training. These concepts are emerging more than ever in the light of the dynamics of music transmission and learning where more than one cultural influence plays a role. This can be through Western classical music traveling to other continents, but perhaps the most interesting cases for studying this phenomenon can be found when world music enters conservatories and schools of music, as this fully exposes the meeting and confrontation among various approaches to music making and learning.

PHOTO 5.3.   Latin jazz was the root of the world music program at Rotterdam Conservatory. Rotterdam, the Netherlands, 2002. Photo: Frank Dries.

World music started taking root in schools of music and conservatories between the 1960s and the 1980s. Among the pioneers were Wesleyan University, Columbia, UCLA, and CalArts in the United States; SOAS and Dartington College of Arts in the United Kingdom; Musikhochschule Basel in Switzerland; and Rotterdam Conservatory in the Netherlands. The phenomenon has since become more widespread. In the context of a 2002 research project, *Sound Links*, funded by the European Commission program Socrates, almost fifty European conservatories indicated some activity in the field of cultural diversity. In-depth study of the most active ones among these demonstrated that the engagement with world music varied from optional, non-credit-bearing activities to full degree courses. The research identified that there were five common "points of entry" for world music: composition, percussion, jazz, pop, and music education departments.[71] This is supported by the history of world music in higher education in the Netherland, taking the three Dutch conservatories most active in world music as examples: the Royal Conservatory in the Hague embraced African music through its percussion department, the Amsterdam Conservatory developed a strong program in cultural diversity after a major curriculum development project in its music education department, and the Rotterdam Conservatory started world music by expanding to Latin jazz from its jazz department.[72]

These programs are fascinating sites for a better understanding of developing multiple musical competencies. While the discussion on bimusicality started by Hood (and continued in Solis)[73] principally concerned gaining *some* practical skill in a world-music tradition as part of a liberal arts degree,[74] others aimed to become proficient or even professional performers in specific forms of world music. Probably the latter had a stronger claim to bimusicality (assuming they had learned another music before); the aim of the performing ethnomusicology ensembles is more a broadening of frames of musical reference, eminently valuable but rarely justifying a claim to competencies in performance that would be taken seriously in the tradition or community itself.

One of the most telling findings from *Sound Links* was that the issue of appropriate approaches and teaching methods was hardly addressed at all. This is remarkable because many of the traditions entering conservatories were based on entirely different precepts from Western classical music in terms of approaches to making, learning, and teaching music. They were in an environment where world musics were treated as static traditions that can only be authentic in their original cultural contexts, with modes of transmission that were aural and holistic (as opposed to notation-based and atomistic), all to be processed into systems that were measurable and accountable. Although many preconceptions were easily disproved for specific traditions in their contemporary "original" contexts, and even more so for those that had successfully taken root across the world, world music did create tension with the dominant educational climate in conservatories. The same is now occurring at a considerable scale in other parts of the world, especially in Asia, where nineteenth-century European models are being applied to music indigenous to their own cultures, with subsequent risks of losing diversity of performance formats, improvisation, and links to other aspects of culture. I have seen striking examples of this in China, Korea, and Vietnam.

Looking at music transmission from a cross-cultural perspective, including world music traditions, has major implications for curriculum and ultimately for the actual musics involved. As the perceived values of any music are embodied in the transmission process, a change in teaching method may result in a change of the tradition itself. In the recent history of Turkish folk music, it was promoted to a product of national pride as a result of the rise of awareness of the value of cultural heritage under Kemal Atatürk. In 1923, the first volume of transcriptions from fifteen different regions was published, the first of a steady stream of publications covering thousands of traditional compositions. Meanwhile, Turkish radio—the state radio in Ankara was established in 1937—rather than the villages became the center of folk-music practice, and radio musicians were expected and trained to play *a prima vista*.[75]

Similar reports come from Bali, where, as Peter Dunbar-Hall told me, senior and highly accomplished musicians from the villages were replaced by less skilled young musicians with diplomas from one of the state music conservatories (personal communication, 2008). This institutionalization of musics that have existed as a vibrant, living tradition for centuries can lead to fixing repertoire into a musical museum, effectively terminating the creativity that many would regard as an essential quality.

Some will argue that the acceptance of jazz in higher education has been a mixed blessing in a similar manner, with too many concessions to the Western classical curriculum structure and a sometimes dry, academic music practice as a result. Institutionalized jazz is being criticized widely for being technically correct but creatively poor. Whyton observes that "rarely are non-educators put on record celebrating the benefits of jazz pedagogy. Rather, they either suggest jazz education is bad and stifles creativity; or that its presence cannot do any harm—hardly a glowing endorsement of educational method by the jazz fraternity."[76] As Håkan Lundström, dean of the Malmö Academy of the Arts in Sweden, remarked about his now well-established jazz department: "Now, it is not one of the radical forces in the school. This happens often when something becomes institutionalised. It gets patterns, forms and shapes."[77]

While there is no need to downplay the success of jazz music in conservatories, there is indeed little evidence that it has become an innovative force in conservatories at large. On the contrary, the curricular emphasis on theory, analysis, history, and similar subjects has led to a new, "academic" approach to what was once a lively, performance-based tradition, with many teachers displaying a static, surprisingly "classical" or even canonical approach to performance and teaching (personal observations, 2001–2002).

Others, however, celebrate the success of jazz as a conservatory degree course. Wouter Turkenburg, head of Jazz Studies at the Royal Conservatory in the Hague and former president of the now defunct International Association of Jazz Educators, argued that jazz does not necessarily copy the dominant educational climate of the institutional environment: "By the mid-nineties, it has become clear that a certain distance was taken from the classical models. Jazz methodology now is able to stand and develop on its own," and "jazz teachers have managed to bring the aural tradition within the walls of the academies and conservatories."[78]

Turkenburg saw the entry of jazz into the conservatory system as a model for world music. He attributed the success of the integration to the fact that "the teaching format was adapted and altered from the existing format of classical music."[79] He argued that "world music stands the best chance to enter the academic music educational system if the path of jazz education is followed. This means by finding a format for world music by adapting and altering the teaching methods known in classical music and jazz."[80]

Conclusion

Although this book is primarily concerned with learning and teaching world music in formal settings, the spectrum from informal to formal learning environments is of considerable importance when we look at the potential and the obstacles faced by music traditions when shifting processes of instruction, educational acts, or environments. This is the case not only in the West but also in many countries where forms of world music originate, where governments actively engage with systems of learning and teaching music to preserve and develop their traditions. Very often, this formal education is based on models developed for Western classical music, which are based on very different sets of priorities.

However, finding these discrepancies in philosophical and practical approaches in institutions does not mean that all new forms of music are at peril when entering formal education. The tensions among systems of transmission do not have to be problems but can be stimulating challenges if openly discussed and intelligently addressed. Opposing forces in the contemporary musical landscape need each other. Particularly in the case of forms of world music, the traditional conditions for music learning and teaching are often shifting in the countries of origin as well.

Much learning of music has depended partially or entirely on community settings. These stimulating learning environments are vulnerable. While many long to restore these, often globalized and mediatized societies have moved on. Then the complex task of recontextualizing these transmission processes into formal environments begins. Traditional musics have to consider adapting their systems of transmission to new realities, while conservatories can find inspiration in methods of world music transmission and learning that adhere less strictly to a single idea of the truth, notation, structure, and authenticity and put greater responsibility on the student. In that sense, with a little creativity, some of the practices that were once regarded as "primitive" or "preliterate" because they had not developed notation, explicit theories, and curricula can now be considered cutting-edge examples of innovative approaches to music learning and teaching and help higher music education carve a niche in the musical complexities of the twenty-first century.

Across the spectrum from informal to formal learning environments, it is clear that a principal concern in shaping music education is the interaction between learner and example, facilitator, peer, or master. To interpret this from an intercultural perspective, the work of Hofstede provides an eminently useful series of continua to understand the interaction between learners and teachers/facilitators as dictated (or inspired) by their context. Figure 5.1 illustrates this final set of choices for the framework for cultural diversity in music education this book aims to define.

When musicians find themselves teaching in culturally diverse environments, they tend to demonstrate one of three responses to challenges to their system of music transmission: adherence to the way of teaching that they experienced or practiced in the culture of origin, complete assimilation of the style of teaching of the host environment, and adopting a mix of the two (or more) traditions of teaching relevant in the new context. This creates a continuum from extreme adherence to traditional styles of music transmission to complete adaptation to the

FIGURE 5.1.   Dimensions of interaction in learning and teaching music (based on Hofstede)

dominant styles of learning and teaching in a new environment. The practices of private teachers and in community settings are less heavily influenced by institutional pressures and may serve as inspiration for devising appropriate new approaches to learning and teaching in formal music education, taking into account the resistance to change in these environments.

The discussions here and in the preceding chapters have an obvious bearing on some of the major issues that have emerged in music and education during the past twenty years, including teacher-centered versus student-centered learning; broadness versus specialization; the order of learning and teaching styles in relation to the learner's musical development; definitions of outcomes and competency-based learning; talent, motivation, and authentic learning; and the creation of stimulating learning environments.[81]

From a contemporary perspective, different styles of structuring and organizing music education can be considered valid, but fitness for purpose and appropriateness for specific contexts must be consciously and conscientiously monitored at all times. In much organization and curriculum, there are still clear remnants of positivist, modernist approaches to learning and teaching, which presuppose that absolute truths exist that can be transmitted in a logical and scientific way. This does not correspond to current philosophical and pedagogical insights, in particular the view that the construction of knowledge is a highly personal one. For music education research, a considerable challenge lies in establishing which ways of organizing learning and teaching world music (and pop, rock, and jazz) can be considered most successful from the perspective of the defined goals of the institution, the community, the teacher, and the individual learner. This has the potential of improving actual practices across the board: music learning and teaching is most likely to be successful when those responsible for shaping the transmission process are fully aware of the implications of their choices, continually monitoring outcomes against perceptions of authorities, institutions, teachers, and learners.

→→ CHAPTER 6 ←←

Toward a Global Understanding
of Learning and Teaching Music

A Framework

*In Rosengård (literally "rose garden"), a highly culturally diverse but rather
bleak suburb of Malmö in Sweden, the secondary school has redesigned
its music program to reflect the musical interests of teenagers from dozens
of different cultures. The music room is well resourced: around the
normal classroom, four small studios have been built, allowing five bands to
practice at once. Each student is invited to bring in a recording of the music
he or she identifies with most. The music teacher takes these home
and arranges them. For the next lesson, the student who has brought in the
music takes the lead in sessions with peers. In the course of one hour, I hear
an Asian love song, Bosnian heavy metal, Turkish arabesk, and Afro pop.
The music program is seen as an important element in the school's efforts
to engage with a challenging population and empowers some of the students
who struggle with language and math to develop prestige and a sense of
self-worth.*

Numerous conscious and subconscious decisions regarding content and approach
lie at the basis of any situation of music transmission. These in turn dictate (or at
least steer) the interaction among learners, teachers (or facilitators), and their
environments. The *what, how, who,* and *where* of music transmission are closely
intertwined. Learning the highly refined and individual music of the qin in China
is different from the communal experience of samba schools in Brazil or the
creative process of a grunge band in Seattle. As a rule, they are well considered,
acknowledging the demands, possibilities, and restrictions of the specific music
and preferred transmission processes.

This may be challenged, however, in rapid or gradual processes of change, such as when music travels over a considerable cultural distance, whether from the eighteenth century to the twenty-first or from Papua New Guinea to New York. Similar challenges may occur when any music moves into institutional environments, where internal rules and external demands (from funding bodies or educational authorities) may weigh more heavily than choices musicians would make on the basis of assessing their environment. In culturally diverse settings, these challenges intensify as the complexity of underlying values and attitudes increases. In many contemporary learning environments, the latter situation is the norm rather than the exception.

In addition to the musical material itself, this complexity largely plays out across four realms: modes of transmission (as explored in chapter 4), issues of context (chapter 3), interaction between learner and teacher/facilitator (chapter 5),

TABLE 6.1. Indicators for modes of transmission

Atomistic/analytical	*Holistic*
• Use of didactic pieces of music such as graded exercises and etudes	• "Real" repertoire serving as the basis for actual transmission
• Explicit music theory	• Implicit music theory
• Substantial amount of speaking and explaining during music transmission	• Relatively little speaking and explanation during music transmission
• Conscious progress from simple to complex	• Intuitive progress from known to unknown
• Curriculum-based, often with formal structures and exams	• Individual path, confusion as consciously or unconsciously used instrument
• Teacher guides and controls learning process in didactic relationship	• Teacher demonstrates, coaches, or may even be absent (through radio, TV, recordings)

Written	*Aural*
• Central body of work exists in prescriptive notation that is used by performers	• No or little notation is used
• Students may be given material to learn in notation without prior exposure to actual sound)	• Tonal material largely improvised (or "restructured")
	• All music and exercises are first or even only presented in actual sound (live or recorded)

Tangible	*Intangible*
• Emphasis on instrumental technique	• Emphasis on expression
• Emphasis on well-defined repertoire	• Emphasis on creativity and improvisation
• Emphasis on theory	• Emphasis on abstract, spiritual, or metaphysical values

This part of the model has been inspired by Van den Bos, "Differences between Western and Non-Western Teaching Methods in Music Education."

and approaches to cultural diversity (chapter 2). While these realms may appear abstract, it is quite feasible to define key choices in each, which can then serve as indicators for the approaches that characterize individual transmission processes. Together, they can provide new insights into specific moments or entire processes of enculturation. This can significantly increase understanding of how music is learned and taught across cultures and settings. In the area of modes of transmission, for example, a distinction can be made between emphasis on atomistic or holistic approaches, predominantly written or largely aural traditions, and focus on more or less tangible aspects of the music being learned. Table 6.1 outlines some indicators for each of these domains.

Much of the information relevant for this table can be gathered readily by extended observation of (or even immersion in) the culture of transmission. It can also be approximated surprisingly well by simply observing one or more lesson situations and interviewing the participants immediately afterward. The next cluster, issues of context (table 6.2) is more difficult to gauge from merely observing a limited number of transmission situations. Attitudes toward the

TABLE 6.2. Indicators for issues of context

Static tradition	*Constant flux*
• Body of work has been in existence for a considerable amount of time	• Musical style is based on a continuous process of change and innovation
• High regard for what is ancient	• Ongoing negotiation between old and new
• Few new additions, closed system	• New contributions form core characteristic
• Music is a sign of distinction for an established class, whether social or religious	• Music is young and/or constantly exposed to new influences, often outside elite culture
• Sometimes less emphasis on aesthetic value (as in healing or ritual music)	• Dynamic references for quality, which develop with new contributions to the style

Original context	*Recontextualized*
• Music is practiced in its place or culture of origin, or a re-creation thereof	• Music has moved to another place or culture and taken new roots there
• Music is practiced at its time of creation	• Music has been transposed to a new era
• Music is practiced in the cultural context in which it originated	• Music has taken root in a new cultural context or social setting

"Reconstructed" authenticity	*"New identity" authenticity*
• Music is practiced in a manner that consciously follows an authoritative vision of re-creating characteristics of the historical, geographical, and/or social circumstances of the origin of the music	• Focus is on being "true to self"; it is taken for granted in the teaching situation that the music practice does not have the same role in society as it did when and where it originated
• Assumed superiority of original	• Critical approach to what is handed down

TABLE 6.3. Indicators for dimensions of interaction

Large power distance	Small power distance
• Teacher undisputedly directs the learning process • Formal words or ways of addressing teacher • Physical distance between teacher and learner	• Learners are valued as peers/equal participants • Colloquial forms of addressing each other • Learner and facilitator close and at same level of physical elevation

Individual central	Collective central
• Conscious focus on individual achievement and development • Tendency toward "art for art's sake" • Emphasis on one-on-one lessons	• Focus on achievement as group • Social aspects important focus of musical practice • Group lessons norm

Strongly gendered	Gender neutral
• Music making exclusive to men or to women • Specific genres exclusive to men or to women • Certain instruments favored by one gender • Musical decision making in the hands of one gender	• Musicking equally by men and women • All genres open to men and women • All instruments played equally across genders • Musical decision making in mixed-sex bodies

Avoiding uncertainty	Tolerating uncertainty
• Music and information about music presented as absolute • Canon and theory clearly defined and unchallenged • Respect for hierarchy and authority • Formalized learning path and pedagogy	• Musical ideas presented, discussed, and shaped to answer the needs of the musical setting • Critical approach to canon and theory • Constant challenge to hierarchy and authority • Acknowledgment of different learning paths/styles

Long-term orientation	Short-term orientation
• Graded progession over years • Emphasis on long hours of practice to make small steps on long road	• Progress steered by quick results • Working toward tangible goals in near future (e.g., performances)

Based on Hofstede, "A Case for Comparing Apples with Oranges."

dynamics of a tradition, different interpretations of authenticity, and recontextualization are not often evident from observing single instances of teaching. Again, while the best strategy is a long immersion in the culture, reading about the music and interviewing learners and culture bearers can also be highly revealing.

In terms of interaction between the learner and the teacher/facilitator, experience, close observation, and/or in-depth interviews can reveal perceptions and realities in these domains, crucial for learning most musics. Some of the indicators that can be observed in this area include those in table 6.3.

Finally, in settings where more than one culture influences the process (in terms of participants, teacher-facilitators, content, or pedagogy), the approach to cultural diversity is a factor of considerable importance, although it is often difficult to grasp. Some information can be obtained from observation or interviews, although there is a risk that the latter may yield politically correct answers rather than reflecting more deeply held values and attitudes of those involved. There are, however, some indicators for various approaches, as shown in table 6.4.

These indicators immediately suggest examples of music that seem to fit neatly in specific columns or categories, such as the strictly organized graded progression through Western classical music as administered globally by the the Associate Board of Royal Schools of Music or, at the other extreme, a free-for-all world percussion improvisation session in a park. On closer examination, however, the choices made in each of these areas are rarely black-and-white. A music transmission process is rarely all aural, all static, or all collective. Consequently, the best way

TABLE 6.4. Indicators for approaches to cultural diversity

Monocultural	Multicultural	Intercultural	Transcultural
• Music is transmitted in the context of a single, dominant music culture • Often a sense of superiority or belief in evolutionary model • Single cultural reference for quality	• Music is transmitted without explicit reference to other musics but within an awareness of several other music cultures existing in a single cultural space • Multiple cultural references for quality	• Music is seen in relation to other musics, compared cross-culturally • May lead to mixing or fusion • Quality is addressed from multiple cultural perspectives	• Music has taken on in-depth characteristic of more than one culture • Likely to have become a genre in its own right • New, fused quality criteria are developed and applied

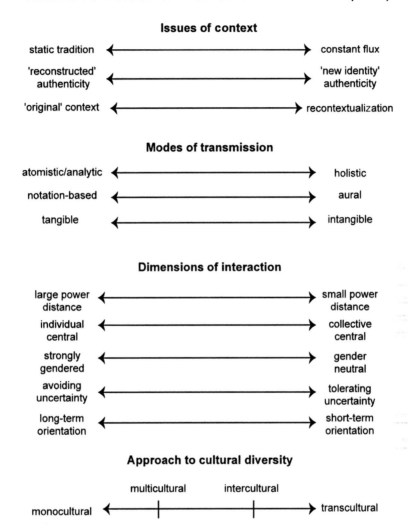

TWELVE CONTINUUM TRANSMISSION FRAMEWORK (TCTF)

Issues of context

static tradition ⟷ constant flux

'reconstructed' authenticity ⟷ 'new identity' authenticity

'original' context ⟷ recontextualization

Modes of transmission

atomistic/analytic ⟷ holistic

notation-based ⟷ aural

tangible ⟷ intangible

Dimensions of interaction

large power distance ⟷ small power distance

individual central ⟷ collective central

strongly gendered ⟷ gender neutral

avoiding uncertainty ⟷ tolerating uncertainty

long-term orientation ⟷ short-term orientation

Approach to cultural diversity

multicultural   intercultural

monocultural ⟷ transcultural

FIGURE 6.1. Framework for understanding music transmission in culturally diverse environments

to represent the various domains discussed is in the form of continua. These can be brought together in a single framework that provides a solid basis for examining and assessing key elements in teaching music across cultures (see figure 6.1).

This framework can be a powerful and effective instrument for a better understanding of music transmission processes, especially when a number of observations are taken into account. First, it is important to establish that the framework can be viewed from four perspectives: the tradition, the institution, the teacher, and the learner. These may be (and in fact often are) at odds with one another. The way these tensions are negotiated is crucial in creating learning environments that will be perceived as successful by all concerned. Second, there are neither "right" nor "wrong" positions on each continuum: the framework is essentially nonprescriptive and nonjudgmental. Positions are likely to vary from tradition to tradition, from teacher to teacher, from student to student, between phases of development, from one individual lesson to another, and even within single lessons.

The aim of the framework is not to establish the "correct" way of teaching for any music but to increase awareness of conscious and subconscious choices, assuming that teaching is more likely to be successful when the institutions-teachers/learners are fully aware of the choices they have and make and are able to adapt to the requirements of different learning situations by choosing a particular position or moving fluidly along the continua.

There is some coherence among the continua: a tendency to the left (atomistic, notation, tangible, static concepts, hierarchical, monocultural) generally points toward formal, institutional settings (such as the Associate Board example); a tendency to the right toward more informal, often community-based processes (the drum extravaganza in the park). When a right-oriented tradition finds itself in a left-oriented environment, there is an increased risk of friction and unsuccessful transmission processes. This may help to explain some of the problems reported from projects trying to introduce community, popular, folk, and world music in European and American formalized environments (see also chapter 5).

Applications of the Framework

One of the greatest risks of any framework is that it might be clever but useless. Some would argue that Alan Lomax's "cantometrics,"[1] which tried to establish universally applicable guidelines for the study of folksong, is an example of this, because it tends both to overcomplicate and to jump to conclusions.[2] I would hope and argue that the framework developed in this book has direct practical applications to increase understanding and improve practices of music education in culturally diverse environments.

The most obvious application of the Twelve Continuum Transmission Framework (TCTF) is to describe given teaching situations, whether they are moments in lessons or entire enculturation processes. Such descriptions of music transmission are preferably based on a full analysis of an observed (or, even better, experienced) teaching process, supported by extensive interviews with the facilitators/teachers and learners. Of the four clusters, methods of transmission and interaction are easiest to deduce from observation. With approaches to tradition, authenticity, and context, issues of interpretation arise: the observer has to deduce or interpret implicit thought patterns and settings, clear indications of which are often absent. In long processes (such as learning the violin or the shakuhachi), these ideas will be transmitted in a sophisticated manner in a combination of verbal and nonverbal communication, but in shorter processes, interviews are essential.[3] Observed approaches to cultural diversity tend to be less ambiguous and can be readily established in most cases, often with support from verbal or written background material.

The graphic representation of a transmission process (with positions marked on each continuum) can provide interesting overviews and comparisons, but on its own it is not sufficient to provide significant insight into a specific situation of music transmission or learning. In spite of its quantitative appearance, the framework primarily serves as a qualitative tool. The *descriptive* component brings to life the transmission process (see the case studies in chapter 7). Not only the position but also the reasoning behind choosing the position on each continuum is crucial, although consistent patterns emerge from comparable traditions and settings.

Description also exposes inevitable researcher bias, which can be caused by a number of factors. One such factor is the level of understanding of the particular tradition: those who are more familiar with a tradition tend to react more strongly to signals enforcing impressions from previous experience. Preconceptions about a particular culture or tradition may also influence positions on one or several of the continua. The exact interpretation of the concepts of tradition, authenticity, and context perhaps causes the largest divergence. Positioning here is influenced by personal background, dominant perceptions of these concepts within each music culture, and the specific references for time and place that are taken for each (for an extended discussion of these issues, see chapter 3).

Another factor that influences positioning is the level of abstraction in thinking about music and society. For many practicing musicians, reflections on the ranges of meanings implied by terminology used in this book are not part of their daily intellectual exercise (nor do they have to be). In addition, translating perceptions of a music transmission practice into specific degrees often proves difficult. For instance, the distinction between "quite aural" and "very aural" is again dictated by observers' norms and their perception of deviation from a norm, which would vary considerably among, for example, a Western classical pianist, a jazz singer, and an African percussionist.

Initial work with the framework indicates that perceptions are likely to be most similar when the framework is applied to the observation of a well-defined, short period in the process of learning and teaching music. A broader range of variation (and a consequently less unambiguous position on the continua) arises when applied to longer processes. This does not devalue the framework: considering the reality of practices of learning and teaching, it stands to reason that we would find alternation among choices over various stages of musical development. However difficult to position and document precisely, the description of longer trajectories, of course, can provide the most valuable information on how musical skills and knowledge are acquired within a specific tradition in a particular setting.

Although the framework has specifically been designed to describe situations of music transmission and learning involving world music traditions in culturally diverse societies, the value of the framework is not limited to those settings. There is considerable potential in applying the framework to more "monocultural" settings. Analyzing the various dimensions of the framework in relation to traditions in their cultures of origin—including world, jazz, pop, and Western classical music—can be quite revealing. In such analyses, some of the continua (e.g., those dealing with cultural diversity) may be less relevant.

Overall, there are four specific areas for which the framework has potential implications: music education in the classroom; professional training of musicians and teachers in institutions such as conservatories, university music departments, and schools of music; (ethno)musicology and music research at large; and music making and learning in communities.

Music Education in the Classroom

For music in schools, world music may well hold both the greatest promise and the greatest challenges. Several authors (e.g., Campbell, Dunbar-Hall, Lundquist, Volk) have commented on the slow growth of vibrant classroom practices that do justice to the present understanding of the complexities involved in realizing successful culturally diverse programs for children of all backgrounds. That should come as no surprise. Considering the vast number of issues and concerns involved in dealing with world music (in this book and in the field) is daunting or even intimidating.

This is complicated further by the vastly different natures of schools, educational systems, and resulting realities. A culturally diverse district might have each school representing this diversity, or white and black schools may be segregated, or the district might employ conscious efforts to obtain the desired "mix," for instance, by transporting students between areas or schools. In the end, however, if one of the purposes of music education is to prepare children to engage with global musical realities, it can be argued that each of those schools has to respond to cultural diversity as a given at local, regional, national, and global levels.

Many initiatives worldwide have already begun to respond to this challenge, which may well be one of the most substantial facing music education. Campbell, for example, refers to "equity pedagogy," which, as she observes, reached the mainstream of educational groups by the mid-1980s. It stimulated teachers "to modify their teaching in ways that could facilitate the academic achievement of students from diverse racial, cultural, ethnic and gender groups."[4] The TCTF is potentially of great practical use in these contexts, as it can make explicit a number of essential differences in learning styles. If the teacher is able to gauge the modes of musical learning best suited to particular students, this can inform conscious choices in the delivery of any material, acknowledging and putting to good use extra skills or difficulties that students may possess.

An issue here, however, is that discussions about approaches to teaching seem to be more alive in circles of academics and policy specialists than in the practice of instrumental and classroom music teachers. In an overview of research, policy, and practice, Cain presents it as an upside-down pyramid, with a wealth of research at the top, a solid anount of policy next, awareness in teacher training much less already, and visionary practice in the classroom still very elementary.[5] Classroom teachers appear to focus more on availability of directly applicable classroom material, which they generally deliver in the manner in which they would deliver courses on Western classical or (more recently) popular music.

Even though the amount and quality of available material have increased substantially, especially in the past ten years, what was true for most classroom music teachers during the landmark Wesleyan Symposium in 1984 seems to be the general picture to this day: "While a study of transmission processes was viewed with intrigue by teacher-participants, it was seen by many as only remotely related to the challenges of teaching in multicultural classroom settings."[6]

This tension between visionary ideas and a practice that takes time to implement these visions is a reality of the sector. This is not because music teachers are unwilling or unable to teach music in the best way possible but because our systems of training teachers, the virtual absence of in-service and life-long learning provisions, and the built-in conservatism of most national curricula, state guidelines, school programs, pedagogies, and teaching materials are not conducive to change. This lack of support prompts many music educators to revert to the familiar, caused by a largely justified apprehensiveness about exploring new ground without the right support or tools. These tools—acknowledging the ideas of other cultures, the voices of culture bearers, new pedagogies (some of which are in fact centuries old)—have become increasingly available over the past twenty-five years, but many still do not feel comfortable applying them. Well-conceived and well-implemented teacher training and professional development can play a key role in removing this obstacle.

In spite of some frustration at the sometimes slow pace of change, there is the realization that as a discipline, music education has traveled far in fifty years. A number of general developments have been conducive to including more world music in school curricula. There has also been a shift of focus from a largely aesthetic to a more praxial approach, from passive listening to reproduction to creative musicking. There has been a shift from enlightening young and disadvantaged minds to the beauty of Western classical music to openness toward empowering young learners to develop their potential through musics from their immediate environment and of their choice.

Policy documents increasingly recognize the importance of cultural diversity. There is a growing awareness that music education based on a single frame of reference and the concept of a zero level at the beginning of formal music education (the child as a musical virgin) is difficult to maintain. The change of musical reality caused by the democratization of music and cultural diversity invites all music educators to consider being more holistic in their approach, making use of the substantial "aural library" that almost all young students have built up by learning holistically, having been exposed to thousands of hours of music as a matter of course in contemporary societies. Initial research suggests substantial importance for holistic and aural learning, even in traditions that use notation extensively. If evidence from predominantly holistically transmitted traditions supports the view that aural/holistic learning is an important force in music enculturation, then it must be taken into account in the design and assessment of all music programs. It would be of great interest to music education at large to determine how much of learning in Western classical music, for instance, can be described in these terms, taking place informally through conscious and subconscious exposure.

These considerations affect receptive, reproductive, and creative music learning in the classroom. In the former, the varying degrees of unfamiliarity with any type of music require strategies that transcend a single cultural frame of reference, for instance by using widely shared themes.[7] In order to reproduce music, it is important to work from sound (and preferably concepts) rather than scored versions of world music. And creating world music is more than running up and down a xylophone scale and calling it rāgas. With the TCTF, the vocabulary, scope, and approach to each of these activities can be widened, particularly for culturally diverse classroom situations, which need a cross-cultural perspective.

Music education systems focusing primarily on teaching practical skills, understanding structures, or developing aesthetic awareness may need to take into account that contextual factors (in the non rigid sense of context) play a significant role in the learning process. Music making reflects a number of crucial choices in actual musical sound and context, and music education both reflects and influences these. It is challenging but not impossible to respond intelligently to this in the classroom. Ultimately, it is possible to imagine—and even to realize—a transcultural music-in-schools program, where many different musics and musical approaches are featured on an equal footing, with sounds, principles, and ideas from a wide variety of cultures. This could allow children to make well-informed choices concerning their musical preferences on the basis of a globally inspired value system, equip them with the tools to explore their culturally diverse musical world, and limit the risk of prejudice and estrangement. Although it is naïve to assume that making music together overcomes all racial tensions, it has been demonstrated to be an effective way of bringing people closer together.[8]

Research can play a crucial role in the further development of successful world music education in schools. In its 1996 *Policy on Musics of the World's Cultures*, the International Society for Music Education recommends: "Existing systems of music education may be reviewed and evaluated as to their efficacy and relevance in the teaching of specific musical cultures." With the TCTF, this process can perhaps be organized more expediently (and include the transmission of Western art music in schools, music schools, and conservatories). It may also inform new research into sociological and psychological aspects of music education. A number of ethnomusicological studies have begun to explore the sociology of learning music from other cultures.[9]

In most institutions for higher music education, the way educational psychology is applied is predominantly based on a traditional approach to learning Western classical music. Educational psychology from a world perspective is a vast challenge but conceivably the only viable way of developing the discipline in line with the educational realities of culturally diverse societies. In the realm of culturally diverse projects, having seen that the various continua can be approached from different perspectives by the three main forces in the process of music transmission (the music, the interaction between student and teacher, and the learning environment), anecdotal evidence suggests that less successful instances of music transmission and learning can be explained from a mismatch in the views of two or more of these "actors." This can be made visible with the TCTF. Research is needed to demonstrate to what extent this is true and whether successful transmission in fact correlates with harmonious views among the players.

If the choices as described in the framework can be shown to contribute to successful transmission of music traditions, then the framework can also be used as a *predictive* tool to forecast whether a particular musical practice or mode of transmission is likely to do well in new settings or is likely to do better when adapted. In this way, problems can be foreseen and addressed in a timely manner. For instance, the frictions with world music in Dutch public music schools in the 1980s[10] could possibly have been attenuated in this way, and indeed the entire issue of learning and teaching aural traditions in music schools and conservatories could have been addressed more effectively from the start.

Going one step farther, those in charge of music transmission may dictate specific choices in music transmission to guarantee success in a new environment. This *prescriptive* use is a contentious area: choices may be conducive to avoid tensions with the new environment but may be less productive in relation to the key musical values of a particular tradition. Musicians may feel compelled to make concessions to an institutional mode of working, which, as we have seen, may itself be outdated. If it is true that the culture of transmission strongly influences the future of music making, it is evident that educators need to strive for optimal awareness and act sensitively in this area. There are no easy solutions to the challenges of realizing vibrant and culturally sensitive music education, but the TCTF can certainly help to focus questions and bring depth to discussions about approach, material, and pedagogies.

Professional Music Training

Bridging music education in schools and professional music training is the professional development of music teachers. From the preceding section, the importance of this area should be evident. In order to ensure that music education in schools keeps pace with developments in society and music itself, all prospective teachers should be equipped with both the conceptual frameworks and the practical tools to address these and be prepared for continual change during their years in education, as Bowman and others have convincingly argued. Bowman also emphasizes the crucial importance of continued professional development for all practicing music teachers.[11] There has been an increase in popular music and music technology in both teacher training and professional development programs, but, barring a few notable exceptions (e.g., Washington, Malmö, Helsinki, Amsterdam, London, Sydney), inductions into world music have often remained at the surface.

While highly skilled professionals are seen as the key ingredient in successful professional music training, the smooth transmission of musical knowledge does not always take place successfully in increasingly complex environments if only that condition is met. Being a musician increasingly means much more than simply playing well and is likely to include highly evolved communicative, project management, and business skills, as well as being able to maintain prestige and dealing with complex community protocols, institutional guidelines, or government regulations. Formalized music education removes some of these obstacles but creates others.

Cultural diversity multiplies the challenges for training professional musicians in terms of place in the musical arena, focus and balance between aspects of the training, structure of the program, and choices in pedagogy. The last mentioned is hardly a new discussion. It can occur through music traveling or when another culture becomes a major influence in the original cultural context of a music tradition, such as with Western culture in the Arab world, as reflected in remarks on the music education system in the 1970s by Habib Hassan Touma:

> Instrumental music and singing do not in any way absolve the students at these music schools from a teaching methodology that Arab musicians have taken over and modified from European methods for violin, flute, etc, so that the student begins from the start with exercises, easy pieces, etc., and only after one or two years starts learning Baschraf-s, Samai-s or Muwaschah-s. However, he has to learn the modal structures by ear or through oral teaching, so without notes, hearing his teacher often,

imitating him and then doing his own modal forms, for one cannot exactly notate Taqsim and Layali, and if one does put them on paper, then the interpretation of the notation never reflects the original music, especially if the performer does not know the music.[12]

Touma's reflections illustrate how cultural diversity presents not only new possibilities but also major challenges to music educators and their environments. Although some may successfully manage to ignore the dynamics of the environment (e.g., by satisfying the needs of governing bodies rather than those of the students or the music culture at large), it may lead to less successful education and ultimately the loss of the basis for existence of institutions. In an age of increasing accountability, processes of evaluation and the ensuing harsh consequences are already occurring, even for schools with a long history, and are likely to become more frequent. Being responsive to change is not a choice; it is a necessity.

One such change is the advent of new music with different values on the doorstep of conservatories. The argument continues about whether institutional environments are savior or downfall for some of these traditions. Assuming the former, it stands to reason that those responsible for music transmission develop sensitivity and explicitly define their position toward each area in the framework. Organizations responsible for music education can use the TCTF to gauge whether how they organize learning and teaching corresponds to the missions they have defined for themselves, their teachers, their students, and their funding bodies: as keepers of a tradition, providers to specific niche markets, or active players in the entire gamut of complex musical realities of the twenty-first century. It is hard to overemphasize the explicit and implicit influence of this positioning. An institution that dedicates itself to maintaining a tradition (such as a traditional Western conservatory) will make different choices from one that professes to maintain and develop specific genres (such as traditional music in many Asian countries), and these choices will be different from those that aim to make groundbreaking contributions to music (as some music technology training institutions do) or simply cater to a market (e.g., beginning keyboard or amateur musical theater). Each of these options is perfectly justifiable, particularly if complementary options exist in the vicinity. However, it is probably unwise to generalize about appropriate learning and teaching styles across these environments. While creativity has been a valuable (re)introduction in teaching Western art music, it may not have a place in the handing down of ancient Vedic hymns; peer learning and creative group processes are convincingly appropriate for popular music[13] but may be less so for learning solo repertoire for the ud or shakuhachi.

A number of the issues mentioned above regarding music in education are worth mentioning in each of these contexts, such as the role of aural learning in the training of professional musicians, the range of pedagogies, and sociological and psychological aspects. For those involved in maintaining and developing traditions, especially in institutional contexts, one of the key issues to be researched is whether and how music traditions change when the system of music transmission is changed, either consciously or by any form of recontextualization. This forms not only an exciting area of research but also one that is eminently practically useful, as institutes for music education are in the continual process of monitoring their efficacy, often without sufficient information about the long-term consequences of their decisions.

Related to this is the link between quality criteria and what is being taught. In looking at various systems of music transmission, there are indications that in some cases, there may be a mismatch between the two. When atomistic approaches dominate, intangibles tend to be underemphasized. An analysis of a conservatory curriculum by an absolute outsider may lead to the conclusion that musicianship in the West revolves around technique and repertoire. This may not be a weakness, if there is assurance that other aspects of musicianship are learned "on the street" or, as is often the case, behind closed doors with the principal teacher. Similarly, in holistic situations, the underlying structures often remain unclear, which may disadvantage learners from analytical backgrounds. In some teaching of world music that I have witnessed in Europe, Australia, and the United States, world musicians may have underused the learning skills that many Westerners bring to any music lesson. The insight into the nature of learning music that the TCTF provides can also influence the setting of priorities by educational and funding authorities. Working from the awareness that many crucial aspects of music learning take place in the realm of intangibles and holistic learning, the increasing insistence of funding bodies on measurable outcomes per well-defined module should be treated with extreme caution and countered with intelligent analyses of the core qualities of musicians as creative practitioners and how they acquire their skills.

(Ethno)musicology

If, as Blacking stated thirty-five years ago, "it is the task of the ethnomusicologist to identify all processes that are relevant to an explanation of musical sound,"[14] in-depth understanding of transmission should probably be high on the list. The systems and processes of learning and teaching music inform insight into social interaction around musical practices and elucidate mechanisms of conservation and/or innovation. But perhaps even more important, they lead straight to what musicians consider to be the core of what they do: not only are technique, repertoire, creativity, and performance skills made explicit, but often reference is made to etiquette, aesthetics, and "intangible" elements of musicianship, which are almost never formulated or expressed in performance. That which flashes before our ears and eyes in a concert is often slowed down, repeated, reconsidered, refined, highlighted, and/or footnoted in transmission processes, like artistic practice in slow motion. As such, transmission constitutes a rich and fertile area of research through which to understand the essence of any music tradition or practice as perceived by its senior representatives.

While there has been an increase in descriptions of transmission processes in individual cultures, a common frame of reference for describing the systems underlying transmission has been lacking. The TCTF can possibly contribute to consistent research into aspects that have been partially addressed to date for many music traditions but rarely comprehensively, such as the balance and interaction between aural/oral learning and notation; varying approaches to tradition, authenticity, and context; and aspects of interaction between learners and teachers/facilitators inside or outside institutional environments. As mentioned above, this can be linked to whether and how music traditions change when the system of music transmission is changed, by recontextualization or conscious choice.

Such studies could also inform the emerging subdiscipline of applied (or engaged) ethnomusicology, which is committed to "giving back" knowledge gained through ethnomusicological study to the music cultures being examined. If, as this book argues, music transmission is a key factor in creating sustainable futures for music cultures, it makes sense to make available findings from studying specific musics to consultants from the culture and maybe also to other stakeholders in the various music cultures in the culture and beyond. With its emphasis on "music in culture" and "music as culture," ethnomusicology can play a central role in contributing to a more complete understanding of domains that, individually and in their interaction, are decisive for the sustainability of any music culture: systems of learning, musicians and communities, contexts and constructs, infrastructure and regulations, and media and the music industry.[15]

Each of these domains overlaps and interrelates in how it affects music cultures, as is evident from much ethnomusicological research over the past few decades. For example, change can be driven by shifts in values and attitudes, technological developments, and/or audience behavior. The manner of music transmission is strongly determined by its (institutional) environment, and media attention, markets, and audiences can often be linked to issues of public perception and prestige.

The power and potential of such a template are easily illustrated by applying it to Western classical opera in the twentieth century, which at first glance would seem to have insurmountable obstacles for sustainability, given its needs in terms of infrastructure (a theater with excellent acoustics, a large stage, and a fly tower), high-level training of the participants (soloists, chorus, orchestra, conductor, director), and audience (refined to appreciate the event, affluent to afford tickets), but which survives by ensuring that a number of key factors are aligned: a rich and interdisciplinary content, very high prestige among those who make decisions on where funds go, excellent and long training opportunities for those who perform, multimillion-dollar theaters that can accommodate and support the production, an elite audience, good exposure in the press, and, at least until recently, a blossoming market for CDs and DVDs.

Other traditions are less fortunate. The beautiful sung poetry with instrumental accompaniment known as ca trù in Vietnam blossomed in villages across the country. Then it moved to the cities, where special ca trù houses came into being. According to Nguyễn Thi Chúc, one of the few surviving masters of the genre, there were ten such houses in Khâm Thiên street in Hanoi when she was young in the 1950s.[16] Some of these houses began offering less widely accepted forms of entertainment as well. Then, with the advent of the Communist government, these immoral places were outlawed, and all of the musicians went back to villages to work in the fields. No prestige, no money, no infrastructure, no training, no audience.

A number of people are now trying to revive this tradition and have just submitted a proposal to UNESCO to have it acknowledged as a masterpiece of Intangible Cultural Heritage. Meanwile, the music is being documented (most notably by the Musicological Institute in Hanoi), small-scale performances can be seen on occasion onstage or in transformed spaces such as small record shops, and some teaching is being organized informally. However, it would certainly not be beyond imagination to reestablish a ca trù house, accessible to both discerning Vietnamese audiences and the cultural tourist trade, which could charge tourists U.S. $25 for an evening of authentic entertainment (rather than the toned-down tourist music in most hotels) and thus feed four musicians, who could spend their non-working hours engaging with schools and the Hanoi Conservatorium to educate the next generation of discerning listeners and performers.

Numerous examples of such practices already exist or are waiting to happen, in communities or in schools, at a national level or very locally. The TCTF facilitates understanding challenges and intricate processes underlying each music tradition and the application of this understanding to the actual transmission of music from one generation to the next in contemporary contexts. As such, it is a potentially highly rewarding instrument for applied ethnomusicology.

Music in Communities

The resilience of music practices is evident from the wealth of music that takes place with little or no formal support: in Tamil communities in London suburbs, Mexican mariachi bands in Portland, African drummers in the *banlieus* of Lyon, and Uruguayan candombe groups in Western Sydney. This demonstrates how strong a force music is in giving people a sense of community, of belonging, of respect, of identity. From the perspective of the TCTF, it is possible to establish that the ways of learning common in community music need not represent the absence of "proper" pedagogical approaches but may constitute well-considered choices.

Some community music activities can provide successful models or inspiration for ensuring vibrant musical practices. Samoan teenagers in Australia easily form community choirs. They sing four-part harmonies beautifully, effortlessly, and without notation. Like musicians in Bali, some of them do not understand the question "How did you learn music?" They feel they never "learned." They grew up in homes where at every family gathering, a brother or uncle would bring out a guitar, and everybody would just started singing. In addition, they sing in church. With the school, this forms a powerful triangle that ensures both a high level of skill and great enjoyment in music making. The value of such examples for music education should not be underestimated. Creating synergy with existing, self-energized models of music making can create substantial advantages over superimposed models.[17]

Rather than seeing these musical practices as remnants of an idealized or irrelevant past, with the TCTF they can serve as inspirations for (re)organizing music education. In the same vein as considering the considerable musical wealth of children as they come into the classroom as the basis for music education, there is a strong case for building upon musical practices and pedagogies that have developed organically within communities. Learning and teaching music in formal environments is always artificial to some degree, but its effectiveness can be improved by learning from examples that exist organically, without outside support, as these must have a strong basis in the community, as well as credibility with the learners to whom they cater.

Conclusion

The Twelve Continuum Transmission Framework has considerable potential as a descriptive, predictive, and even prescriptive tool. At the core of the framework is the aim to gain greater understanding of past, present, and future processes of learning and teaching music in culturally diverse environments. The scope and implications of these concepts and their application are challenging but not impossible. It is largely within the control of musicians, learners, educators, and institutions to take these into account when shaping music education for the future.

Exploring a number of key concepts, ideas, and practices of cultural diversity in music learning and teaching from this new perspective—and applying the framework to make these concepts visible in relation to specific instances of music transmission—will aid in furthering the discussion of learning and teaching music in various settings. This can lead to a more fruitful dialogue among musicians, music educators, and ethnomusicologists in understanding and building vibrant cultures of transmission.

CHAPTER 7

Music Cultures in Motion
A Case Study

Bamboo flute in hand, Indian maestro Hariprasad Chaurasia sits on a simple wooden chair in the attic room of a former Dutch harbor building. He teaches in an annex of the Rotterdam Conservatory, located in the heart of ancient Delfshaven, now one of the most culturally diverse suburbs in the world. At his feet, five students from four different countries, enrolled in the Indian classical music degree, sit cross-legged on the ground with their flutes. Chaurasia starts playing the ascending and descending outline of the rāga Bihag. The students follow. Then, phrase by phrase, the slow introductory section of the rāga, known as ālāp, is explored through improvisation, with Chaurasia leading, and all of the students following in unison or sometimes one by one. Occasionally, a student varies a phrase slightly, which may be met with a subtle nod or a mild grimace from the guru. Hardly a word is spoken; nothing is explained. Yet it is very clear to all present that this is a remarkably concentrated and successful music lesson and, to the informed observer, a beautiful illustration of how aural traditions can be taught and learned.

A framework to capture visible and less visible processes of music education comes to life in its practical application. In order to demonstrate the potential and limitations of the Twelve Continuum Transmission Framework (TCTF), I will briefly examine practices from a country that by virtue of its cultural diversity, central position for international travel, population density, history of tolerance, and commitment to funding arts and arts education, has been a breeding ground for some well-advanced practices: the Netherlands. Focusing on actual practice will also give a strong voice to the key players in the process: accomplished musicians who have learned in one system and are now teaching in another.

137

World Music Education in the Netherlands

Like many European countries, the Netherlands has a dubious track record of imperialism and colonialism. With the United Kingdom and Portugal, it was one of the main players in the slave trade (and the last country to abolish it); it colonized Indonesia extensively, cruelly and very profitably for several centuries; and it gave the world the word *apartheid*, which persisted much too close to recent history as well. On the other hand, the Netherlands has been a country of great openness and tolerance. It welcomed the French Huguenots and the Portuguese Jews and has been very welcoming to asylum seekers and war refugees.

In the 1960s, along with many other European countries, it started to attract migrant workers to meet the demand for unskilled labor in its growing economy after World War II. This brought major influxes of people from Turkey and Morocco and, later, Capeverdians. In the 1970s, another major group of immigrants arrived when Surinam (which the Dutch had traded with the British for New Amsterdam, now also known as New York) became independent and its population was given the choice between Dutch and Surinami citizenship. The Surinamis who came to the Netherlands belonged to two major groups: Creoles (black descendants from the slave trade) and Hindustanis (Indians who came to Surinam to work as contract laborers after slavery was abolished). Finally, migrants from the Cape Verdes and refugees from many other countries arrived in large numbers. From the early 1980s, once it was clear that most migrant workers (called guest workers at the time) were not intending to return to their countries but preferred to build a future in their new environment, general and arts policies were developed to accommodate this new reality into the well-developed cultural infrastructure of the country.

In the Netherlands, almost three million out of the population of sixteen million are now considered to be of non-Dutch origin.[1] Of these people, almost one million represent a significantly different cultural background. Substantial concentrations of people from Turkey, Morocco, and Surinam in particular live in and around the cities. This brings the average of non-Dutch schoolchildren to more than fifty percent in cities such as Amsterdam and Rotterdam. This has transformed dealing with cultural diversity from a benevolent gesture into a market reality. In addition, the "indigenous" population, white Dutch people, have become increasingly interested in non-Western cultures, fueled by immigration, travel, and media exposure. This opened the road for synergy between existing and new population groups.

In table 7.1, six identifiable stages in Dutch cultural diversity policies are summarized, stretching out over twenty-five years. They suggest a movement from multicultural to intercultural toward transcultural between 1982 and 2008. However, meanwhile, in the aftermath of the events of September 11, 2001, a

1982–1988: Werkgroep Kunstuitingen Migranten

This period saw a special task force installed at the Netherlands Arts Council on what was then termed "artistic expressions of migrants." During these years, the emphasis was on activities of minorities in their own cultural circuits: a multicultural approach. "Minority artists" felt they were undervalued, and only few found their way to mainstream arts funding. This period concludes with the 1989 publication of *De Kunst van het Artisjokken Eten* (The Art of Eating Artichokes), by the National Arts Council (Raad voor de Kunst), a critical document on culturally diverse arts policies in the Netherlands.

After that, Dutch arts policy—and the division of subsidies—was organized in four-year plans, the so-called *Kunstenplanperiodes*. The philosophy behind this system was that to develop new practice, arts institutions needed to be given time and financial security to experiment and choose new paths, without the pressure of having to prove themselves to merit a continuation of the grant every year.

1989–1992: Room for multicultural expression

Around 1990, national and local governments devoted a substantial amount of money and effort toward integrating "minority arts" into existing institutes as part of "*sociale vernieuwing*" (literally, "social Innovation"). Projects integrating world music into public music schools were started all over the Netherlands. Funding bodies required a minimum of commitment from the institutes. The projects could usually be funded externally, so they did not interfere with the regular concerns of the institution. Few of these initiatives survived beyond the additional funding. The approach was toward organizational integration but would need to be termed multicultural in content, as the cultures were approached separately.

1993–1996: Integration and participation

During this period, the concepts of integration and participation were central to government policy. Secretary of State d'Ancona presented her views in a 1992 document called *Investeren in Integreren* (Investing in Integration). She stressed the responsibilities of the established arts world to incorporate cultural diversity into the work of their institutions. This represented a continuation of the multicultural approach, with some openings for intercultural.

1997–2000: Interculturality and fusion

The cultural policies of Secretary of State Nuis were formulated in 1996 in *Pantser of Ruggengraat* (Armour or Spine). Influenced mostly by the prevalent thoughts in the literary scene, he devoted a great deal of attention to an intercultural approach to arts from a culturally diverse perspective (not unlike the British Arts Council) and left relatively little room for expressions of separate cultures.

2001–2004: Cultural diversity and youth

In 1999, van der Ploeg, the incoming secretary of state, announced that he intended to put great emphasis on cultural diversity during his term in office. He published a policy document on the subject, *Ruim Baan voor Culturele Diversiteit* (Making Way for Cultural Diversity), in 1999. His policies included an emphasis on youth culture (which he justifiably considered as becoming increasingly transcultural through eclectic cultural choices of young people), accepting that the meeting of cultures is sometimes less than harmonious, as evidenced in his 2000 policy paper, *Cultuur als Confrontatie* (Culture As Confrontation). He left room for both expressions of distinct cultures and mixing: a combination of multicultural, intercultural, and transcultural approaches.

(Continued)

TABLE 7.1.   (*Continued*)

2005–2008: Cultural diversity integrated?

The Dutch Arts Council distanced itself from the interventionist politics of van der Ploeg and pleaded for returning the responsibility of making choices to the subsidised institutions. Minister van der Laan acknowledged the artistic value of cultural diversity in addition to its potential for increasing participation in the arts. Cultural diversity was assumed to be integrated into the cultural fiber of the Netherlands. Some may regard this as a transcultural view, others as an excuse to ignore cultural diversity in the offerings of key arts organizations.

controversy about the "failure" of multicultural societies erupted in the Nether-lands, fueled by the murders of right-wing politician Pim Fortuyn and controver-sial cinematographer Theo van Gogh. In the discussions, aspects of social failure, such as unemployment and limited integration of people who are at risk of getting lost between the cultures of their background and the new country, were not always clearly distinguished from aspects of cultural or musical integration. This led to several steps back for explicit policies on cultural diversity in the Netherlands.

Music Traditions

In addition to an internationally acclaimed scene for Western art music (from classical to contemporary) and substantial activity in improvised and popular music, the rich cultural diversity of the population has led to a vibrant world music scene in the Netherlands, ranging from unpublicized concerts of Iranian or Azerbaijani masters through Turkish and Hindu weddings to curated series in prominent concert venues and large outdoor festivals. Prominent among these musics are Latin American music, African music, Capeverdian music, Turkish music, Moroccan music, Indian music, and Indonesian gamelan, as well as hip-hop and R&B. Most of these have also gained a presence in music education in informal, nonformal, and formal environments.

Foremost among the formal is Rotterdam Conservatory, which developed full degree courses in five specific forms of world music: Latin, flamenco, North Indian classical, tango, and Turkish folk. The Rotterdam world music department, established in 1990, is based on "the prevailing vision that professional music education should reflect global changes in culture and society."[2] Rotterdam Conservatory was among the first in the Netherlands to set up departments for jazz (1978) and popular music (1988).

The choice of traditions being taught was motivated less by ethnic represen-tativity than by the answers to three practical questions, which Joep Bor, initiator and long-term head of the department, formulated as follows:

(1) Will the programme attract and continue to attract a sufficient number of talented and motivated students? (2) Can we assemble a team of highly qualified and cooperative teachers and a coordinator who knows the ins and outs of the field? And (3) is it possible to teach this type of music in a Western conservatory setting?[3]

When these questions were answered in the affirmative, a curriculum was designed based on the specific practical and theoretical demands of the tradition, largely structured along lines of a typical conservatory curriculum, with individual classes in the main subject, ensemble, subsidiary instruments, music theory, history, languages, workshops in other music traditions, and educational theory and practice. Acknowledged master musicians such as Paco Peña (flamenco), Hariprasad Chaurasia (bansuri), Gustavo Beytelmann (tango), and Talip Özkan (saz) were attracted to take artistic leadership over the program. All but Chaurasia teach with a heavy bias toward notation. Their teaching ranges from tangible to intangible aspects of their respective areas of musical expertise.

The central position of one-on-one teaching for the main subject/instrument in fact approximates the master-disciple relationship that is common in most of these traditions in their cultures of origin. An important support role is played by "bridging musicians" who are less senior in the tradition but have cultural competencies that span the backgrounds of masters and learners. Although the degree courses have been developed through trial and error, they have produced a number of musicians who are successful as performers or teachers (and sometimes both) in a number of traditions, notably Latin music and flamenco guitar. The department is now integrated into the World Music & Dance Centre and continues to have a student population of about one hundred students, divided over the five cultural areas mentioned.

Within this wider context, I will examine three examples of music transmission using the TCTF developed in chapter 6. These samples focus on music traditions and transmission settings that can be found not only in the Netherlands but in many culturally diverse environments: West African percussion (djembe) in a community music setting, Balinese gamelan (gong kebyar) in the training of music teachers who will work with schoolchildren, and classical music from North India (bansuri) in a dedicated music degree course. Although all three are recontextualized traditions (rather than fusion or new music), they represent a broad spectrum of approaches to musical structure, social context, and thinking about music transmission.

Each of the traditions has been well established in the West, with a history of more than forty years on European and American soil.[4] They entered Western society through different channels. Djembe conquered the West through a combination of recordings, interest from Africa travelers, and a number of West African musicians traveling and settling. The interest in gamelan can be traced back to a colonial past and the works of scholars and musicians such as Claude Debussy,

Colin McPhee, Jaap Kunst, and Ki Mantle Hood.[5] Indian music became firmly established after the immense popularity of the music in the West during the late 1960s and early 1970s, although interest in live Indian music can be traced back to the 1950s and even the first decades of the twentieth century, while serious theoretical interest goes back to the eighteenth century.[6]

The three forms of music are comparable in the sense that they have all influenced Western music and engaged in fusion experiments but simultaneously continued to exist as distinct traditions that have become recontextualized. The relative continuity over decades of these traditions makes it possible to consider processes of learning and teaching in new environments over a longer period of time and to compare them with transmission processes in the cultures of origin.

For consistency of approach, each case study has a one-hour session as its basis. In order to ensure a balanced picture, however, I have drawn on other classes I observed in each of the traditions chosen. This substantially reduces the risk of idiosyncrasies, incidents being interpreted as generalizations, and other mis-understandings clouding the picture. Prolonged exposure also made it possible to use a variety of sources as background material: descriptions by scholars, interviews with teachers, reports by learners, observations of practice, didactic methods, formal curricula, and sound and video recordings. With this diversity of sources and the ensuing opportunities for triangulation, while inevitably idiosyncratic, the picture that emerges is likely to be reasonably representative.

Example 1: Djembe for Western Amateurs

One of the most widespread forms of instrument-specific world music education is African percussion. The djembe in particular, with its main proponents hailing from Mali and Guinea, has become vastly popular in the West.[7] There are three obvious reasons for this: Africa is seen—rightly or wrongly—as the drumming continent; Mandinka percussion music is accessible and exciting to broad audiences, and, perhaps most important, the djembe itself has a low initial threshold in terms of playing technique. While a conga or a tabla requires substantial amounts of practice to produce a resonant sound, the response of the djembe is very direct, leading to instant gratification during the first lessons. This is an important factor in attracting students to attend and continue beyond initial workshops, which is where the interest in much other world music ends.

As one of many possible examples illustrating this phenomenon, the following pages describe the work of Ponda O'Bryan, a teacher of Dutch Surinami descent, who is widely regarded as the central person in bringing the djembe to music education in the Netherlands. He represents the type of "musical ambassa-dor" increasingly found in world music scenes: an accomplished musician from the home culture who has immersed himself in another culture and can consequently serve as a bridge for new learners "out of context." O'Bryan has played a key role in training both students and a next generation of trainers in this tradition in the Netherlands. He has been teaching privately, at public music schools, and as a guest teacher at several conservatories.

The central point of reference for the analysis that follows is an advanced class that was held as part of his private practice. It took place on the evening of July 3, 2003, at Melody Line, a studio in Amsterdam. There were seven students: two men in their thirties and five women in their forties and early fifties. The students in O'Bryan's studio have been learning drumming for four to seven years, and their teacher considers them quite advanced.

In the observed lesson, O'Bryan taught "Tama," a male dance which he characterizes as a dundumba (dundum) rhythm from the Korusa region in Upper Guinea. It is a fairly complicated rhythm, with seven different parts, played with three bass drums (dundum, saimbang, and kenkeni), three accompanying djembes, and a solo djembe. In a slightly simplified form, it can also be played with only five drummers. The students had been playing this particular rhythm for five weeks before the recorded lesson, with one ninety-minute lesson a week. Key sources for this case study include a video recording of the class[8] and a video interview with O'Bryan after the lesson.[9] The findings were checked against regular observation of O'Bryan's work in his private practice, the Amsterdam Music School, and several school projects over a period of twelve years, as well as many informal conversations.

Issues of Context

As a tradition, Mandinka djembe percussion is characterized by a specific repertoire of traditional rhythms. Each of these has its fixed patterns in the cycle, its own name and appropriate ensemble, and its own relation to social events. All but the last are maintained in O'Bryan's djembe lessons. He describes a number of varying characteristics of the tradition in West African percussion:

> Each region has its own styles and dialects. Particular rhythms are played only in certain regions, and the ensemble can be different as well.... Sometimes the same rhythms have a different name, or different rhythms have the same name in various regions. Then there are the instruments that are being used. Some use bells, some use no bells, sizes of djembe differ, and some use cow instead of goat skin: that gives a different sound. Next there is the technique of playing, for instance where exactly on the skin the slap is played. Other factors are the sound, the tempo, and the improvisations.

This suggests a considerable degree of variance and flexibility within the tradition. Most musicians learn in a single regional tradition, which may be defined less ambiguously. O'Bryan, as an outsider, is an exception, as he has branched out from his teacher, Famadou Konaté (from the Korusa region), into various other styles of djembe playing. Considering the various traditions as a whole, O'Bryan sees them as stable but not static:

> The regions influence each other. First, only in Korusa they used three dumdums. Now, the other regions are copying that. Musicians meet and influence each other. So it is always evolving. But it goes very slowly. The old is greatly respected in Africa, so the tradition largely stays the same over time.

At a national level, however, O'Bryan observes more rapid and substantial change:

> In the last forty or fifty years, there is a new style, the African ballet. In this style, the tradition is made art. They make arrangements, choreographies with the dance, new steps to the dances. That changes very fast. I would not call it a tradition, but it is based on the tradition, and it is played in the African context. But this music is for the stage, while the traditional drumming is for the villages. Ballet drummers are not able to play in the ceremonies, and traditional drummers don't know how to play with the ballet. They have become separate. One is the source, the other what came from it. The tradition is very fixed, ballet moves very fast, it constantly takes on new things.

This illustrates how a relatively static tradition and a form with a new identity can exist side by side in contemporary West African settings. O'Bryan's approach would tend toward the former, but this is qualified somewhat by the fact that he emphatically does not present the music in association with its original social function. Djembe music is strongly linked to specific events in African village life: weddings, naming ceremonies, circumcision, and so on. In the Netherlands, this context is mentioned, but no efforts are undertaken to reproduce it in any way. Still, O'Bryan asserts that context in quite important to him:

> In my classes with Westerners, I always tell them what a particular rhythm is for, and often I show them videos. But for many of my students, just knowing where it comes from is enough. They come for the fun of playing and the beauty of the music itself. With dance, I don't do so much. I tell my advanced students to try to play with dance classes in the Netherlands. That is very good for them. Also because the rhythms are often played faster. But you also get the energy from the dancers. So it is

important when you are advanced. When you are a beginner, it can help
you understand the beat of the music, but I usually just tell them where
[the beat] is.

From this, it appears that the context is considered important but is only referred
to verbally in the highly contrasting setting of a music studio in an Amsterdam
suburb. Considering the vast difference between the original context and
the setting of O'Bryan's classes, his practice would qualify as decidedly recontextualized.

   O'Bryan has a clear perception of authenticity. In his teaching practice, he tries
to remain true to the values of the music he learned from his teachers in West
Africa, including respecting repertoire that is not suitable to be taught in noncer-
emonial settings:

> I am attached to traditional playing. So the way you see us play in the
> classes is the same when you see it in the region where it is from. Only
> they will play it a little bit richer in the patterns of the sambaing, the
> dumdum, and the djembes, where there is freedom in the music. They
> have been playing these rhythms for many years, and often hours at a
> time, so they can put all kinds of subtle things inside. I go back every
> year and see all the ceremonies, I can see how they play, and how it
> relates to the dance, so I can tell the students the truth about it. There are
> some rhythms I have learned there that I will not play in class. These
> are ritual and religious rhythms that are not played like that in Africa,
> either.

O'Bryan indicates that his students often experiment with new settings for
djembe:

> We live in modern times, and there are many things happening. I think
> that is all OK, but I go to the source. It's fine when my students play with
> a band or something. But I don't teach that. Only if I see someone
> playing in a modern context, but they don't know the basics of the
> instrument, I don't like it. It's like playing free jazz without having
> learned to play the piano. You shouldn't try to reinvent the wheel. But
> once you have the skills, you are free.

O'Bryan indicates a strong tendency toward authenticity in the sense of being true
to the original. However, the setting far away from Africa gives it aspects of a new
identity. Across the issues of context, O'Bryan takes a well-considered position,
attaching considerable value to the tradition as he learned it in Africa but aware of
the variables there and in the new teaching context.

Learning Process

Djembe has always been transmitted without notation in West Africa. The lessons
in the West generally reflect this practice. Occasionally, djembe students trained in
Western music feel the need to write the rhythms as an aide-mémoire, but the
general practice is to memorize the basic patterns and learn the structures for
improvisation. Recordings are often used to support this process; teaching rooms
are commonly a jungle of microphone wires. O'Bryan knows how to write music,
but he sees limited use for it:

> You can write how it is played theoretically, but there are certain things
> you can only learn from a master. For instance, you can write something
> down as a triplet, but it is never really played like a triplet. I know people
> who understand the structure, but to get the real feel takes a lot of time.
> It has to ripen, like an apple. There are a few students who can write, but
> I don't stop the class for them. I can also write music myself, as I went to
> Rotterdam Conservatory for a few years, but I did not learn from my
> masters like that myself. I will start a class for rhythm notation for those
> that are interested. You don't need it to play African percussion, but it can
> be useful when you need to remember a lot of rhythms in a short time.
> On the other hand, I have children who play at the same level, and they
> never write anything.

In other words, O'Bryan chooses a method of transmission that strongly leans
toward aural, although he does not exclude the use or usefulness of notation for
particular settings of learning the djembe repertoire, particularly the nontraditional
setting of learning many rhythms over a short span of time. His remark about
children is striking and consistent with my observations on how "naturally"
children pick up African rhythms, presumably because they do not have to
translate rhythms into conscious understanding first and into hand movements
after; they are integrated.

While historically the music is learned through immersion, with an absolute
minimum of explanation, O'Bryan's lessons in the Netherlands make use of the
analytical capabilities of both teacher and students. Playing remains the core of the
lessons, but the pieces are built up step by step in a logical order. In this setting,
there is no formal lesson plan, but the teacher does have a very clear picture of how
he expects students to develop:

> In Africa, they don't stop and explain what went well or wrong during the
> classes like I do. Most of the learning takes place during the ceremonies.
> So it's happening during the playing. They just grow in the music.
> There may be some explaining at times. For instance, after playing at a
> ceremony, one of the accompanying djembe players can ask the master,

"What was this pattern the solo drum was doing, or that?" But the explanation will be very short. A lot of the teaching we do in Europe is only short sounds in Africa; if I say, first do a tone and then a slap, they just say, *tun tan,* and if you play *tan tun,* they will tell you *tun tan* once more. By that time, you'd better get it. They don't have much patience with the students; sometimes they even beat them if they are not playing well.

While his lessons may seem very loosely organized, O'Bryan in fact structures his material quite carefully:

I already played some rhythms from the same family with them, so I first show them what's the same. There are three patterns which are identical in the entire family. Then I show them the "melody," which is played on the sambaing. Then I bring in the countermelody on the dumdum. We play that awhile, and then I start to rotate, so that everybody gets to play and understand every pattern of the rhythm. Then we go to the solo parts. I do some explaining, but most of it is playing.

In observing the lesson, it becomes clear that there is very little spoken explanation indeed. Barring quick shifts from instrument to instrument, O'Bryan keeps the rhythm going almost constantly, listens to the whole, but subtly singles out individuals in order to correct them, making eye contact and indicating patterns or emphases on his djembe or dumdum for the student to copy. In this way, the overall picture is one of holistic transmission with atomistic and analytical accents in specific actions of the teacher and the general conception of the lesson.

At beginning levels, the emphasis is on tangible aspects of playing, although aspects such as tonal quality emerge early on:

I work on sound quality from the beginning. But it is largely a matter of time. It takes quite long to get the right sound. And it's quite individual. It is related to the shape of the hands: some people have long, slender hands, others short ones. So they need to find their own sound. Adults seem to need more time than children, whose hands are more flexible.

Improvisation is an important aspect of the creativity of the mature musician, which O'Bryan addresses with his advanced students, and he allows children to experiment with it as well:

I also teach them how to improvise. But that takes a lot of time. I give them standard phrases and some of my own solos. Then they can see how they can approach the melody of the rhythm. Not everybody feels the freedom to improvise; the kids are quite free, they will do something, even if it is wrong.

At later stages, the deeper musical qualities of djembe music emerge. O'Bryan mentions the important aspect of the "flow" of the rhythm during the lesson, and afterward comments further on this subject, referring to specific episodes in the course of the session:

> In the right combination, it got very close. It was the second or third combination [change of students over instruments], when the lady with the glasses was playing the sambaing. If we have trouble getting the flow, I leave out patterns until we get it in a simpler form, and then I add them again. When I teach, I hear all the different parts in my head, like a chord. If one is off, you hear it immediately, and you try to correct it.

The latter corresponds to what I have observed of several African percussionists, who will speak about their music while hearing all parts and their interrelationships, not unlike a conductor of a choir or ensemble of Western classical music.

The reference for right and wrong in djembe music, as we have seen before, cannot be found in books, but it is very clear:

> There is no written theory in Africa, and the tradition is too young in the West to have books on this. But the masters know exactly what is right and what is wrong. There are rules to improvisation. First, you deal with the melody of the music. Then, you deal with the dance. If there are dancers, there are certain appropriate traditional phrases and solo improvisation. There is freedom but within restrictions.

A great deal of attention goes to playing the right pattern at the right time in the structure, which is quite tangible, but the aim of "getting in the flow" underlies many of the corrections and comments. From observing the lesson, a balance that leans slightly toward tangible aspects of transmission can be deduced.

Dimensions of Interaction

In Africa, patterns of interaction are well defined. Knight describes how learning is organized in another main tradition within Mandinka communities:

> Jaliya . . . is learned through apprenticeship. For the boy, who will most likely learn the instrument his father plays, this means between seven and ten years spent with a recognised master—usually from age ten, and usually not with the father, since a non-family member can deal more strictly and objectively with a student.[10]

O'Bryan echoes this when he comments on his observations of learning djembe in Africa:

Students can start learning both formally and informally. Sometimes, when an ensemble is incomplete, they can just pick someone to assist. In that way, he can grow in the system if he likes it. The other way—when you really want to learn—is that the elder people that see a kid with intelligence for rhythm, they bring him to a master. Then he is given some cola nuts as a sign of respect, and he is asked if he wants to train the child. There is a natural selection. When a student does not have the particular type of intellect to understand the music, or is too slow to pick up, then the master will just ignore him. I know some people in the West think otherwise, but not everybody in Africa has the talent to become a good drummer.

While the interaction in the Netherlands is very egalitarian, there appears to be a considerable power distance between learner and teacher in the culture of origin. In spite of the highly individual nature of contemporary Dutch society, the music making is unmistakably collective because of the nature of the ensemble: the rhythmic patterns only make sense in relation to one another: "One monkey, no show," as O'Bryan once expressed it succinctly.[11] In this form of Mandinke percussion, the drums are being played exclusively by men. The women dance. Ironically, in much of Europe, mature-age women form the majority of djembe students. This represents a significant shift from a strongly gendered to a gender-neutral practice. Finally, while the focus of many Western players is immediate gratification or preparing for a performance in the near future, long-term orientation is evident in O'Bryan's description of the progression through the various instruments in Africa:

> They begin with the bass drums. The first is the kenkenni. That is the time-keeping instrument. When people are playing, they just look for a young kid around, and if the kid is intelligent, if he has the musical ear to understand the basic pattern in the music, they keep him on the kenkenni. This is the lowest level. Then, maybe after two years, bit by bit, he can start changing to the other instruments. He can go to the sambaing, to the dundumba, then the accompanying djembes. Gradual- ly, he can start going to the different festivities and ceremonies with his master and finally become a master himself.

Approach to Cultural Diversity

With an African djembe teacher of Surinami descent instructing a group of Dutch learners in a community center in Amsterdam, there can be little doubt that cultural diversity plays a role here. But the interaction remains limited to a single culture being taught to a group from another culture. This would qualify as multicultural.

Conclusions

Considering O'Bryan's practice as exemplified by the observed lesson as a whole, it can be concluded that he appears to have successfully recontextualized a holistic, aural tradition with a strong contextual bond to social and ritual events into a new teaching environment.

Although he regularly returns to Africa to study, perform, and observe recent developments, O'Bryan has a fairly static view of the tradition he feels he represents. This may be an expression of the "convert phenomenon," the tendency of newcomers to a tradition to be more inclined to adhere to time-honored concepts than those who have grown up in the tradition. He resolves the challenge to context practically: although he sees it as important, he also realizes the impossibility of reproducing the context in the learning and teaching context of a private practice in Amsterdam and compromises by at least pointing out the context of each rhythm. It is difficult to establish O'Bryan's exact views on authenticity beyond following the musical aspects of the tradition; it seems that some of his students are more intent on creating a new identity for the music.

While maintaining the attractive aspects of a holistic experience for the students, O'Bryan has elegantly added analytical aspects to it. The aural modes of transmission are maintained almost completely. There seems to be a fairly strong emphasis on tangible aspects of learning, which may be accounted for by the lack of familiarity with the basic rhythms among learners in the Netherlands. The concept and importance of the intangible "flow" form a counterbalance to this tendency.

In terms of interaction, O'Bryan is very friendly with the students but exerts unchallenged authority throughout the lesson, not leaving much room for uncertainty, creativity, or self-exploration even at this advanced level. Throughout the lessons and discussions, he emphasizes the collective and only singles out an individual if he or she is at risk of falling out of the group. He treats the mixed-sex group as gender-neutral, which is evidenced by all players rotating around all of the instruments.

In the lessons, no effort is made to connect African music to other aspects of musical life in the Netherlands. O'Bryan positions it as a separate culture within the culturally diverse landscape, which would qualify it as a multicultural approach, with minor overtones of intercultural because of the intended use of the music of some of his students in fusion music. This translates into the picture shown in figure 7.1.

TWELVE CONTINUUM TRANSMISSION FRAMEWORK (TCTF)

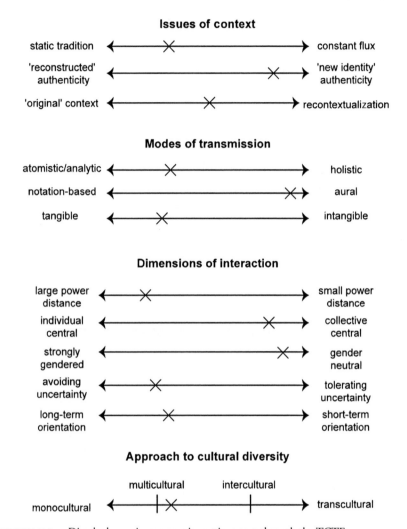

Issues of context

static tradition ⟷⨯⟶ constant flux

'reconstructed' authenticity ⟷⨯⟶ 'new identity' authenticity

'original' context ⟷⨯⟶ recontextualization

Modes of transmission

atomistic/analytic ⟷⨯⟶ holistic

notation-based ⟷⨯⟶ aural

tangible ⟷⨯⟶ intangible

Dimensions of interaction

large power distance ⟷⨯⟶ small power distance

individual central ⟷⨯⟶ collective central

strongly gendered ⟷⨯⟶ gender neutral

avoiding uncertainty ⟷⨯⟶ tolerating uncertainty

long-term orientation ⟷⨯⟶ short-term orientation

Approach to cultural diversity

multicultural   intercultural

monocultural ⟷|⨯———|⟶ transcultural

FIGURE 7.1.   Djembe lesson in community settings seen through the TCTF

Example 2: Balinese Gamelan in Teacher Training

In gamelan music, there is a broad distinction between religious music and music for entertainment. While the former is sometimes translated into the latter, the reverse movement does not occur. The large orchestra known as gong kebyar is the principal reference for contemporary gamelan music in Bali. Although it is less than a hundred years old as a form with its own repertoire, it is firmly based in earlier traditions in the dynamic musical life of Bali. But even now, the repertoire changes quickly; only a few pieces from more than a few decades ago are being regularly performed.[12] Several systems of enculturation exist side by side in Indonesia. There are the traditional systems of learning within a group or village on the one hand and, on the other, a network of conservatories in major urban areas such as Den Pasar (STSI), Surakarta (ASTI), Bandung, and Jogyakarta. According to some of the students there, these music institutes merely formalize what they have already learned in the traditional settings, but nowadays they are certainly a force of considerable influence on musical practice.[13]

Gamelan has become highly popular as a form of world music for schools across the West. It represent a culture that is far removed from the familiar soundscapes of most students, yet it is readily accessible. Moreover, it enables young learners through collaboration to play a piece of music that sounds reasonably coherent after a workshop as short as a single hour. In the 1990s, the Royal Tropical Institute in Amsterdam ran a successful school project featuring such workshops called "Invisible Guests," referring to the close association of music and spirituality in Bali. Many hundreds of primary students participated, as they continue to do with similar projects elsewhere, particularly in the UK and the United States.

Facilitating such workshops is within range for Western-trained music teachers. This description focuses on lessons in Balinese gong kebyar given to a group of Dutch music education students of the Conservatorium of Amsterdam by the traditionally trained specialist I Ketut Gedé Rudita. The lessons took place between November 1998 and February 1999. Source material included a reader for the students, personal observations of one of the lessons, a video of the final performance, and interviews with and a final report by Vonck,[14] the coordinator of the project and a seasoned player and teacher of Balinese music herself.

Issues of Context

Considering approaches to tradition, Ketut seems to work from a clear, fairly static concept of Balinese music during the workshops. But, as Vonck explains, the music in Bali itself allows a considerable degree of change:

> Every village or *banjar* (neighborhood) has its own style. But they do not exist in isolation. In fact, they borrow things they like from other areas. This means quite a lot of changes. Pieces can also disappear completely. I went back to Bali with a piece that was recorded around 1930, and nobody knew it anymore. And even gender wayang pieces I recorded 20 years ago in a particular regional style are not played anymore.

> Balinese music is an uninterrupted tradition, but it changes constantly. The leader of the ensemble is the motor behind this change. If you want to learn something in an old style, you have to find an old master. The young people won't know it. The amount of change also depends on the type of music. Religious music, for instance, the music for the wayang, does not change noticeably. But dance music and entertainment music, such as gong kebyar, does change quite a lot. Only at STSI, [the "gamelan conservatory"] things become standardized, because it is linked to a single teacher. There the tradition becomes static.

Therefore, the tradition can be perceived as in flux but "frozen" for this teaching situation.

While Ketut himself did not even consider referring to a context that was completely obvious to himself, Vonck considers this a factor of major importance in teaching Balinese gamelan in the West:

> Context is essential. This is my conviction and my experience. Recently, I went to Bali with some of my students, and when they saw the context, they asked me: "Why didn't you explain these things before?" But you can't explain everything. You have to see and experience it. There are so many aspects to context: the days you honor your instruments, the ritual you do before every performance. These are aspects of the unity, . . . creating an atmosphere. I also include correct behavior, such as taking off shoes and not stepping over the instruments. These are important as well.
>
> Context is inseparable from the music, but what you play is the music itself. It is important for the players but less so for an audience, although we do often choose to work in thematic projects, so we get in as much context as possible. Religious music, such as gender wayang, requires more awareness of context. In that music, the dalang is like a priest. Gong kebyar needs less. In the end, it is viable without context but better with. I think context also stresses the value of the music and its equality to Western classical music. In Western music, we don't need the context, because we have it.

A number of theoretical classes and references to literature were included in the course structure in order to make the students in the Netherlands aware of context. However, little was done to try to *re-create* the context of the particular pieces being studied, conceivably because the original context might be experienced as too foreign. This, as I have argued before, may lead to a sense of estrangement rather than connection with the music. The balance is toward a recontextualized setting.

Vonck comments on the different approach to authenticity between Bali and the West:

Balinese musicians claim they are authentic, but they are not, certainly not in the historical sense. I accept the way the Balinese deal with it. Authenticity is what they do when they do it right. There is not a single standard. The concept may play a role for Western learners. In the Netherlands, we try to stay close to the original. I don't feel qualified to make changes when we play traditional music.

Here we have a fascinating example of a Westerner defining authenticity in a more restricted manner than those for whom the music is the first reference. The living tradition seems to allow for a considerable degree of variation that is still considered authentic, rather than using as a reference some ancient framework. However, in this setting, for perfectly legitimate reasons, the balance is toward a reconstructed authenticity.

Learning Process

During Ketut's lessons, no notation was used. This corresponds to the practice in Bali. Vonck explains: "In learning, it is not used at all, or anywhere else in the musical process. Everything is memorized. Composers say they use notation, but in fact even they only write down the core melody. The rest is reconstructed from memory." This qualifies Balinese gamelan as an almost entirely aural tradition.

In Bali, the traditional system of learning to play gong kebyar is almost exclusively through absorption. This takes extreme forms in the perception of music transmission and learning:

In Bali, people do not learn music; they just sit down and play. At least, this is what they say. In Bali, children are taken to rehearsals from an early age. They sit on the laps of their fathers (or sometimes nowadays their mothers) and just absorb the music. After some years, when their father has to go to the bathroom during a rehearsal, for instance, they simply take over. It sounds like a very romantic story, but I have seen it to be true. So music learning in Bali is predominantly an unconscious process, quite unlike the conscious process in the West.

Only if you want to go beyond just playing in a gong kebyar orchestra, if you want to be a specialist, for instance, on the kendang [drum], you go to an expert. You select this expert yourself. If you like his *pukulan* [strokes], you ask him to teach you. For instance, if you want to be a specialist in barong dances, in which the strokes have to be heavy and thick, you find someone who can do that. The normal system of learning is that you become part of his group. But you don't have a single teacher; you can shop around for the styles and skills you like.

The tradition of learning holistically, of a leader of an ensemble taking for granted that the members actually know the music already, led to confrontational situations in Amsterdam:

> It was a disaster. The transmission almost stopped. It was a major culture shock for Ketut, who had no teaching experience and had never experienced people before who did not know the music. Moreover, he basically spoke no English when he came over. And the Dutch students expected a lot of explanation. Instead, while he was teaching, he just looked into the air and probably prayed that the students would get it. But if he gave a cue to an *angsel*, a break, to his surprise, nobody followed. His teaching was completely holistic in the Balinese way. It didn't connect at all. In the end, he was saved by his musicality and his charisma.

It is interesting to note that even when faced with noncomprehension, Ketut did not shift to a more analytical or atomistic method of teaching. Holistic learning appears to have been his only frame of reference.

Because the learning process is so emphatically holistic, Vonck finds it difficult to determine a balance on the continuum from tangible to intangible. Yet she refers to aspects of both:

> This is hard to answer. As I said before, they already know the music when they start "learning," so in a way, it is just a matter of finding out where the notes are. In fact, the core of playing in a gamelan ensemble is something they call *seka*. This word is composed of two words, *sa* and *eka*, both meaning "one." The idea behind this is that the entire group plays like one. In this unity, all aspects of the music, including the dynamics, are absorbed. I have never heard a teacher say, "This part needs to be played soft, and that louder." In fact, most Balinese do not have a teaching system. In all my years in Bali, I have only met two or three teachers who had developed a teaching method. It is very rare.

On the basis of this, we can conclude that the ultimate goal of Balinese music teaching in this area is intangible, which is even stronger in religious contexts. Of course, tangible aspects are learned, particularly in the field of the precision in timing and speed that is required to play the interlocking patterns, but emphasis on technique and theory seems to be absent from any explicit aspects of learning. In the situation in the Netherlands, however, tangible aspects needed to be included in order to bring the students to some practical understanding of the music. This brings the balance to the middle for this specific teaching situation.

Dimensions of Interaction

Although the drummer is the undisputed leader in the gamelan ensemble, the distance seems to be less defined than in, say, a Western orchestra. It is difficult to define the position of the drummer as a teacher, because there is no explicit acknowledgment or even awareness of learners and teachers. There is no doubt that the collective is central in playing Balinese gamelan; it is strongly community-based. Men predominantly play the instruments in Bali, but there seems to be no high barrier against women playing, and Peter Dunbar-Hall observes that gamelans with female players are gaining ground in Bali. While the practice slowly shifts toward more gender-neutral in Bali, the session in Amsterdam is completely so, with the slight overrepresentation of women typical for music education students.

The tradition is firmly established in players' memories and hands in Bali, so there is little uncertainty there; in the workshops, uncertainty was considerable because of unfamiliarity; this was hardly intentional, however. While the aim of the workshops was short-term (the performance at the end), the orientation in Bali seems to be on very long-term participation in the culture of the village.

Approach to Cultural Diversity

Vonck has a clear picture of where she places gamelan education in the Netherlands:

> The main reference for the small group of about 30 people actively involved in Balinese gamelan is the tradition. In fusion projects, that is another matter. We played with Western musicians, and in multidisciplinary settings. But that is not a part of the gamelan lessons here. First you have to know the tradition; then you can explore. This can be still linked to the tradition or completely separate.

Although there are some examples of intercultural use of gamelan, such as the twelve-tone gamelan introduced by composer-performer Sinta Wullur, and suggestions exist of transcultural use in the sense of gaining transferable skills by participants from the conservatory, the musical reality of virtually all gamelan transmission in the Netherlands is aimed at realizing a "pure" Indonesian cultural product in the Netherlands, without significant interaction with the outside world. That would make this exercise qualify as multicultural.

The practice of teaching Balinese music in Bali itself provides a fascinating example of an extreme in holistic learning, to the point where it goes beyond any awareness of learning. When transplanted to a Western conservatory, this can cause a clash between different cultures of music learning and teaching. In a way, this case study represents a meeting of extremes: institutionalized

Western music, and its emphasis on analysis and notation, with the almost entirely holistic/aural Balinese tradition. The Dutch experience can be summarized as in figure 7.2.

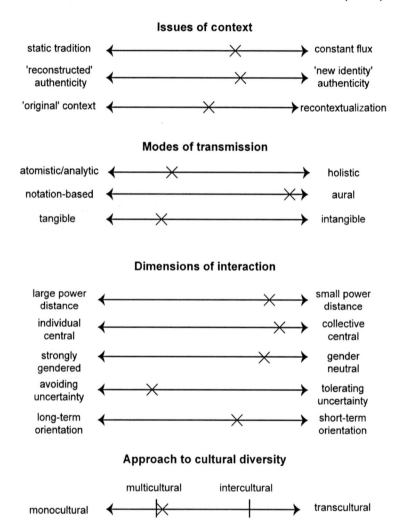

FIGURE 7.2.   Gong Kebyar workshop for music education students in the TCTF

Conclusions

The first cluster offers particularly valuable insights. Few of the traditions discussed so far are transmitted in a manner so purely holistic and aural. Music making in Bali places considerable emphasis on intangible aspects (including gods, demons, good and evil), although it may never be made explicit in the transmission of the music. This is a fascinating extreme example in which an analytical or even predictive application of the TCTF could have anticipated the incompatibility of learning and teaching styles, including assumptions about previously acquired knowledge and skills.

The description of musical practice in Bali presents a picture of a tradition with a solid basis but at the same time in a considerable state of flux. In its place of origin, it is strongly linked to its context. However, it does not appear to strive for re-creating an authenticity of the past. When it is moved to a conservatory in the Netherlands with essentially total beginners, priorities shift. The tradition can easily be taken to be static, the context is only re-created theoretically, and the attempt seems to be to make "authentic" Balinese music in the sense of being true to the originals in its culture of origin. In this way, the modest Balinese music practice in the Amsterdam Conservatory can be seen as a separate island of Indonesian culture in a sea of music from all over the world. Consequently, it is again multicultural in the terminology of this study.

Example 3: Indian Music As a Degree Course in a Conservatory

Indian music or, more precisely, the tradition known as Hindustani or North Indian classical music, has been in the awareness of Westerners for more than two hundred years through some early publications such as those by Jones (1796) and Willard (1834).[15] Having moved from Hindu temples to Muslim courts to public performances for the cultural elite in India, it also did well in a fourth major change of context: the expansion to the West.[16] In spite of preconceptions of many Westerners that were drawn to it from the 1960s, direct religious connections are not the central feature of Indian classical music today. Not unlike Western classical music, Hindustani music is essentially a refined, worldly music. Indian music schools sprung up across the Western world from the late 1960s, and engaged many Westerners in learning this demanding art form.

One of the most prominent contemporary North Indian classical musicians is Pandit Hariprasad Chaurasia, an exponent of the bansuri, or bamboo flute. Unlike many of his peers and predecessors, Chaurasia does not come from a long line of flautists. His father was a famous wrestler, who hoped that his son would follow in his footsteps. The young Chaurasia had a strong love of music, however, and after hearing a flute recital by Pandit Bholanath, he was so impressed that he changed his focus to studying the flute. From age nineteen, he played for All India Radio, first in Orissa and later in Mumbai. There he studied with Shrimati Annapurna Devi, daughter of the legendary Ustad Allauddin Khan (who also taught Ali Akbar Khan and Ravi Shankar).

With Devi, Chaurasia established the basis for an impressive career, developing a style that was respectful of tradition yet innovative. During a lifetime of performances, he has become one of India's most respected classical musicians, earning numerous prestigious national and international awards. He has collaborated with several Western musicians, including John McLaughlin and Jan Gabarek, and has also composed music for a number of Indian films. Chaurasia heads the Indian music department at CODarts/ World Music & Dance Centre in Rotterdam. This section documents an advanced group lesson featuring the evening rāga Bihag within the context of a degree course, which he has been teaching since 1991. This specific lesson, followed by an interview, was recorded and observed on May 8, 2003.[17]

Issues of Context

Although he himself has been involved in musical projects mixing traditions, Chaurasia emphatically does not use non-Indian cultural influences in his teaching. He believes that students are coming to him to learn pure classical music, which is also the music he learned. However, he does not consider the tradition that he teaches static but rather in constant flux on a firm basis of unchangeable aspects, namely, the fixed parts of compositions and the treatment of the tonal material of the rāga.

For a senior musician, Chaurasia has an uncommonly positive approach to the music of the young generation: "It has very much changed; it is becoming more and more beautiful. The younger generation are making it more and more beautiful.... They are creating their own thing." Chaurasia expresses the view that merely repeating one's predecessors is not enough: creativity is an essential aspect of the North Indian tradition: "This is the beauty in classical music." However, the material he teaches is strongly traditional. His movements in Bihag are very similar to those in renditions of most traditional masters. Therefore, his approach to this area holds the middle area between static tradition and constant flux, with perhaps a slight leaning toward the former.

In the interview, Chaurasia gives strong hints of trying to re-create an Indian context, but he also seems to be aware of new realities: "I'm trying to make them Indian. When they pick up the bamboo, they should look like Indian. Their sound should sound like Indian. That's what I'm trying to do." But he relates this less to context than to actual musical skills and properties. And he indicates that he spends little time on teaching his students about behavioral codes among musicians, which he finds they pick up themselves from being exposed to Indian culture away from the conservatory.

In India, Chaurasia spends time discussing the background of the music in terms of stories about famous musicians. In Europe, he concentrates on the sound. He says the students get the background on Indian culture through television. This may seem a somewhat meager source of in-depth understanding; perhaps Chaurasia deems a modest understanding of Indian culture sufficient. Chaurasia does not see any problem in one of the great questions and challenges of multicultural music practice: students from other cultures learning Indian music. He mentions that there are a number of Western musicians who have reached a high level of proficiency: "If you close your eyes, you will feel that this music is played by Indians," provided they have learned properly. There is a leaning toward re-creating a musical rather than a cultural context for the students.

Authenticity is a complicated issue in the context of Hindustani music. Chaurasia sees little use in trying to reconstruct the music from the past, as this is widely considered poor musicianship. On the other hand, great value is attached to remaining true to certain rules and values, particularly in early musicianship, with an emphatic personal stamp at more advanced stages of learning. In this way, North Indian music can be considered to take on a new identity with every new generation of musicians in a way that strives for "truth to self," while retaining considerable historical authenticity.

Learning Process

The transmission process observed is entirely aural. This is how Chaurasia prefers the music transmission to take place. But he does observe that Westerners take time to learn in this way, because they are not used to it. He relates memorizing music to the way it is developed in performance, by stating that the remembered piece of music in the mind forms the basis for improvisation. At the same time, Chaurasia is sensitive to the situation of the students at the conservatory: "I don't want anybody to use [notation], but I'm not here all the time, so they have to record, and they have to write." He indicates that he does attach value to writing as a means to ensure preservation of the material.

Rather strikingly, he prefers writing to recording, because he ascribes greater longevity to written music than to sound recordings, presumably based on the vulnerability of reel-to-reel and cassette tapes (particularly in India). In general, this picture shows a strong emphasis on aural transmission but some use of notation as support. On the continuum, the balance is very much toward the right. The recorded lesson shows an almost entirely holistic approach.

It is tempting but not accurate to call his approach entirely holistic, however. Chaurasia consciously shows the development of the rāga in slow motion. "When I teach them, I go very slowly. I show them how to go from note to note." This actually implies a more analytical strategy. The same goes for the fast improvisations known as *tans*. Chaurasia indicated that he does not explain the structure of these to the students but gives them examples so they can work out the structure for themselves. Although it is not demonstrated in the lesson, Chaurasia indicates in the interview that he checks and corrects improvisations by the students, until they do not make certain mistakes, for instance in prescribed note order when they create new free or fixed improvisations. He also corrects mistakes in approach to sound, as when the quality of the tone is derived from Western music.

Chaurasia makes clear that he explains theoretical aspects of music as well: "Sometimes I explain about the rāga. When I start teaching the rāga, I explain about the *chalan*, about *asthayi* and *antara*, about *vadi, samvadi*, about the timing of the rāgas." The discussion of timing occurs briefly at the end of the lesson, when he asks the group at what time of day the particular rāga should be played. Although the picture is somewhat clouded by the structure of the curriculum, in which analytical aspects of the training of the musician (such as history and analysis) are being addressed in specific modules outside the instrumental lessons, we can establish that in this case study, the emphasis is clearly on a holistic approach, to the right of the continuum, but it does display some elements of analytical approaches.

As Chaurasia spends most of the lesson showing the students the way through the melodic material of the rāga, the emphasis seems to be on tangible aspects, but there are several pointers toward the intangible as well. Chaurasia indicates that the reason for playing with the students (rather than singing the music, which is common among Indian instrumentalists when teaching) is sound production and color:

> I play with them, so they can get the sound of the instrument, the beauty
> of the notes, and they can also watch me, how I blow. This is a
> very difficult part: how I blow and how I make my fingers move on the
> flute. . . . You have to lift half finger to get half notes and then to create
> microtones through your blowing. So they have to watch when I play.
> If I just sing, they will never have the idea of the technique of the
> instrument.

In addressing advanced issues of interpretation of rāga, he uses a metaphor to illustrate how one is allowed to take certain liberties when interpreting a rāga: when you see the moon temporarily hidden from view by clouds, then it looks even brighter when it reappears. This is called *avir bhav, tiru bhav*. In a further comment, he goes into the metaphysical: "They also have to understand that you don't have to tune the instrument, but you have to tune yourself. The instrument itself, the flute, does not need to be tuned, but if you are not tuned here [inside], then you cannot play in tune."

Comments like these are quite common in Indian classical music transmission. As in many other traditions, metaphor is used frequently to make the student understand aspects of the music that defy description. On the basis of this particular example, the emphasis seems to lie in the middle area between tangible and intangible.

Dimensions of Interaction

The class on the video bears some resemblance to any group teaching at a conservatory, but it also has some specific Indian aspects. On the superficial level, we see the students sitting on the floor. This is necessary for some instruments, such as the sitar and the tanpura and is a reflection of the traditional concert practice, during which the artists always sit on the floor. Chaurasia sits on a chair. It is not uncommon for a guru to be in a slightly elevated position, such as on a small dais, when he is teaching, both improving the visual contact with a group of students and underlining his status. Although some musicians are quite egalitarian in how they relate to students, the guru is not an equal. In this case, however, as I discovered while discussing this with Joep Bor, the founder of this program, the elevated position was attributable primarily to a much more mundane reason: the master has a knee problem. Although the setting is Western and contemporary, Chaurasia chooses to refer to his system of teaching at the Rotterdam Conservatory as *guru-śiṣya-paramparā*, the traditional system of transmission in India.

While the lesson observed is a group event and students play in unison for a substantial part of the lesson, there is no doubt that the focus is on the individual for this essentially solo tradition. In India, the flute is strongly associated with Krishna (a reincarnation of the god Vishnu) and is traditionally played by males, but both there and in the West, women increasingly play and perform on this instrument. There is no stigma attached. With an improvisatory style in which most of the rules governing these improvisations are implicit rather than explicit, there is considerable uncertainty. Chaurasia does not make any comments beyond a noncommittal "very good" at the attempts of the students to follow him or improvise. He echoes this in the interview: "I don't explain much, but I am playing." Learning Indian music is emphatically a long-term endeavor: the short-term rewards for beginning students are negligible. Apprenticeship basically continues until the guru passes away. One could even argue that reincarnation is a necessity for achieving mastery in this tradition!

Approach to Cultural Diversity

The situation regarding the approach to cultural diversity is very clear. Chaurasia gives evidence of an emphatic attempt to re-create a little India in Rotterdam. Within the idiom of this discussion, that would be called a multicultural approach. Chaurasia does refer to his own intercultural musical experience, but this is not what the students are coming for, and it is allowed among students but not especially stimulated. That indicates a position on the continuum just to the right of multicultural (see figure 7.3).

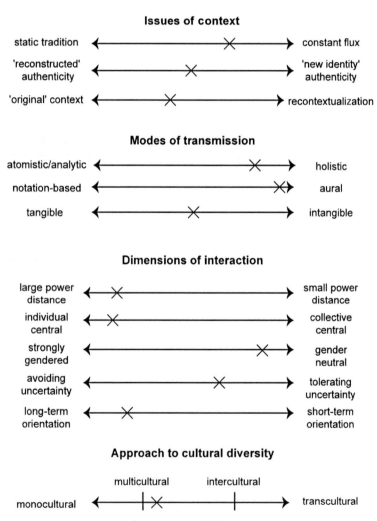

TWELVE CONTINUUM TRANSMISSION FRAMEWORK (TCTF)

Issues of context

static tradition ←———————✕———————→ constant flux

'reconstructed' authenticity ←————✕————→ 'new identity' authenticity

'original' context ←————✕————→ recontextualization

Modes of transmission

atomistic/analytic ←————————✕———→ holistic

notation-based ←———————————✕→ aural

tangible ←————✕————→ intangible

Dimensions of interaction

large power distance ←✕—————————→ small power distance

individual central ←✕—————————→ collective central

strongly gendered ←——————————✕—→ gender neutral

avoiding uncertainty ←————————✕———→ tolerating uncertainty

long-term orientation ←—✕————————→ short-term orientation

Approach to cultural diversity

multicultural   intercultural

monocultural ←——|✕————————|——→ transcultural

FIGURE 7.3.   Degree course in *bansuri* in the TCTF

Conclusions

This pattern—along with the discussions about each continuum—demonstrates that the system of music transmission used by Chaurasia is quite close to the traditional system used in India, while his views demonstrate clear awareness of the new setting and the type of students he deals with in the West. The conservatory setting has not had a great deal of influence on the teaching practice, except for, ironically, the reinstitution of one-to-one teaching, considered an essential feature of guru-śisya-paramparā.

Indian classical music exists in relative isolation within the conservatory context. Its specific musical characteristics dictate separate modules for almost every subject. (In Latin jazz and tango, for example, some theoretical and practical subjects may be shared with jazz and Western classical music, respectively.) This may be a strength and a weakness, an opportunity and a threat at once for a solid position within the institution.

In the end, North Indian classical music at the Rotterdam Conservatory has retained its character as a *musique savante*, with a focus on one-to-one education by settling in a system that already supports this. A major difference from Western methods of teaching is the insistence on aural and holistic transmission, with less emphasis on tangible aspects. This is partly compensated for by teaching support subjects, but it remains the essence of the transmission practice, which, ironically, as established at the end of chapter 5, is more in line with contemporary, constructivist thinking on education than much of the positivist approach that still can be found at the basis of organization and curriculum in traditional conservatories.

The setup and practices at Rotterdam and other conservatories continue to raise questions about appropriate methods of teaching and the placing of traditions. From the short description above, a picture emerges of the world music department at the Rotterdam Conservatory aiming to be intercultural, but it is predominantly multicultural in focusing on individual traditions. The approach to tradition is fairly static in the prominence of established musical practices in the cultures of origin over innovation, authenticity is sought in the sense of spirit rather than historical reconstruction, and the conservatory environment necessitates far-reaching recontextualization, with little effort to re-create aspects of the original context of the musical practices in question.

The way the curricula have been set up, with formulated modular units that correspond to the norms set by the Dutch higher education authorities, tends toward the atomistic/analytical. Overall, the programs would average out in a middle position between tangible and intangible aspects of music, with theoretical subjects stressing the former and many of the one-on-one vocal/instrumental classes including less tangible elements of musical practice, whether it be the "feel" of the clave in Latin music, the subtle intonation through srutis in Indian rāgas, or the spirit of duende in flamenco guitar playing.

Conclusion

The most striking insight that emerges from these examples and the case study of the Netherlands as a whole is that in spite of the complex issues surrounding cultural diversity in music education, actual practices, if given the space and support they need, seem to be able to find sensitive and commonsense solutions to most challenges, leading to satisfying learning and teaching experiences for all involved.

While the examples above all focus on instrument-specific training, very similar experiences can be reported from projects in the classroom. For instance, as a spin-off of the Amsterdam World Music School, a project called "Drumming around the World" featuring three "world drummers" on djembe, darbuka, and congas (briefly discussed in chapter 5) ran successfully for years on a project basis, while "The Music Club" was a longitudinal exercise of six teachers across five disciplines (including classical, pop, and world music) to work intensely with children in a disadvantaged and highly culturally diverse primary school.[18] A final initiative worth mentioning is the custom-built "Flying Gamelan," which was ordered from Java and designed to ensure easy transport from school to school, allowing access to the actual sound and playing techniques of gamelan to hundreds of children a year. All three projects used a broad variety of pedagogical approaches, flexible approaches to authenticity and tried to build on the natural forms of interaction of the children.

The TCTF seems to provide a useful basis for in-depth documentation and description for such examples of learning and teaching world music in new contexts. In each of the three instrument-specific settings, patterns can be discerned where the "incoming" tradition creates (or is given) room to flourish more or less on its own terms. There are some areas where friction occurs, such as the extremely holistic approach to learning in Balinese gamelan. In others, aspects of the music are sacrificed in the new environment, such as the cultural context in African percussion and flux in Balinese gamelan. The classroom examples highlight the possibility of framing external expertise into projects that fit in yet add value to the school activities and curriculum. Each of these settings would be labeled primarily multicultural: they create little islands of another culture within the community, classroom, and studio setting, rather than reaching out to other musical forms. This is the reality of much world-music activity in the Netherlands, as it is across the world.

What is most important, however, is that applying the TCTF to an in-depth case study and some specific samples provides an eminently useful template to describe what is going on both at the surface level and at the level of values and attitudes. It paints a fairly detailed picture of synergies and frictions in settings for learning and teaching music "out of context." It provides an excellent basis for planning, negotiating, and realizing world music education in culturally diverse environments, especially in the case of aural, holistic traditions entering formal music education.

Epilogue

Shaping Music Education from a Global Perspective

I n this book, I have tried to explore a rich array of issues arising from cultural diversity in music education (or transmission in world music). Some of these are obvious; others have deep implications for thinking, designing, and realizing music education across the board. The seven angles that have informed this journey reveal different perspectives. The auto-ethnographic account related the increasingly common experience that preconceived notions about music making and learning cannot be transplanted to other cultures at random. The exploration of terminology showed that the words used to refer to aspects of cultural diversity in music are not random, have deeper implications in terms of values and attitudes, and change over time.

The closer look at tradition, authenticity, and context revealed a somewhat liberating fluidity in each of these concepts. The exploratory analysis of what is considered important in music making and learning is far from absolute but rather illustrates how these vary greatly from culture to culture and from setting to setting. This certainly holds true for music traditions in different stages of formalized and institutionalized transmission, which is not synonymous with well-conceived and appropriate for contemporary contexts. In drawing together these considerations into a framework, the multitude of conscious and subconscious choices in any situation of music learning and teaching becomes clear. An extended case study shows how this can lead to deeper and sometimes surprising insights into the interplay of practice and ideas in music learning and teaching across cultures.

These reflections provide music educators with a powerful set of tools to plan, design, implement, and evaluate music education that is truly inclusive in terms of content and delivery. Mindful of Patricia Campbell's insightful and compassionate account of the imaginary teacher Ms. Benson, who naively tries and fails to engage a culturally diverse classroom in making world music (reprinted as appendix 5 in this book),[1] I realize that the multitude of concerns and subtleties of approach raised here may seem a little intimidating at times; but I hope that they inspire passionate engagement rather than being dismissed as "too much and too hard."

At an individual level, those who wish to move forward may be wise to remember that "a journey of a thousand songs begins with a single tune."[2] When teachers or children hear new music and start to engage with it, tapping feet, feeling the melody go around in their heads, they are already in. What follows is a process of defining and refining one's position, which may involve acquiring knowledge and skills, analyzing, practicing, conversations, reading, listening, and often a great deal of joy and humor.

The following seven practical, hands-on suggestions are written primarily with the realities of classroom music teachers in mind, but they can easily be translated into actions for teacher trainers, music education researchers, and ethnomusicologists, as well as those in government, policy, curriculum development, or leadership positions. I hope that they can assist in making some of the ideas in this book happen where it counts most: in classrooms, studios, and community settings across the world.

1. If you want to learn about world music, communicate with musicians and communities around you. It is not necessary to go to inland Borneo or outback Australia to do fieldwork for cultural diversity in music education. The opportunities are around the corner. Most communities from other cultures are extremely welcoming and generous, even if they have major grief from a recent or more distant past (be it war, suppression, racism, colonialism, or slavery). A dialogue approached with integrity and some cultural sensitivity can lead to highly rewarding experiences or even revelations (see appendix B for sample questions).

2. If you take cultural diversity in music education seriously, request and use in-service training, professional development, study leave, or refresher time to develop insights, knowledge, and skills that will help realize vibrant learning experiences. Locate and access learning material designed for the classroom with solid background information. Do not depend on transcriptions if you do not know the music well; always try to find recordings. But most important, try to find people who make or listen to the music and speak to them; invite them into the classroom. Working with communities can bring major new pedagogical ideas, new dimensions, and added credibility to a music lesson or program that may otherwise fail to engage and convince.

3. Do not try to master too many musics. Over a period of several years, concentrate on maybe two or three (in addition to your own). Choose musics that you feel genuinely interested in, and try to select musics that have very different sounds and background, perhaps a traditional one and a

contemporary one. Read about them, and especially listen to recordings as much and as often as possible (even while walking the dog or doing the dishes). If possible, try to attend live performances and speak to audiences, communities, and musicians.

4. Be aware of tradition, authenticity, and context, but do not get stifled by these concepts. Read about them, think about them, and boldly present the recontextualized version of the music you have chosen to work with in the classroom. The core of music is not correctness but its power to move people. Acknowledge differences with originals, and proceed to create meaningful experiences.

5. When planning introductions to world music, consider alternatives to single lessons dedicated to world music amid lessons on baroque and classical music and to the multilesson geographical introductions. At all levels of education, there are formats that are more inclusive and more engaging: for instance, discussing music from all over the world on the basis of themes such as music of the royal courts, music and love, or music and resistance. Remember to include contemporary musics in the mix (see appendix C for a possible template).

6. Engage with curriculum. While most educators see curriculum as a given constraint on their work, it should be a support for delivering the best, most inspiring, and most relevant music to young learners. If it isn't, it should be changed. Challenge shortcomings in terms of repertoire balance or pedagogical approaches within your working environment, and be around the table (literally or via the Internet) when it is discussed at the state or national level.

7. Address the diversity of learning styles and strengths within any educational setting. Students from other cultures may have trouble learning music through notation or analysis yet excel in understanding and remembering complicated music by ear. Some may learn best through abstract presentations of the material, while others gain most from a hands-on approach. These are well-known principles that require additional sensitivity and can be put to even more effective use in culturally diverse environments.

From a global perspective, music learning and teaching appear to be at a crossroads. Key stakeholders can either withdraw into seemingly safe fortresses (in thought or stone) or embrace the complexities and challenges of contemporary cultural realities and move forward on the basis of constructive dialogue among musicians, learners, music educators, and (ethno)musicologists from all over the world. We have at our disposal an enormous diversity and beauty in forms of musical expression. For all of the challenges that cultural diversity brings to societies at large around the world, in music, with a little effort and sensitivity, there is the opportunity to explore, celebrate, and help sustain this diversity.

Emergency Guidelines in Case
of World Music

In the summary of the final report of *Sound Links*, a project investigating cultural diversity in higher music education funded by the European Commission, the project team decided to communicate some of the key findings as a variation on the fire warnings encountered in every hotel room around the world. These might be of some use to those interested in engaging with cultural diversity.

WHAT TO DO IN CASE CULTURAL DIVERSITY ENTERS YOUR INSTITUTION

1. Open all doors and windows. Receive the new influences in the same spirit of **curiosity and receptiveness** that have been at the core of most major developments in the history of music across the globe.
2. Set realistic, tangible **aims and targets** for pilot projects or long-term initiatives, and relate them to the key motivation for including these activities in terms of artistic, personal, and organizational outcomes.
3. Be aware that cultural diversity does not refer only to many musical sounds and structures but also to a wealth of approaches to **teaching and learning** that can benefit the entire institution.
4. Quality criteria are complicated within traditional conservatory subjects; activities in cultural diversity call for an even more **flexible set of criteria**, with fitness for purpose and relevance to context.
5. The success of cultural diversity in higher music education also depends on its **position in the structure**, ranging from optional workshops to credited parts of the core curriculum.
6. Cultural diversity has been high on the cultural and political agenda for some time. Placing it carefully in the **political and funding climate** will benefit the activities and the institution at large.

---

7. As a new area of development, cultural diversity lends itself very well to **making connections** in the community surrounding the institute, in the national arts world, and in international networks.

8. Experience shows that successful initiatives in cultural diversity center around inspired people, well supported in the hierarchy. This has implications for **leadership, organization, and management.**

9. Cultural diversity may lead to the formation of isolated islands within the institution. Constantly involving **staff and students** in planning, process, and results will help to avert this danger.

10. It is relatively easy to realize a single, successful initiative. The greater challenge lies in ensuring **sustainability** by creating a climate that will contribute to an open and inspiring learning environment.

Reprinted with permission from the 2003 final report of *Sound Links* (Kors, Saraber, and Schippers).

Sample Questions for Interviewing World Musicians on Learning and Teaching

(90–120 minutes)

1. Can you tell me something about your own musical history?
   - Earliest remembered musical experiences?
   - Beginning to learn music (formally or informally)?
   - Formal musical training in your main tradition?
   - Musical training in other traditions (including Western art music)
2. From whom or where did you learn music in your main area of expertise?
   - At an institution for professional music training?
   - With a master in your particular tradition?
   - As part of a community in which this music is made as a matter of course?
   - Did your training lead to a formal qualification or recognition?
3. How did you learn music in your main area of expertise?
   - By rote as part of an aural tradition or through a formalized teaching program?
   - From scores, radio, recordings, or Web-based resources?
   - What was the balance between using notation and aural transmission (including recording)?
   - What was the balance between atomistic and holistic teaching?
   - What was the balance between emphasis on tangible and less tangible elements?
4. What are your attitudes toward various aspects of the music tradition you represent?
   - Do you see your tradition as fixed or constantly in movement?
   - What do you consider authentic in your music?
   - What do you consider to be appropriate contexts for your music?
5. What place does your music tradition have in the musical landscape?
   - In contemporary settings?
   - In its historical settings (various phases of its development)?

- Where do you see it placed in the near future, five years from now, twenty years from now?

6. Is a sustainable future of the music tradition you represent currently being supported?
   - By government policies (and funding)?
   - By performing arts organizations or venues?
   - By the media or recording industry?
   - By the tourism industry?
   - By universities or research institutes?
   - By conservatories or music schools?
   - By music programs in schools?

7. What are the implications of each of these forms of support for the music itself?
   - Does it change the position of the music in the community or society?
   - Does it change aspects or the essence of the tradition (if yes, which and in what ways)?

8. How do you envision the best way of creating a sustainable future for your music?

Example of a Series of Classes on World Music with a Thematic Approach

The series below is based on a lecture cycle for music education students at the Amsterdam Conservatory, designed in 2000 by Huib Schippers and Adri Schreuder to deliver an alternative to geography-based introductions to world music and refined in various settings since. It fulfills three conditions that are important in the context of cultural diversity in music education: it naturally includes music of all periods, styles, and genres, including Western classical music; it highlights music as a dynamic phenomenon that interacts with (changes in) society; and it provides students from all backgrounds with opportunities to connect themes and ideas to music they are familiar with. With the first six themes presenting various contexts for music and the latter six offering links to emotions and social factors, this course is a highly concentrated "History of the Musics of the World," which can be delivered at most levels of education with slight variations in musical examples (most of which are readily available through online sources in audio and—even better—video formats).

1. Music and the Supernatural

Many cultures attribute divine or supernatural beginnings to music or even musical beginnings to the world. We find this in the Indian concept of the primal sound *aum* at the heart of creation; in Pythagoras's "harmony of the spheres"; in the legend that the different maqams of Arab music came from the rock that Abraham hit with his stick; and in the traditional belief that the African kora was given to the first *jali* by a spirit in a well. There are hundred of stories of this kind.

As a logical consequence, music has come to be seen as an appropriate means to accompany ritual or even to communicate directly with higher powers. This does not extend only to the low overtone singing of Tibetan monks, the rain dances of Native Americans, or the mystic union sought by the Whirling Dervishes. The Catholic mass has a section that calls out directly to God, *Kyrie eleison* ("Lord have mercy"); J. S. Bach wrote *Ich ruf zu dir, Herr Jesu Christ* ("I call out to you, Lord Jesus Christ"); and Janis Joplin wailed, "Oh Lord, won't you buy me a Mercedes-Benz."

2. Music and the Royal Courts

Court music has been a massive phenomenon and influence in music for more than fifteen centuries. Often, court music developed from religious traditions, sometimes taking inspiration from folk music. Its key characteristics are that it tends to be *refined* (what the French so poetically call *musiques savantes*, literally "knowing musics"); often unashamedly *elitist* (only for the king and those close to him); and a sign of *prestige/distinction*, down to the rather childish but very frequent "I've got more (or better) court musicians than you." The last mentioned has greatly helped musicians' employment prospects through the ages.

It is quite exciting to make a fourteenth-century journey across the world from the European courts in Europe, to the kingdom of Mail (which covered an area roughly as large as western Europe), to the courts in Istanbul, Baghdad, or Tehran, to the courts in India, to those in Indonesia, China, and Japan. The music sounds very different, but the setting and accompanying expected way of listening are remarkably similar, as are the stories of chivalry and courtly intrigue, of great courage in the face of danger, and of cowardly kings who ordered their court musicians to compose songs about their imagined heroic deeds.

3. Music and the Middle Classes

With the decline of courts (over a period of roughly hundred-fifty years from the time of the French Revolution in 1789), music "went public." Court music found new audiences among the intellectual, cultural, and often financial elites. As these elites were also prominent in government, the state became the chief patron of the arts in many countries: concert halls were built, orchestras were formed, and formal music education was organized. National radio often became the new patron of orchestras (e.g., in Australia) or of the masters of rāga (in India).

Recordings exist from the time when many of these changes took place, so there are numerous musical examples of the shifts of audience and the music that accompanied this change. Current orchestral practice stems from this period. A little later, most strikingly in the twentieth century, initiatives were taken to educate the "common people" to appreciate fine music, in most instances the ideological basis of our current systems and continued ethos of music education.

4. Music and Travel

Music has always traveled with people. This has led to a number of phenomena: the establishment of dominant forms of music in other cultures by beauty, power, or money;

enriching musical life by adding new cultural presences or influences; and cross-fertilization by in-depth exchange among musicians.

This theme lends itself to exploring expansionism and colonialism, not only by Europeans but also by Muslims, who occupied a territory stretching from Morocco to China within a hundred years after the death of Muhammad in 632, spreading musical genres and instruments. The stories of exoticism—such as Debussy being fascinated and inspired by Indonesian gamelan at the Paris World Exhibition in 1889—also belong to this theme, as does the fascination with African drumming (traditionally an all-male activity) by Western women from the 1980s. The story of musical styles developing in ports (often in houses of ill repute); of Spanish and African musical elements mixing into Cuban son and later salsa; of world musicians from Turkey and Azerbaijan on tour; of the violin in European, North African, and South Indian music—all of these are fascinating illustrations of music traveling across the globe.

5. Music and Fusion

Where musics and musicians meet, encounters in sound take place. Fusion can be inspired by a variety of motivations. The most desirable are probably musical curiosity and the will to improve oneself as a musician. Other common motives may involve financial gain or career (a particular form of fusion secures a job or pays better) or power relations (the oppressed adopt music of the colonial force or the economically strong). But mostly, exploring new musical horizons is the main driver.

Fusion can take many forms. It may entail using an instrument from another culture, direct quotation from melodic structures, inspiration from rhythmic ideas, imitation of (perceived) sound quality, using themes from history or other arts, taking religious/spiritual inspiration, or simply getting together onstage or in the studio. In many cases, it can be argued that the process is more interesting than the product: it is exciting to see musicians exploring one another's musical idiom, but often the result highlights rather than bridges the gap between sound cultures.

6. Music and Technology

In retrospect, the technological developments of the past fifty years have probably changed the face of music production and dissemination more than any technological, religious, social, or political change ever before. Music recordings and then broadcasting have become principal means of music consumption; amplification has made it possible to reach vast audiences with a single concert; and the video clip has emerged as a new, interdisciplinary format, first via television and from the Web to iPods, computers, and phones. This has become the prime provider of music to young people today. It is relatively simple to create an overview of the various stages of this rapid development.

7. Music and Love

Love has possibly been the most powerful inspiration for creating music. The intense and ineffable emotions that come with strong attraction lend themselves well to expression in sound, from country to opera, from Bulgarian love song to Indian film music. It is interesting to note that the pain of love has probably yielded more (and more lasting) music than the joys of love.

This theme opens the road to juxtapose Maria Callas and Hank Williams, the legendary Egyptian singer Oum Kolsoum and the ironic love songs of African tribal women. Jazz, rock, and pop catalogues offer several thousands of other examples.

8. Music and Death

While music is strongly associated with love, it also plays a key role in how we deal with death. In addition to Irish keening and laments from the Pacific Islands, there are fabulous requiems in the Western classical traditions and heartrending songs in the popular traditions.

9. Music and Nature

After love, nature is probably the most common source of inspiration for music. There are Indian rāgas dedicated to the rainy season (with the chance of cloudburst if it is sung really well at other times of the year), beautiful blue rivers inspire European composers, and a silent meditation on waves inform the Japanese shakuhachi player.

10. Music and Place

While most music travels quite well, much of is has a strong link to place. Many popular songs have place names in them, which anchor them in association with San Francisco in the 1960s or the province of Oriente in Cuba. The music of Indigenous Australians is deeply rooted in place, and avant-garde works are increasingly site-specific.

11. Music and Dissent

Music has been the carrier of protest through the ages, from the subtle irony of medieval jesters to the cutting texts of contemporary hip-hop singers. The Indonesian dalang has the rare freedom to criticize the government from behind his wayang screen, and youths revolt against the status quo in the voices of Bob Dylan in the United States, Mercedes Sosa in

Latin America, and a stadium full of AMC members clamoring for democracy in South Africa under apartheid.

12. *Music and Commerce*

Money has always been important in music. While there are many amateurs and semiprofessionals, thousands of musicians want and need to make a living from their art. The payment can be very direct: successful praise singers in Africa and qawwali singers in Pakistan have their instruments covered in bank bills at the end of a performance. Others get paid discreetly after a performance or even receive a monthly salary as a rather abstract sign of appreciation. The most influential players in music and money have been the major record companies, many of which are now rapidly reorienting themselves as their "ownership" of artists and copyright claims may become a thing of the past. Enter online models with much more direct control by the artist of what he or she wants to do and what can be delegated.

Five Domains of Musical Sustainability in Contemporary Contexts

Systems of learning music	Systems of learning are central to the sustainability of most music cultures. In this domain balances are assessed between informal and formal training, notation-based and aural learning, holistic and analytical approaches, and emphasis on tangible and less tangible aspects of musicking. It explores contemporary developments in learning and teaching (from master-disciple relationships to systems based on cutting-edge Web technology), and how non-musical activities, philosophies and approaches intersect with learning and teaching. These issues play a key role from the level of community initiatives to the highest level of institutionalized professional training.
Musicians and communities	This domain involves the role and position of musicians and the basis of the tradition within the community. It looks at the everyday realities in the existence of creative musicians, including the role of technology, media, and travel, and issues of remuneration through performances, teaching, portfolio careers, community support, tenured employment, freelancing, and non-musical activities. Cross-cultural influences and the role of the diaspora are also examined, as well as the interaction among musicians within the community.
Contexts and constructs	This domain assesses the social and cultural contexts of musical traditions. It examines the realities of and the attitudes to recontextualisation, cross-cultural influences, authenticity and context, and explicit and implicit approaches to cultural diversity resulting from travel, migration or media, as well as obstacles such

as poverty, prejudice, racism, stigma, restrictive religious attitudes, and issues of appropriation. It also looks at the underlying values and attitudes (constructs) steering musical directions. These include musical tastes, aesthetics, cosmologies, socially and individually constructed identities, gender issues, and (perceived) prestige, which is often underestimated as a factor in musical survival.

Infrastructure and regulations

This domain primarily relates to the 'hardware' of music: places to perform, compose, practice and learn, all of which are essential for music to survive, as well virtual spaces for creation, collaboration, learning, and dissemination. Other aspects included in this domain are the availability and/or manufacturing of instruments and other tangible resources. Also examined here is the extent to which regulations are conducive or obstructive to a blossoming musical heritage, including artists' rights, copyright laws, sound restrictions, laws limiting artistic expression, and challenging circumstances such as obstacles that can arise from totalitarian regimes, persecution, civil unrest, war or the displacement of music or people.

Media and the music industry

This domain addresses large-scale dissemination and commercial aspects of music. Most musicians and musical styles depend in one way or another on the music industry for their survival. In the past hundred years, the distribution of music has increasingly involved recordings, radio, television and the Internet (e.g. podcasts, YouTube, MySpace). At the same time, many acoustic and live forms of delivery have changed under the influence of internal and external factors, leading to a wealth of new performance formats. This domain examines the ever-changing modes of distributing, publicizing, and supporting music, including the role of audiences (including consumers of recorded product), patrons, sponsors, funding bodies, and governments that 'buy' or 'buy into' artistic product.

The World Music Adventures of Primary Teacher Ms. Benson

PATRICIA SHEHAN CAMPBELL

Ms. Benson is teaching at Lakemount Elementary School in a suburban American community, where the school children are "mildly diverse," with 20 percent African American, 10 percent Hispanic (mostly Mexican), another 10 percent whose parents or grandparents arrived from Vietnam or the Philippines, a few from Somalia, Eritrea, and Ethiopia, and all the rest who claim first- to fifth-generation European heritage. A "multiculti" American music teacher (the designation given by some for those teachers who are prone to feature varied cultural perspectives on a concept or subject, such as the study of poetry, or governmental practices, or music), she is very real, as are her children, but the names have been changed to protect the innocent. She knows the diversity of the children she teaches through the languages they speak, the religious and seasonal holidays they celebrate, the foods they bring from home in their brown bags, and the songs and recordings that they bring to share with her at music time.

Lakemount is a far cry from Ms. Benson's own monocultural experience as a school child some twenty years ago, and she is keen to allow her music program to reflect the diversity of the school community. It is nearly the time of the winter program (once called Christmas, but no longer) and Ms. Benson has been rehearsing her 10- and 11-year-old fifth grade students on the music that will comprise a "Festival of Lights" concert. She has selected a carol for Christmas, a xylophone arrangement of a song from an Indian Divali celebration, a dance with recorded music to honor St. Lucia's Day, a Hanukkah song with descant for recorders, a drumming piece with sung melody for Kwanzaa, a singing game for Thailand's Loy Kratong, and a circle dance with recorder-and-drum accompaniment for Winter Solstice. This repertoire is quite multifarious, and Ms. Benson is eager to celebrate diversity through song, dance, and instrumental music with the children, their parents, and the entire school community.

As she is distributing the recorders and drums for the Solstice song, Jamal murmurs something about "honky music." Several other boys join in chanting, "We won't play that h-o-n-k-y music," and they wave their arms rhythmically as their fingers spread, poke, and point in every direction. They are rhythmic, but they are loud, and Ms. Benson worries that their gestures might be gang- or street-related and offensive to other children. She orders them to stop. Jamal (an African-American boy) protests, "That song is lame. It's so white." Ms. Benson nervously replies in a sweet tone, "But we've already done your music, so you can do ours." The hip-hop boys hold their recorders to their mouths but, in protest, they do not play. (Among the concerns of this scene is the teacher's erroneous interpretation that only an African-American boy would call hip-hop music his own, as if it were not a generational genre that extends beyond a given race or ethnicity—as it most certainly is.)

The class is invited next to review the song for Divali. The children take their places by the wood and metal xylophones, and Ms. Benson conducts the singers and players through several repetitions of the unison song. Shanta, who arrived two years ago from India, raises her hand to inform the class, "We really don't have xylophones in India." Ms. Benson grimaces, several children look at each other and roll their eyes, and although she carries on with the song's arrangement as planned, she is feeling uneasy inside. (Expressions and gestures can convey exasperation, superiority, or intolerance, and the teacher should be able to read the signals that may indicate bias, prejudice, and disrespect. When something is awry, a quiet vigilance and a talking-to may be necessary, so that students can be made aware of the need to accept opinions of others and respond appropriately to them.)

"Okay, let's see what we remember of the Loy Kratong. Partner up so we can sing and perform the actions." Ms. Benson walks up to Isaias and Kaleta and pairs them up. They are not pleased with the arrangement and will not join hands in the opening position. While others sing and play the partner game, the two boys stand stiffly facing each other, silently glowering. Later, Ms. Benson learns that Isaias is from Ethiopia and Kaleta is from Eritrea, two warring nations with deep-seated feelings of animosity toward one another that spreads from adults to children. (Teachers need to know the cultural relations of the families of their children, and they do so by making observations, talking with their teaching colleagues, and keeping abreast of what may be transpiring out in the community that surrounds the school.)

"Why aren't we doing 'Feliz Navidad'?" asks Marisol. Ms. Benson recognizes that she has committed another faux pas in her selection of repertoire. She had assumed that the Hispanic children would know "The First Noel" because it is a Catholic hymn, and they are all Catholic ... aren't they? There is not enough time for the entire class to learn another song, so she invites Marisol, Maria, and Ramona to sing it in the winter program by themselves. The girls look shy yet pleased at the prospect of being featured, until Katerina and Anna complain, "What about us? Can we play one of our Ukrainian songs on our accordions?" As their classroom teacher arrives at the door to pick up her class, Ms. Benson realizes that the class has disintegrated into cultural enclaves and animosities that she never would have predicted. She is beginning to think that an "All-American" program might be safer next time around. (How does one interpret "All-American" in these times, when nations have gone multicultural, intercultural, and global in their composite populations? For Americans come in every size, shape, and hue, and reverting to an early image of the nation as Anglo-American, or constraining music to a European-based repertoire, is regressive and not in keeping with the cultural diversity of a population transformed.)

Ms. Benson is, like Mary with her little lamb, "as white as snow." She is trying hard, and is well-intentioned in her attempts not to perpetuate the monocultural, white-dominant repertoire of her own early experiences. She deserves an "A" for effort, despite the bumbling ways in which principles of cultural diversity have played themselves out in her practice. She is pumped and primed with a belief in music as a tool for social responsibility and social justice, and for playing out the meaning of a cultural democracy. She is intent on moving young people center-stage in their understanding of the world's people, their cultural ideals and artistic expressions. Yet Ms. Benson is living dangerously in her attempts at "teaching world musics." She goes to music teachers' workshops, holds memberships in two teachers' organizations, spends nights googling for music of many lands. She's negotiating cultures: her own, her children's, and those of the music traditions themselves (which may or may not match those of the children she teaches). She's playing catch-up to a training she never had, talking to teachers in teacher-culture who share their "successes"—many of which are equally uncertain and not completely true to any one culture.

Acknowledgment

This text appeared previously in *Musiké* 3 (2007): *Networks and Islands: World Music and Dance Education*, ed. by Ninja Kors, and has been reprinted with permission from the author.

acculturation   adoption and assimilation of an alien culture.

ālāp   nonmetric exposition of a rāga in Indian music.

analytic   structured, step-by-step approach to presenting material to be learned.

angsel   dramatic rhythmic break in Balinese music.

arabesk   form of syncretic Turkish urban popular music.

āsheq   Turkish bard or minstrel (literally "lover").

atomistic   pedagogical approach that breaks material down into small parts.

aural   received by ear (whether produced orally, by instruments, or through recordings), in contrast with notation-based transmission.

authenticity   striving for historical correctness, original context, or trueness to self.

avir bhav, tiru bhav   playing with expression of a rāga (literally "out of mood," "into mood").

bağlama (saz)   long-necked Turkish folk lute.

balo(phone)   African xylophone.

bandoneón   Argentine button accordion used in tango music.

bānsuri   Indian bamboo flute.

bayaka   tribe of pygmies of the rain forests of central Africa.

bhangra   popular, Indian-derived dance song style that developed in the United Kingdom.

bimusicality   state of having a musical frame of reference or musical skills from two cultures.

bol(s)   word(s) or syllable(s) representing drum strokes or dance steps in India.

canon   body of works that serves as a reference in a music tradition.

ca trù   Vietnamese form of sung poetry with instrumental accompaniment.

chansonnier   popular singer in a traditional style of French music.

chŏngak   court music of Korea (literally "proper music").

community music   musical practices taking community engagement as a starting point.

context   temporal, acoustic, ideological, or social environment of music.

cross-cultural   involving application of ideas, methods, or musics to other cultures.

culture bearer   person who represents a specific (musical) culture by birth or enculturation.

cultural diversity   presence of more than a single culture in any context.

cumbia   Colombian musical style and folk dance.

dalang   puppeteer in Indonesian shadow puppet theater.

darbūka   goblet-shaped, single-headed drum found throughout the Arab world.

djembe   large Wassoulou goblet-shaped drum from West Africa.

duende   reference to the soul or spirit of flamenco music.

dundun   bass drum in djembe ensemble, also reference to the largest of three drums (sometimes *dundumba*)

enculturation   process of conscious or unconscious conditioning by means of which people achieve competence in their culture.

Ewe   Kwa-speaking people of Ghana and Togo.

filmī gīt   film songs recorded for commercial Indian films; the pop music of India.

flamenco   song, dance, and guitar style developed in Andalusia (southern Spain).

gā   people of southeastern Ghana; also used to refer to their music.

gagaku   Japanese court music and dance.

gamelan   Indonesian orchestra consisting mostly of struck idiophones.

gamelan gong kebyar   Balinese dynamic modern gamelan style.

gat   instrumental composition in North Indian classical music.

gordang sembilan   nine-drum ensemble of the Mandailing people of Sumatra.

griot   See *jali.*

guellal   North African cylindrical drum.

guru-śisya-paramparā   master-disciple tradition in India.

hālau   Hawaiian school, academy, or group.

highlife   popular West African musical genre, combining pop and traditional rhythms.

Hindustani music   classical music of North India (as opposed to the South Indian Carnatic tradition).

holistic   approach to teaching using actual musical practice as a direct source.

huju   Shanghai opera.

iemoto   system of familial generations in traditional Japanese arts.

intercultural   facilitating contact between cultures through work, school, and so on.

isicathamiya   step-dancing choirs that blend ragtime and indigenous part singing from South Africa.

jali   professional musician among the Mandinka (West Africa).

jig   lively Irish, English, and Scottish dance.

jor   solo vocal or instrumental section with a recurring pulse in ālāp.

kawina   oldest Creole music from Surinam, still widely practiced across generations.

kenkeni   smallest of three dunduns, bass drums in a djembe ensemble.

khyal   preeminent Hindustani vocal genre since the eighteenth century.

kompang   Malay, single-headed frame drum of Arab origin.

kora   Mandinka harp-lute (West Africa).

koto   Japanese board zither having 13 strings.

Mandinka   people including Manding, Malinké, Mandingo, Maninka.

maqām   generic term for melodic mode in the Arab world.

mbira shona   plucked lamellophone (Zimbabwe).

monocultural   using a single (dominant) culture as the frame of reference.

muğam   Azerbaijani art music, based on maqām.

multicultural   working from an acceptance of cultural differences and separation.

musica popular brasileira (MPB)   popular Brazilian music.

oral   by listening or word of mouth (rather than by notation); better *aural.*

p'ansori   Korean musical storytelling, narrated folk music.

qin   seven-stringed plucked zither from China.

rāga   Indian modal system, melodic resource for composition and improvisation.

raï   form of energetic contemporary Algerian music, originating in northern African youth counterculture.

rasa   aesthetic sentiment called forth by Indian performing arts.

sanbang   middle-sized of three dunduns, bass drums in a djembe ensemble.

salsa   Afro-Hispanic Caribbean song and dance form, rooted in Cuban son.

samba (batucada)   form of popular Brazilian music and dance with prominent percussion.

sambhangra   fusion of samba batucada and bhangra.

sarod   short, unfretted, plucked Indian lute.

saz   literally "instrument"; often used to refer to Turkish bağlama.

seka   sense of unity in communal music making in Bali and Lombok.

shakuhachi   Japanese notched vertical bamboo flute.

shôga   system for learning Japanese music consisting of syllables or mnemonics.

sitar   long-necked, fretted, plucked lute from India.

solfeggio   more commonly *solfège;* fixed do system of sol-fa syllables.

son   Cuban song tradition.

śrti (sruti)   microtone, drone, or intonation in Indian classical music.

svara   scale degree or pitch in Indian music.

syômyô   Japanese Buddhist chant.

tabla   North Indian small drums played in a pair.

tala   organization of time, rhythm, and meter in Indian music; a metric cycle.

tān   improvisatory melodic phrase in Indian classical music.

tango   Argentine nostalgic, melancholic music and dance.

tanpura   long-necked, unfretted, plucked drone lute from India.

tarab   intangible essence of Arab music.

thumri   light classical Hindustani vocal or instrumental form and style.

tradition   relation to the past through canon, rules, practice, or context.

transcultural   profound merging of several cultures and value systems.

ud   plucked Arab lute found throughout the Middle East.

ustad-śagird   Muslim term for master-disciple relation in India (Turkish: *usta-cirak*).

wayang   shadow puppetry of Indonesia.

world beat   hybrid music with Western production values.

world music   phenomenon of music taking root outside its culture of origin.

NOTES

Prologue

1. Cook, *Music*, 15.
2. Small, *Musicking*, 9.
3. See McCarthy, *Passing It On*, 4.
4. Merriam, *The Anthropology of Music*, 145.
5. McCarthy, *Passing It On*.
6. Volk, "Multiculturalism."
7. Choate, *Documentary Report of the Tanglewood Symposium*.
8. Draper, *Music 2.0*.

Chapter 1: Journeys in Music

1. Perlman, "Indonesia: Sumatra."
2. *Times of India*, Ahmedabad, January 7, 1988; *Times of India*, Mumbai, December 11, 1993.
3. Aubert, *The Music of the Other*, 80.
4. See Gutzwiller, "Teaching Methods of Traditional World Music," 73.
5. See Nzewi, "Acquiring Knowledge of the Musical Arts," 25.
6. See Marett, *Songs, Dreamings, and Ghosts*.
7. Cf. Dunbar-Hall and Gibson, *Deadly Sounds, Deadly Places*.
8. Rice, *May It Fill Your Soul*, 114–117.

Chapter 2: Positioning "World Music" in Education

1. Johnson and Johnson, *Congorilla*. This excerpt is available online at http://www.oup.facingthemusic.

2. See McCarthy, "The Role of ISME in the Promotion of Multicultural Music Education."

3. See Slobin, *Subcultural Sounds*; Taylor, *Beyond Exoticism.*

4. Sweeney, *Directory of World Music*, ix.

5. Taylor, *Beyond Exoticism*, 113–121.

6. Brown, "World Music, As It Was in the Beginning."

7. Hood, "The Challenge of Bi-Musicality" and "The Birthpangs of Bimusicality."

8. Kunst, *Music in Java*, vii.

9. Hood, "The Birthpangs of Bimusicality," 56.

10. Brown, "World Music, As It Was in the Beginning," 7.

11. Ibid., 10.

12. Solis, *Performing Ethnomusicology.*

13. Bohlman, *World Music*; Bor, "And Then There Was World Music and World Dance."

14. Sweeney, *Directory of World Music*; Taylor, *Beyond Exoticism.*

15. Nettl, "Ethnomusicology: Definitions, Directions, and Problems," 1.

16. Sweeney, *Directory of World Music*, ix.

17. *OED* Online, www.oed.com (accessed September 10, 2008).

18. Bohlman, "World Music at the 'End of History,'" 2.

19. Aubert, *The Music of the Other*, 50 n.

20. Haydon, *Introduction to Musicology.*

21. Schneider, "Primitive Music."

22. *OED* Online, http://www.oed.com (accessed September 10, 2008).

23. See Hopkins, *Aural Thinking in Norway*, 34.

24. See Agawu, "Representing African Music," 1.

25. Said, *Orientalism*, 40.

26. Burkholder, Grout, and Palisca, *A History of Western Music.*

27. Aubert, *The Music of the Other*, 20–22.

28. Slobin, *Subcultural Sounds*, 4.

29. Aubert, *The Music of the Other*, 48–49.

30. Taylor, *Beyond Exoticism*, 161–183.

31. Dunbar-Hall and Gibson, *Deadly Sounds, Deadly Places*, 95–116.

32. Bohlman, *World Music*, vii.

33. Taylor, *Beyond Exoticism*, 140–144.

34. Stockhausen, "World Music," 11.

35. Berendt, *Nada Brahma: De Wereld is Geluid* and *Ons Derde Oor.*

36. Letts, "Music"; Campbell, "Music, the Universal Language."

37. Cited in Volk, *Music, Education and Multiculturalism*, 48–49.

38. Brown, "World Music, As It Was in the Beginning," 8.

39. *OED* Online, http://www.oed.com (accessed September 10, 2008).

40. Bohlman, "World Music at the 'End of History,'" 4–5.

41. Brown, "World Music, As It Was in the Beginning," 8.

42. Taylor, *Beyond Exoticism*, 119.

43. Blacking, *A False Trail for the Arts?* 11.

44. Lübke, *Der Musikwagen.*

45. Aubert, *The Music of the Other*, 1–3.

46. Melchers, *Muziek, een Wereldtaal*.

47. Cited in Rutherford, "The Third Space," 211.

48. Yehudi Menuhin, *Classical Indian Music*, Decca LP LXT5600, 1960.

49. Swanwick, *Music, Mind and Education*, 97.

50. Ibid., 47.

51. Wellesz, "Introduction," xviii.

52. Reimer, *A Philosophy of Music Education*, 179.

53. Ibid., 191.

54. Reimer, "The Need to Face the Issues," 3–11.

55. Elliott, *Music Matters*, 207.

56. Ibid., 209.

57. Volk, *Music, Education and Multiculturalism*, 11–12.

58. Elliott, "Philosophical Perspectives on Research," 86.

59. Bourdieu, *Distinction*, 328.

60. Cook, *Music*, 42–43.

61. Hood, "The Challenge of Bi-Musicality."

62. Merriam, *The Anthropology of Music*.

63. Blacking, *How Musical Is Man?*

64. Nettl, "How Do You Get to Carnegie Hall?" 324.

65. Nettl, "Recent Directions in Ethnomusicology," 388.

66. Myers, *Ethnomusicology*, 31.

67. Solis, *Performing Ethnomusicology*.

68. Trimillos, "Subject, Object and the Ethnomusicology Ensemble," 28–40.

69. Szego, "A Conspectus of Ethnographic Research," 710.

70. Rice, "Bi-Musicality."

71. Rice, "The Ethnomusicology of Music Learning and Teaching," 80.

72. Szego, "A Conspectus of Ethnographic Research," 710.

73. Booth, "The Transmission of a Classical Improvisatory Performance Practice."

74. Trimillos, "The Formalized Transmission of Culture."

75. Neuman, *The Life of Music in North India*.

76. Berliner, *The Soul of Mbira*.

77. Hopkins, *Aural Thinking in Norway*.

78. Rice, *May It Fill Your Soul*.

79. Brinner, *Knowing Music, Making Music*.

80. McCarthy, *Passing It On*.

81. Wong, *Sounding the Center*.

82. Dunbar-Hall, "Training, Community and Systemic Music Education."

83. Howard, *Creating Korean Music*.

84. Lieth-Phillipp and Gutzwiller, *Teaching Musics of the World*; Campbell et al., *Cultural Diversity in Music Education*.

85. See Cain, "Philosophy, Policy, Practice."

Chapter 3: The Myth of Authentic Traditions in Context

1. *OED* Online.

2. In Hobsbawm and Ranger, *The Invention of Tradition*, 3.

3. Willemsen, *Woordenboek Filosofie*.

4. Cook, *Music*, 30.

5. Ibid., 31.

6. Marett, "Japan: Court Music."

7. Bor, *The Raga Guide*, 1–2.

8. Morgan, "Rethinking Musical Culture," 45.

9. Ibid., 46.

10. Brinner, *Knowing Music, Making Music*, 30.

11. Morgan, "Rethinking Musical Culture," 60.

12. Hobsbawm and Ranger, *The Invention of Tradition*, 2.

13. See Rouget, *Music and Trance*.

14. Merriam, *The Anthropology of Music*, 64.

15. See Howard, "Teaching Musics of the World," 268, 276.

16. Schippers, "Sustainable Futures for Musical Traditions."

17. Aubert, *The Music of the Other*, 10.

18. Hobsbawm and Ranger, *The Invention of Tradition*, 1.

19. See Drummond, "What Do You Mean, Mozart Didn't Wear Tails?"

20. Miner, *Sitar and Sarod in the 18th and 19th Century*, 18–24.

21. Bor, "On the Decline and Revival of Hindu Music."

22. Aubert, *The Music of the Other*, 18–19.

23. Bohlman, "Traditional Music and Cultural Identity."

24. Mautner, *A Dictionary of Philosophy*, 39.

25. Cook, *Music*, 13.

26. Butt, "Authenticity."

27. Taylor, *Global Pop*, 21.

28. Ibid.

29. Cook, *Music*, 11.

30. Taylor, *Global Pop*, 126–136.

31. Ibid., 143.

32. Johnson, "Authenticity: Who Needs It?"

33. Mills, *Music in the School*, 154.

34. Lundquist, "Music, Culture, Curriculum, and Instruction," 634.

35. Campbell, "Music, Education and Community in a Multicultural Society," 68.

36. Ibid., 69.

37. Campbell, "Culture Bearers in the Classroom."

38. Nettl, "Ethnomusicology: Definitions, Directions, and Problems," 1, 7.

39. Myers, *Ethnomusicology*, 3.

40. Swanwick, *Music, Mind and Education*, 107.

41. Cited in Campbell, "Music, Education and Community in a Multicultural Society," 69.

42. Neuman, *The Life of Music in North India*.

43. Reimer, *A Philosophy of Music Education*; Swanwick, *Music, Mind and Education*; Elliott, *Music Matters*.

44. See Drummond, "What Do You Mean, Mozart Didn't Wear Tails?" 22–24.

45. Volk, *Music, Education and Multiculturalism*, 9.

46. Slobin, *Subcultural Sounds*, 20.

Chapter 4: Global Perspectives on Learning and Teaching Music

1. Vonck, "*Bali, Muziek en Dans in Theorie en Praktijk.*"

2. Nettl, "How Do You Get to Carnegie Hall?" 324.

3. Rice, "Transmission."

4. Plummeridge, "Schools."

5. Green, *Music, Informal Learning and the School*, 7; Lebler, "Student-as-Master?"

6. Berliner, *Thinking in Jazz*, 36–59; cf. Whyton, "Birth of the School."

7. International Society for Music Education, *Policy on Musics of the World's Culture*.

8. Nketia, "Cultural Diversity and Music Education in Ghana," 55.

9. Nzewi, "Acquiring Knowledge of the Musical Arts in Traditional Society," 20.

10. Flolu, "Music Education in Ghana," 171.

11. Sangeet Research Academy, *Indian Music and the West*.

12. Sangeet Research Academy, *Teaching of Indian Music*.

13. Neuman, *The Life of Music in North India*, 45.

14. Slawek, *Sitar Technique in Nibaddh Forms*, 2; see Slawek, "The Classical Master-Disciple Tradition," 457–460.

15. Rice, *May It Fill Your Soul*, 64.

16. Brinner, *Knowing Music, Making Music*, 39.

17. Ibid., 38.

18. Goormaghtigh, *L'Art du Q'in*, 30. Trans. by Schippers.

19. Goormaghtigh, "'*L'Air du Roi Wen,*'" 153.

20. Cited in Ross, "The Sonata Seminar."

21. Persson, "Brilliant Performers As Teachers," 10.

22. Feld, "'Flow Like a Waterfall,'" 42.

23. Ellingson, "Notation," 157.

24. Howard, "Performing Ethnomusicology."

25. See Brinner, *Knowing Music, Making Music*, 35–38.

26. Daniélou, *The Ragas of Northern Indian Music*, 28.

27. "Philosophy of Music: Formalism."

28. Ibid.

29. Blum, "Analysis of Musical Style," 166.

30. Ibid., 213.

31. See Solis, *Performing Ethnomusicology*.

32. Hood, "The Challenge of Bi-Musicality," 58.

33. See, e.g., Emmerson, *Around a Rondo*.

34. Bazzana, *Glenn Gould*, 36–51.

35. Juslin, "Five Facets of Musical Experience," 274.

36. Hood, "The Challenge of Bi-Musicality," 58.

37. LOKV, *One Monkey, No Show*.

38. See Schippers, "'As If a Little Bird Is Sitting on Your Finger.'"

39. Mark, *Music Education: Source Readings*, 3–17.

40. Cited in Volk, *Music, Education and Multiculturalism*, 27.

41. Shankar, *My Music, My Life*, 11.

42. Schippers, "Swara Samrat, Emperor of Melody," 89.

43. See, e.g., Bouquet, *Raga, Rai en Arabesk*.

44. Van den Bos, "Differences between Western and Non-Western Teaching Methods," 175.

45. Elliott, *Music Matters*.

46. Pruett and Slavens, *Research Guide to Musicology*, 34.

47. Cook, *Music*, 62.

48. This is based on a conservative estimate of an average of 25 hours of "musicking" per week for 50 weeks a year from the age of eight (not downplaying the vast importance of what happens before), generating an aural library of 32 × 50 × 25 = 40,000 hours. This is a conservative estimate; the actual figure for most professional musicians is likely to be much higher.

49. Schippers, "A Synergy of Contradictions"; see Emmerson, *Around a Rondo*.

50. Cook, *Music*, 59.

51. Ibid., 60.

52. Ellingson, "Notation," 139.

53. Rice, "Transmission."

54. Hughes, "Japan: Court Music."

55. Tracey, *Ngoma*.

56. Flolu, "Music Education in Ghana," 171.

57. Schippers, "Swara Samrat, Emperor of Melody."

58. Mathieson, "Mimesis."

59. Burkholder, "Modelling."

60. Grout, *A History of Western Music*, 416.

61. Schuon, "Principles and Criteria of Art," 66.

62. Campbell, "Music, Education and Community in a Multicultural Society," 60.

63. Cited in Abeles, Hoffer, and Klotman, *Foundations of Music Education*, 11.

64. Volk, *Music, Education and Multiculturalism*, 31.

65. Abeles, Hoffer, and Klotman, *Foundations of Music Education*, 11.

66. Pressley, *Reading Instruction That Works*.

67. Abeles, Hoffer, and Klotman, *Foundations of Music Education*, 11.

68. Berliner, *The Soul of Mbira*, 139.

69. Cited in Howard, "Teaching SamulNori," 16.

70. Berliner, *Thinking in Jazz*, 22.

71. Yung, "Teachers: East Asia & North America," 18.

72. Van der Meer, *Hindustani Music in the 20th Century*, 139.

73. Blacking, *How Musical Is Man?* 10.

74. Ibid., 8–9.

75. Neighbour, *The Inner Apprentice*.

76. Valcke, *Onderwijskunde als Ontwerpwetenschap*.

77. Hood, "The Challenge of Bi-Musicality," 56.

78. In LOKV, *One Monkey, No Show*.

79. I have encountered such assignments in a number of institutions, including the Rotterdam Conservatory Popleiding (Curriculum 2001–2002) and Bachelor of Popular Music (BPM) at Queensland Conservatorium, Griffith University.

Chapter 5: Communities, Curricula, and Conservatories

1. Blacking, *How Musical Is Man?*
2. Wong, *Sounding the Center*, 62–70.
3. See Green, *Music, Informal Learning and the School*, 5.
4. See ibid.
5. Saether, "The Oral University."
6. Higgins, "Boundary-Walkers," 8.
7. Johnson, Headey, and Jensen, *Communities, Social Capital and Public Policy*, 12.
8. Amit and Rapport, *The Trouble with Community.*
9. Cahill, *The Community Music Handbook*, v.
10. Ibid. vii.
11. Letts, "Music," 27.
12. Higgins, "Boundary-Walkers," 7.
13. Cahill, *The Community Music Handbook*, vii.
14. Veblen and Olsson, "Community Music," 730.
15. Higgins, "Safety without Safety," 65.
16. Higgins, "Boundary-Walkers," 7.
17. Erb, "Music for a Better Community," 446.
18. Veblen and Olsson, "Community Music," 1.
19. Ibid., 730–753.
20. International Society for Music Education, Community Music Commission, "Vision."
21. Elliott, Higgins, and Veblen, "Editorial," 3.
22. Veblen, "Community Music and Praxialism."
23. Zeserson, "A Passionate Exchange."
24. Bartleet et al, *Sound Links.*
25. Higgins, "Boundary-Walkers," 85.
26. Weber, "The Role of the Conservatory."
27. See, e.g., Hargreaves, Welch, Purves, and Marshall, "The Identities of Music Teachers," 181.
28. Hallam, "Novice Musicians' Approaches to Practice and Performance"; Jorgensen, "Student Learning in Higher Instrumental Education."
29. Turkenburg, "Classical and Jazz Music Compared to World and Pop Music in Music Education," 167.
30. See Berliner, *Thinking in Jazz.*
31. Hofstede, "A Case for Comparing Apples with Oranges."
32. Trimillos, "The Formalized Transmission of Culture"; Trimillos, "Subject, Object and the Ethnomusicology Ensemble."
33. McCarthy, *Passing It On*, 5.
34. Blacking, "A False Trail for the Arts?" 10.
35. Jorgensen, "Philosophical Issues in Curriculum," 49.
36. Ibid., 55.
37. Cited in Abeles, Hoffer, and Klotman, *Foundations of Music Education*, 11.
38. Daverio, "Herbart, Johann Friedrich."

39. Volk, *Music, Education and Multiculturalism*, 26–27.

40. Bent and Pople, "Analysis: History 1840–1910."

41. Volk, *Music, Education and Multiculturalism*, 31.

42. Ibid., 27.5

43. Ibid., 31.

44. Campbell, "Ethnomusicology, Education and World Music Pedagogy," 33–41.

45. Flolu, "Music Education in Ghana," 165.

46. Ibid., 171.

47. Ibid., 172.

48. See Campbell, "Musica Exotica, Multiculturalism and School Music"; Campbell, *Music in Cultural Context*; Campbell, "Culture Bearers in the Classroom"; and Schippers, *One Monkey, No Show*.

49. Van Amstel, *World Music Teaching Material*.

50. Campbell, "Culture Bearers in the Classroom."

51. Hood, "Preface," x.

52. Hood, "The Challenge of Bi-Musicality," 55.

53. Conservatorium van Amsterdam, *Intercultural Curriculum Project*.

54. Van Amstel, *World Music Teaching Material*.

55. Mills, *Music in the School*, 148–154.

56. Weber, "The Role of the Conservatory."

57. Vereniging voor Kunstzinnige Vorming, *A Survey of Teaching World Music Initiatives in the Netherlands*.

58. Schippers, "A Synergy of Contradictions," 13.

59. Ibid., 14–15.

60. Campbell, "Ethnomusicology, Education and World Music Pedagogy," 33.

61. Schippers, "A Synergy of Contradictions."

62. Abeles, Hoffer, and Klotman, *Foundations of Music Education*, 7.

63. Weber, "The Role of the Conservatory."

64. Abeles, Hoffer, and Klotman, *Foundations of Music Education*, 7.

65. Cook, *Music*, 85.

66. Ibid., 94.

67. Krebs, Siouti, Apitzsch, and Wenk, Disciplinary Barriers between the Social Sciences and Humanities, 3.

68. Nettl, *Heartland Excursions*.

69. Slobin, "The Wesleyan Way," 46, 54.

70. Sloboda, "The Acquisition of Musical Performance Expertise," 110.

71. Kors, Saraber, and Schippers, *Sound Links*, 11.

72. Bor, "Global Music Education at the Rotterdam Conservatory."

73. Solis, *Performing Ethnomusicology*.

74. For critical reflections on this model, see Bailey, "Learning to Perform as a Research Technique in Ethnomusicology"; and Trimillos, "Subject, Object and the Ethnomusicology Ensemble."

75. Markoff, "Aspects of Turkish Folk Music Theory," 79.

76. Whyton, "Birth of the School," 68–69.

77. Traasdahl, *Music Education in a Multicultural Society*, 173.

78. Turkenburg, "Classical and Jazz Music Compared to World and Pop Music in Music Education," 167.

79. Ibid., 166.

80. Ibid., 168.

81. Valcke, *Onderwijskunde als Ontwerpwetenschap*; Colwell and Richardson, *The New Handbook of Research on Music Teaching and Learning*.

Chapter 6: Toward a Global Understanding of Learning and Teaching Music

1. Lomax, *Cantometrics*.

2. Thieme, "Cantometrics."

3. See appendix 2 for an example of a questionnaire for semistructured interviews on these issues.

4. Campbell, "Musica Exotica, Multiculturalism and School Music," 70.

5. Cain, "Philosophy, Policy, Practice."

6. Campbell, "Musica Exotica, Multiculturalism and School Music," 69.

7. For an example of a themed series of lessons, see appendix 3.

8. See Skyllstad, "The Resonant Community."

9. See, e.g., Neuman, *The Life of Music in North India*; Rice, *May It Fill Your Soul*.

10. Vereniging voor Kunstzinnige Vorming, *A Survey of Teaching World Music Initiatives in the Netherlands*.

11. Bowman, "Re-tooling Foundations to Address 21st Century Realities."

12. Touma, *Die Musik der Araber*, 138–139. Trans. by Schippers.

13. See Green, *Music, Informal Learning and the School*; Lebler, "Student-as-Master?"

14. Blacking, *How Musical Is Man?* 17.

15. See appendix 4 for a more detailed breakdown of these areas, which may also serve to inform introductions to specific musical cultures in music education.

16. Hue, "How Your Mind, Your Heart Works."

17. See Green, *How Popular Musicians Learn*.

Chapter 7: Music Cultures in Motion

1. Centraal Bureau voor Statistiek, 2008.

2. Bor, *The Raga Guide*, 4.

3. Ibid., 6.

4. See Hood, "The Challenge of Bi-Musicality"; Brown, "World Music, As It Was in the Beginning"; Farrell, *Indian Music and the West*; and Bor, "And Then There Was World Music and World Dance."

5. Heins, "132 Jaar Gamelan in Nederland."

6. Farrell, *Indian Music and the West*; Bor, "And Then There Was World Music and World Dance."

7. In fact, the djembe has gained such popularity in the Netherlands that the country may now have one of the highest djembe density indices (DDIs) outside West Africa. O'Bryan ("Most of It Is Playing") estimates that there are 10,000 djembes in the Netherlands, which has a surface of 41,526 square kilometers, leading to a DDI of 240.8 djembes per 1,000 square kilometers.

8. Excerpts of this session can be accessed through the Oxford University Press Web site http://www.oup.com/us/facingthemusic

9. O'Bryan, "Most of It Is Playing."

10. Knight, "Music in Africa," 4.

11. LOKV, *One Monkey, No Show.*

12. Tenzer, *Balinese Music,* 77–79.

13. Schippers, *One Monkey, No Show,* 56–58.

14. Vonck, "In Bali, People Do Not Learn Music" (interview); and "*Bali, Muziek en Dans in Theorie en Praktijk*" (report).

15. Bor, "And Then There Was World Music and World Dance."

16. Farrell, *Indian Music and the West.*

17. Chaurasia, "If You Are Not Tuned Here, You Cannot Play in Tune." Excerpts of this session can be accessed through the Oxford University Press Web site, http://www.oup.com/us/facingthemusic

18. Muziekschool Amsterdam, *MuziekClub in de Dapperschool.*

Epilogue

1. Campbell, "Ethnomusicology, Education and World Music Pedagogy."

2. After Lao Tse: "A journey of a thousand miles begins with a single step."

Abeles, Harold F., Charles R. Hoffer, and Robert H. Klotman. *Foundations of Music Education.* New York: Simon & Schuster/Macmillan, 1995.

Adler, Guido. "*Umfang, Methode und Ziel der Musikwissenschaft.*" *Vierteljahresschrift für Musikwissenschaft* 1 (1885): 5–20.

Agawu, Kofi. "Defining and Interpreting African Music." In *Musical Arts in Africa: Theory, Practice and Education*, ed. by Anri Herbst, Meki Nzewi, and Kofi Agawu, 1–12. Pretoria: University of South Africa, 2003.

———. *Representing African Music: Postcolonial Notes, Queries, Positions.* New York: Routledge, 2003.

Amit, Vered, Nigel Rapport. *The Trouble with Community: Anthropological Reflections on Movement, Identity and Collectivity.* London: Pluto, 2002.

Apel, Willi. *Harvard Dictionary of Music.* Cambridge, Mass.: Harvard University Press, 1944.

Appadurai, Arjun. *Modernity at Large: Cultural Dimensions of Globalization.* Minneapolis: University of Minnesota Press, 1996.

Association of European Conservatories (AEC). *Music Education in a Multicultural European Society.* Video. Birmingham, U.K.: Birmingham Conservatory, 2000.

Au, Sook Kyung. "The Education of Musicians in the Republic of Korea." *International Music Education: ISME Yearbook* 2 (1974): 21–28.

Aubert, Laurent. *The Music of the Other: New Challenges for Ethnomusicology in a Global Age*, trans. by Carla Ribeiro. Aldershot, U.K.: Ashgate, 2007.

Bailey, John. "Learning to Perform as a Research Technique in Ethnomusicology." *British Journal of Ethnomusicology* 10, no. 2 (2001): 85–98.

Banks, James A. *An Introduction to Multicultural Education*, 3rd ed. Boston: Allyn & Bacon, 2002.

——. "Multicultural Education: Historical Development, Dimensions, and Practice." In *Handbook of Research on Multicultural Music Education*, ed. by James A. Banks and C. A. McGee. New York: Simon & Schuster-Macmillan, 1995.

Bartleet, Brydie-Leigh, Peter Dunbar-Hall, Richard Letts, and Huib Schippers. *Sound Links: Community Music in Australia*. Brisbane: Queensland Conservatorium Research Centre, 2009.

Baumann, Max Peter. "The Local and the Global: Traditional Musical Instruments and Globalisation." In *The World of Music* 42, no. 3 (2000): 121–144.

Bazzana, Kevin. *Glenn Gould: The Performer in the Work*. Oxford, U.K.: Clarendon Press, 1997.

Bebey, Francis. *African Music: A People's Art*. Westport, Conn.: Lawrence Hill, 1975.

Bent, Ian D., and Anthony Pople. "Analysis: History 1840–1910." *Grove Music Online*, edited by Laura Macy (2008). http://www.grovemusic.com (accessed September 24, 2008).

Berendt, Ernst Joachim. *Nada Brahma: De Wereld is Geluid*. The Hague: East West Publications, 1983.

——. *Ons Derde Oor: Luisteren naar de Wereld*. The Hague: East West Publications, 1985.

Bergeron, Katherine. "Prologue: Disciplining Music." In *Disciplining Music: Musicology and Its Canons*, ed. by Katherine Bergeron and Philip V. Bohlman. Chicago: University of Chicago Press, 1992.

Berliner, Paul F. *The Soul of Mbira*. Chicago: University of Chicago Press, 1982.

——. *Thinking in Jazz: The Infinite Art of Improvisation*. Chicago: University of Chicago Press, 1994.

Blacking, John. *A Commonsense View of All Music*. Cambridge, U.K.: Cambridge University Press, 1987.

——. "A False Trail for the Arts? 'Multicultural' Music Education and the Denial of Individual Creativity." Unpublished and undated typescript.

——. *How Musical Is Man?* Seattle: University of Washington Press, 1973.

——. *Music, Culture & Experience: Selected Papers*, ed. by Reginald Byron. Chicago: University of Chicago Press, 1995.

Blum, Stephen. "Analysis of Musical Style." In *Ethnomusicology: An Introduction*, ed. by Helen Myers, 165–218. London: Macmillan Press, 1992.

Bohlmann, Philip V. "Ethnomusicology III: Post-1945 Developments." *Grove Music Online*, edited by Laura Macy (2008). http://www.grovemusic.com (accessed February 12, 2008).

Bohlman, Philip V. "Traditional Music and Cultural Identity: Persistent Paradigm in the History of Ethnomusicology." *Yearbook for Traditional Music* 20, no. 1 (1988): 26–42.

——. *World Music: A Very Short Introduction*. New York: Oxford University Press, 2002.

——. "World Music at the 'End of History.'" *Ethnomusicology* 46, no. 1 (2000): 1–32.

Booth, Gregory D. "The North Indian Oral Tradition: Lessons for Music Education." *International Journal for Music Education* 9 (1987): 7–9.

——. "The Transmission of a Classical Improvisatory Performance Practice." *International Journal for Music Education* 26 (1995): 14–26.

Bor, Joep. "And Then There Was World Music and World Dance." Inaugural lecture, University of Leiden, 2008.

———. "Global Music Education at the Rotterdam Conservatory." Lecture at UCLA, School of the Arts and Architecture, May 7, 1999.

———. "On the Decline and Revival of Hindu Music." Unpublished manuscript.

———. *The Raga Guide: A Survey of 74 Hindustani Ragas*. London: Nimbus, 1999.

———. "Studying World Music: The Next Phase." In *Teaching Musics of the World*, ed. by Margot Lieth-Philipp and Andreas Gutzwiller, 61–81. Affalterbach, Germany: Philipp Verlag, 1995.

Bouquet, Bert. *Raga, Rai en Arabesk*. Utrecht, Netherlands: LOKV, 1990.

Bourdieu, Pierre. *Distinction: A Social Critique of the Judgement of Taste*. London: Routledge, 1984.

Bowman, Wayne D. "Educating Musically." In *New Handbook of Research in Music Teaching and Learning*, ed. by Richard Colwell and Carol Richardson, 63–84. New York: Oxford University Press, 2002.

———. *Philosophical Perspectives on Music*. New York: Oxford University Press, 1998.

———. "The Problem of Aesthetics and Multiculturalism in Music Education." *Canadian Music Educator* 34, no. 5 (1993): 23–30.

———. "Re-tooling Foundations to Address 21st Century Realities: Music Education Amidst Diversity, Plurality, and Change." *Action, Criticism and Theory for Music Education* 2, no. 2 (2003): 2–29.

Boyce-Tilman, June. "A Framework for Intercultural Dialogue in Music." In *World Musics in Education*, ed. by Malcolm Floyd, 43–94. Hants, U.K.: Ashgate, 1996.

Boynton, Susan. "Aspects of Orality and Formularity in Gregorian Chant, by Theodore Karp." *Journal of the American Musicological Society* 53, no. 1 (2000): 141–151.

Brinner, Benjamin. *Knowing Music, Making Music: Javanese Gamelan and the Theory of Musical Competence and Interaction*. Chicago: University of Chicago Press, 1995.

Broughton, Simon, ed. *World Music: The Rough Guide*, vols. 1 and 2. London: Rough Guides, 1999 and 2000.

Brown, Robert E. "World Music, As It Was in the Beginning, Is Now and Really Should Be." In *Teaching Musics of the World*, ed. by Margot Lieth-Philipp and Andreas Gutzwiller, 7–18. Affalterbach, Germany: Philipp Verlag, 1995.

Burkholder, J. Peter, Donald J. Grout, and Claude V. Palisca. *A History of Western Music*. New York: Norton, 2005.

Burkholder, J. Peter. "Modelling." *Grove Music Online*, edited by Laura Macy (2008). http://www.grovemusic.com (accessed February 12, 2008).

Butt, John. "Authenticity." *Grove Music Online*, edited by Laura Macy (2008). http://www.grovemusic.com (accessed February 12, 2008).

Cahill, Ann. *The Community Music Handbook: A Practical Guide*. Sydney: Currency Press, 1998.

Cain, Melissa. "Philosophy, Policy, Practice: Visions and Realities of Cultural Diversity in Selected Primary Music Classrooms in Brisbane and Singapore." Ph.D. confirmation document. Queensland Conservatorium Griffith University, Brisbane, Australia, 2008.

Caird, George, Martin Prchal, and Richard Shrewsbury, eds. *Music Education in a Multicultural European Society: Final Project Publication*. Utrecht, Netherlands: Association of European Conservatories, 2000.

Campbell, Patricia Shehan. "Culture Bearers in the Classroom: Scenarios from the Pacific Northwest." Lecture transcript, 1998.

———. "Ethnomusicology, Education and World Music Pedagogy: Across the Pond." *Musiké* 3 (2007): 33–44.

———. "In Study of Expressive Cultures: The Pathway of a White Middle-Class Music Teacher." In *World Musics and Music Education: Facing the Issues*, ed. by Bennett Reimer, 239–258. Reston, Va.: Music Educators National Conference, 2002.

———, ed. *Music in Cultural Context: Eight Views on World Music Education*. Reston, Va.: Music Educators National Conference, 1999.

———. "Music, Education and Community in a Multicultural Society." In *Cross Currents: Setting an Agenda for Music Education in Community Culture*, ed. by Marie McCarthy, 4–33. Danbury: University of Maryland, 1996.

———. "Music, the Universal Language: Fact or Fallacy?" *International Journal of Music Education* 29 (1997): 32–39.

———. "Musica Exotica, Multiculturalism and School Music." *Quarterly Journal of Music Teaching and Learning* 5, no. 2 (1994): 65–75.

———. *Teaching Music Globally: Experiencing Music, Expressing Culture*. Oxford, U.K.: Oxford University Press, 2004.

Campbell, Patricia Shehan, John Drummond, Peter Dunbar-Hall, Keith Howard, Huib Schippers, Trevor Wiggins, eds. *Cultural Diversity in Music Education: Directions and Challenges for the 21st Century*. Brisbane: Australian Academic Press, 2005.

Centraal Bureau voor Statistiek. *Bevolking*. http://statline.cbs.nl/StatWeb/publication/? VW=T&DM=SLNL&PA=37325&HD=090623-0009 (accessed May 12, 2009).

Chaurasia, Hariprasad. "If You Are Not Tuned Here, You Cannot Play in Tune." Interview with Huib Schippers, Rotterdam Conservatory, Rotterdam, May 8, 2003.

Choate, Robert A. *Documentary Report of the Tanglewood Symposium*. Washington, D.C.: Music Educators National Conference, 1968.

Colwell, Richard, Carol Richardson, eds. *The New Handbook of Research on Music Teaching and Learning*. New York: Oxford University Press, 2002.

Cook, Nicholas. *Music: A Very Short Introduction*. Oxford, U.K.: Oxford University Press, 1998.

Cultuur als Confrontatie (Culture As Confrontation). The Hague: Ministerie van OCW, 2000.

Daniélou, Alain. "The Education of Musicians and Their Public in Asian Countries." *International Music Education: ISME Yearbook* 2 (1974).

———. *The Ragas of Northern Indian Music*. New Delhi: Munshiram Manoharlal, 1980.

Daverio, John. "Herbart, Johann Friedrich." *Grove Music Online*, edited by Laura Macy (2008). http://www.grovemusic.com (accessed February 12, 2008).

Davison, Annette. "Report on the Critical Study Day on 'Authenticity.'" *Popular Music* 20, no. 2 (2001): 263–264.

De Kunst van het Artisjokken Eten (The Art of Eating Artichokes). The Hague: Ministerie van OCW, 1989.

Dewey, John. "The Aims of Education, and Pragmatism and Culture: Science, and Technology, Art and Religion." In *The Essential Dewey*, vol. 1. Bloomington: Indiana University Press, 1934.

Draper, Paul. "Music 2.0." Queensland Conservatorium Research Centre Twilight Lecture, October 27, 2007. Podcast http://www29.griffith.edu.au/radioimersd/content/ blogcategory/16/28/ (accessed August 26, 2008).

Drummond, John. "Cultural Diversity in Music Education: Why Bother?" In *Cultural Diversity in Music Education: Directions and Challenges for the 21st Century*, ed. by Patricia Shehan Campbell, John Drummond, Peter Dunbar-Hall, Keith Howard, Huib Schippers, and Trevor Wiggins, 1–11. Brisbane: Australian Academic Press, 2005.

———. "What Do You Mean, Mozart Didn't Wear Tails?" In *The Musician's Role: New Challenges*, ed. by Giacomo M. Oliva, 11–28. Lund, Sweden: Malmö Academy of Music, 2000.

Dunbar-Hall, Peter. "The Ambiguous Nature of Multicultural Music Education: Learning Music through Multicultural Content, or Learning Multiculturalism through Music." In *World Musics and Music Education: Facing the Issues*, ed. by Bennett Reimer, 57–69. Reston, Va.: Music Educators National Conference, 2002.

———. "Concept or Context? Teaching and Learning Balinese Gamelan and the Universalist-Pluralist Debate." *Music Education Research* 2, no. 2 (2000): 127–139.

———. "Training, Community and Systemic Music Education: The Aesthetics of Balinese Music in Different Pedagogic Settings." In *Cultural Diversity in Music Education: Directions and Challenges for the 21st Century*, ed. by Patricia Shehan Campbell, John Drummond, Peter Dunbar-Hall, Keith Howard, Huib Schippers, and Trevor Wiggins, 125–132. Brisbane: Australian Academic Press, 2005.

Dunbar-Hall, Peter, and Chris Gibson. *Deadly Sounds, Deadly Places: Contemporary Aboriginal Music in Australia*. Sydney: University of New South Wales Press, 2004.

Ellingson, Ter. "Notation." In *Ethnomusicology: An Introduction*, ed. by Helen Myers, 376–399. London: Macmillan Press, 1992.

Elliott, David J. "Key Concepts in Multicultural Music Education." *International Journal of Music Education* 13 (1989): 11–18.

———. *Music Matters: A New Philosophy of Music Education*. New York: Oxford University Press, 1995.

———. "Musical Diversity and Music Education: Principles and Practices." *Canadian Music Educator* 39, no. 2 (1998): 11.

———. "Philosophical Perspectives on Research." In *The New Handbook of Research on Music Teaching and Learning*, ed. by Richard Colwell and Carol Richardson, 85–102. New York: Oxford University Press, 2002.

Elliott, David J., Lee Higgins, and Kari K. Veblen. "Editorial." *International Journal of Community Music* 1, no. 1 (2008): 3–4.

Emmerson, Stephen. *Around a Rondo: The Art of Interpretation*. DVD. Brisbane, Australia: Queensland Conservatorium Research Centre, 2006.

Erb, J. Lawrence. "Music for a Better Community." *Music Quarterly* 12, no. 3 (1926): 441–448.

Erlmann, Veit. "Aesthetics of the Global Imagination: Reflections on World Music in the 1990s." *Public Culture* 8 (1996): 467–88.

Farrell, Gerry. *Indian Music and the West*. Oxford, U.K.: Clarendon Press, 1997.

Feld, Steven. "'Flow Like a Waterfall': The Metaphors of Kaluli Musical Theory." *Yearbook for Traditional Music* 13 (1981): 22–47.

Flolu, James. "Music Education in Ghana: The Way Forward." In *World Musics in Education*, ed. by Malcolm Floyd, 157–185. Hants, U.K.: Ashgate, 1996.

Floyd, Malcolm, ed. *World Musics in Education*. Hants, U.K. Ashgate, 1996.

Folkestadt, Goran. "The Local and the Global in Music Learning: Considering the Interaction between Formal and Informal Settings." In *Cultural Diversity in Music Education: Directions and Challenges for the 21st Century*, ed. by Patricia Shehan Campbell, John Drummond, Peter Dunbar-Hall, Keith Howard, Huib Schippers, and Trevor Wiggins, 23–28. Brisbane: Australian Academic Press, 2005.

Frith, Simon, ed. *World Music, Politics and Social Change*. Manchester, U.K.: Manchester University Press, 1989.

Goehr, Lydia, and Andrew Bowie. "Philosophy of Music—Formalism." *Grove Music Online*, edited by Laura Macy (2008). http://www.grovemusic.com (accessed September 1, 2008).

Goormaghtigh, George. "'L'Air du Roi Wen' et 'L'Immortel des Eaux': Aspects de la Musique des Lettres Chinois." In *De Bouche à L'Oreille: Cahiers de Musiques Traditionelles*, ed. by Laurent Aubert, vol. 1: 144–156. Geneva: Ateliers d'Ethnomusicologie, 1988.

———. *L'Art du Q'in: Deux Textes d'Esthetique Musicales Chinoise*. Brussels: Institut Belge des Hautes Etudes Chinoises, 1990.

Green, Lucy. *How Popular Musicians Learn: A Way Ahead for Music Education*. Aldershot, U.K.: Ashgate, 2002.

———. *Music, Informal Learning and the School: A New Classroom Pedagogy*. Aldershot, U.K.: Ashgate Publishers, 2008.

Grout, Donald J. *A History of Western Music*, 3rd ed. New York: Norton, 1980.

Grove Music Online. Laura Macy, ed. http://www.grovemusic.com (accessed February 12, 2008).

Gutzwiller, Andreas. "Teaching Methods of Traditional Japanese Music." In *Teaching World Music*, ed. by Huib Schippers, 71–77. Utrecht, Netherlands: VKV, 1992.

Hallam, Sue. "Novice Musicians' Approaches to Practice and Performance: Learning New Music." *Newsletter of the European Society for the Cognitive Sciences of Music* 6 (1994): 2–10.

Hanslick, Eduard. *The Beautiful in Music: A Contribution to the Revival of Musical Aesthetics*, trans. by Gustave Cohen. London: Novello, 1854.

Hargreaves, David J., Graham Welch, Ross Purves, and Nigel Marshall. "The Identities of Music Teachers." In *Proceedings of the 5th Triennial ESCOM Conference*, ed. by Reinhard Kopiez, Andreas C. Lehmann, Irving Wolther, and C. Wolf, 178–181. Hanover, Germany: Hanover University of Music and Dance, 2003.

Harnish, David, Ted Solis, and J. Lawrence Witzleben. "A Bridge to Java: Four Decades of Teaching Gamelan in America." In *Performing Ethnomusicology: Teaching and Representation in World Music Ensembles*, ed. by Ted Solis, 53–68. Berkeley: University of California Press, 2004.

Haydon, Glen. *Introduction to Musicology: A Survey of the Fields, Systematic & Historical, of Musical Knowledge & Research*. New York: Prentice-Hall, 1941.

Heins, Ernst. "132 Jaar Gamelan in Nederland." *Wereldmuziek* 2 (1989): 4–8.

Higgins, Lee. "Boundary-Walkers: Contexts and Concepts of Community Music." Doctoral dissertation. University of Limerick, Ireland, 2006.

————, and Gordon Ross. "ConCussion: A Synthesis of Old and New Technologies." *Music Education Research* 2, no. 1 (2000): 87–93.

————. "Safety without Safety: Participation, the Workshop, and the Welcome." *Networks and Islands: World Music and Dance Education* 3 (2007): 65–84.

Hobsbawm, Eric, and Terence O. Ranger, eds. *The Invention of Tradition.* Cambridge, U.K.: Cambridge University Press, 1983.

Hofstede, Geert. "A Case for Comparing Apples with Oranges: International Differences in Values." *International Journal of Comparative Sociology* 39 (1998). http://www.questia.com (accessed November 18, 2003).

Hood, Ki Mantle. "The Birthpangs of Bimusicality." In *Teaching Musics of the World,* ed. by Margot Lieth-Philipp and Andreas Gutzwiller, 56–60. Affalterbach, Germany: Philipp Verlag, 1995.

————. "The Challenge of Bi-Musicality." *Ethnomusicology* 4 (1960): 55–59.

————. "Preface." In *Musics of Many Cultures: An Introduction,* ed. by Elizabeth May, ix–x. Los Angeles: University of California Press, 1983.

Hopkins, Pandora. *Aural Thinking in Norway: Performance and Communication with the Hardingfele.* New York: Human Sciences Press, 1986.

Howard, Keith. *Creating Korean Music: Tradition, Innovation, and the Discourse of Identity.* London: Ashgate, 2006.

————. "P'ansori." In *Korean Music: A Listening Guide,* 83–93. Seoul: National Center for Traditional Performing Arts, 1999.

————. "Performing Ethnomusicology: Exploring How Teaching Performance Undermines the Ethnomusicologist within University Music Training." *Musiké* 3(2007): 25–32.

————. *Preserving Korean Music: Intangible Cultural Properties as Icons of Identity.* London: Ashgate, 2006.

————. "Teaching Musics of the World: Perspectives." In *Teaching Musics of the World,* ed. by Margot Lieth-Philipp and Andreas Gutzwiller, 267–288. Affalterbach, Germany: Philipp Verlag, 1995.

————. "Teaching SamulNori: Challenges in the Transmission of Korean Percussion." In *Cultural Diversity in Music Education: Directions and Challenges for the 21st Century,* ed. by Patricia Shehan Campbell, John Drummond, Peter Dunbar-Hall, Keith Howard, Huib Schippers, and Trevor Wiggins, 131–141. Brisbane: Australian Academic Press, 2005.

Howard, Keith, and Dutiro, Chartwell, eds. *Zimbabwean Mbira Music on an International Stage: Chartwell Dutiro's Life in Music.* London: Ashgate, 2007.

Huè, Pham Thi. "How Your Mind, Your Heart Works." Interview with Huib Schippers, Hanoi, January 2007.

Hughes, David W. "Japan: Court Music. III. Notation Systems. 4. Oral Mnemonics." *Grove Music Online,* edited by Laura Macy (2008). http://www.grovemusic.com (accessed September 1, 2008).

International Society for Music Education. *Policy on Musics of the World's Cultures.* Reading, U.K.: ISME, 1996.

International Society for Music Education, Community Music Commission. Vision. http://www.isme.org/en/community-music-activity/community-music-activity-cma.html (accessed October 10, 2008).

Investeren in Integreren (Investing in Integration). The Hague: Ministerie van OCW, 1992.

Johnson, David, Bruce Headey, and Ben Jensen. *Communities, Social Capital and Public Policy: A Literature Review.* Canberra, Australia: Department of Family and Community Services, 2005.

Johnson, Martin, and Osa Johnson. *Congorilla* (documentary film), 1932.

Johnson, Sherry. "Authenticity: Who Needs It?" *British Journal of Music Education* 17, no. 3 (2000): 277–286.

Jorgensen, Estelle R. *The Art of Teaching Music.* Bloomington: Indiana University Press, 2008.

———. "Philosophical Issues in Curriculum." In *The New Handbook of Research on Music Teaching and Learning,* ed. by Richard Colwell and Carol Richardson, 48–62. New York: Oxford University Press, 2002.

———. "Reflections on Futures for Music Education Philosophy." *Philosophy of Music Education Review* 14, no. 1 (2006): 15–22.

———. *Transforming Music Education.* Bloomington: Indiana University Press, 2003.

Jorgensen, Harald. "Student Learning in Higher Instrumental Education: Who Is Responsible?" *British Journal of Music Education* 17, no. 1 (2000): 67–77.

Juslin, Patrick N. "Five Facets of Musical Experience: A Psychologist's Perspective on Music Performance." *Psychology of Music* 31, no. 3 (2003): 273–302.

Kartomi, Margaret J., and Stephen Blum, eds. *Music-Cultures in Contact: Convergences and Collisions.* Melbourne: Gordon and Breach, 1994.

Keil, Charles, and Steven Feld. *Music Grooves: Essays and Dialogues.* Chicago: University of Chicago Press, 1994.

Knight, Roderic. "Music in Africa: The Manding Context." In *Performance Practice: Ethnomusicological Perspectives,* ed. by Gerard Béhague, 75–82. Westport, Conn.: Greenwood Press, 1984.

Koizumi, Fumio. "Three Important Aspects in the Training of Professionals of Japanese Traditional Music." *International Music Education: ISME Yearbook* 2 (1974): 15–16.

Kors, Ninja. "Islands, Networks and Webs: Current Issues in Today's Debate." *Musiké* 3 (2007): 1–10.

Kors, Ninja, Laurien Saraber, and Huib Schippers. *Sound Links: Cultural Diversity, Mobility and Employability in Music Education.* Rotterdam: Academy of Music and Dance, 2003.

Krebs, R., I. Siouti, U. Apitzsch, and S. Wenk. "Disciplinary Barriers between the Social Sciences and Humanities: National Report on Germany." http://www.hull.ac.uk/researchintegration/National%20Report%20Germany.pdf (accessed November 29, 2006).

Kunst, Jaap. *Music in Java.* The Hague: Martinus Nijhoff, 1973.

Ladzekpo, Alfred. "Don't Play the Notes, Just Play the Sounds." In *Teaching World Music,* ed. by Huib Schippers. Utrecht, Netherlands: VKV, 1992.

Lebler, Don. "Student-as-Master? Reflections on a Learning Innovation in Popular Music." *International Journal of Music Education* 25, no. 3 (2007): 205–221.

Letts, Richard. "Music: Universal Language between All Nations?" *International Journal of Music Education* 29 (1997): 22–31.

Lieth-Philipp, Margot, and Andreas Gutzwiller, eds. *Teaching Musics of the World.* Affalterbach, Germany: Philipp Verlag, 1995.

LOKV Netherlands Institute for Arts Education. *One Monkey, No Show: World Music Education in the Netherlands.* Video. Rhizome Productions, Utrecht, Netherlands, 1995.

Lomax, Alan, et al. *Cantometrics: A Method in Musical Anthropology.* Berkeley: University of California Press, 1976.

Lübke, Edelgard. *Der Musikwagen: Musik Verstehen, Verstehen durch Musik.* Kassel, Germany: Gustav Bosse Verlag, 1994.

Lundquist, Barbara R. "Music, Culture, Curriculum, and Instruction." In *The New Handbook of Research on Music Teaching and Learning,* ed. by Richard Colwell and Carol Richardson, 626–647. New York: Oxford University Press, 2002.

Lundquist, Barbara R., and C. Kati Szego, eds. *Musics of the World's Cultures: A Source Book for Music Educators.* Reading, U.K.: ISME/CIRCME, 1998.

McCarthy, Marie. *Passing It On: The Transmission of Music in Irish Culture.* Cork: Cork University Press, 1999.

———. "The Role of ISME in the Promotion of Multicultural Music Education." *International Journal for Music Education* 29 (1997): 81–93.

———. "Social and Cultural Contexts of Music Teaching and Learning: An Introduction." In *The New Handbook of Research on Music Teaching and Learning,* ed. by Richard Colwell and Carol Richardson, 563–565. New York: Oxford University Press, 2002.

Magriel, Nicolas. "Westerners and Indian Art Music." In *Teaching of Indian Music,* edited by Arvind Parikh, 159–166. Bombay: Sangeet Research Academy, 1998.

Manuel, Peter. *Popular Musics of the Non-Western World.* New York: Oxford University Press, 1998.

Marett, Allen. *Songs, Dreamings, and Ghosts: The Wangga of North Australia.* Middletown, Conn.: Wesleyan University Press, 2005.

Marett, Allen. "Japan: Court Music." *Grove Music Online,* edited by Laura Macy (2008). http://www.grovemusic.com (accessed September 27, 2008).

Mark, Michael L., *Music Education: Source Readings for Ancient Greece to Today.* New York: Routledge, 2008.

Markoff, Irene. "Aspects of Turkish Folk Music Theory." In *The Garland Encyclopedia of World Music,* vol. 6, ed. by Virginia Danielson, Scott Marcus, and Dwight Reynolds, 77–88. New York: Routledge, 2002.

Marsh, Kathryn. "Going behind the Doors: The Role of Fieldwork in Changing Tertiary Students' Attitudes to World Music Education." In *Cultural Diversity in Music Education: Directions and Challenges for the 21st Century,* ed. by Patricia Shehan Campbell, John Drummond, Peter Dunbar-Hall, Keith Howard, Huib Schippers, and Trevor Wiggins, 34–37. Brisbane: Australian Academic Press, 2005.

Mason, Andrew. *Community, Solidarity and Belonging: Levels of Community and Their Normative Significance.* New York: Cambridge University Press, 2000.

Mathiesen, Thomas J. "Mimesis." *Grove Music Online,* edited by Laura Macy (2008). http://www.grovemusic.com (accessed September 23, 2008).

Mautner, Thomas. *A Dictionary of Philosophy.* Cambridge, Mass.: Blackwell, 1995.

Melchers, Marita. *Muziek, een Wereldtaal.* Amsterdam: Amsterdamse Hogeschool voor de Kunsten, 1996.

Merriam, Alan P. *The Anthropology of Music.* Bloomington, Ind.: Northwestern University Press, 1964.

Mills, Janet. *Music in the School.* Oxford, U.K.: Oxford University Press, 2005.

Miner, Allyn. *Sitar and Sarod in the 18th and 19th Century.* Wilhelmshaven, Germany: Florian Noetzel Verlag, 1993.

Morgan, Robert P. "Rethinking Musical Culture: Canonic Reformulations in a Post-Tonal Age." In *Disciplining Music: Musicology and Its Canons,* ed. by Katherine Bergeron and Philip V. Bohlman, 43–64. Chicago: University of Chicago Press, 1992.

Mundi, Simon. "Music and Globalisation." In *Globalization and Indian Music,* ed. By Arvind Parikh, 16–20. Mumbai: Sangeet Research Academy, 2002.

Muziekschool Amsterdam. *MuziekClub in de Dapperschool.* Video documentary. Home Theatre BV, 1996.

Myers, Helen, ed. *Ethnomusicology: An Introduction.* London: Macmillan Press, 1992.

Neighbour, R. *The Inner Apprentice.* Plymouth, U.K.: Petroc Press, 1992.

Nettl, Bruno. "An Ethnomusicological Perspective." *International Journal of Music Education* 23, no. 2 (2005): 131–133.

———. "Ethnomusicology: Definitions, Directions, and Problems." In *Musics of Many Cultures: An Introduction,* ed. by Elizabeth May, 1–7. Berkeley: University of California Press, 1980.

———. "Ethnomusicology and the Teaching of World Music." *International Journal of Music Education* (1992): 3–8.

———. *Heartland Excursions.* Urbana, Ill.: University of Chicago Press, 1995.

———. "How Do You Get to Carnegie Hall?" In *The Study of Ethnomusicology: Twenty-nine Issues and Concepts.* Chicago: University of Illinois Press, 1983.

———. "Recent Directions in Ethnomusicology." In *Ethnomusicology: An Introduction,* ed. by Helen Myers, 376–399. London: Macmillan Press, 1992.

Neuman, Daniel M. *The Life of Music in North India,* 2nd ed. Chicago: University of Chicago Press, 1990.

Nketia, J. H. Kwabena. "Community-Oriented Education of Musicians in African Countries." *International Music Education:, ISME Yearbook* 2 (1974): 38–42.

———. "Continuity of Traditional Instruction." Unpublished typescript.

———. "Cultural Diversity and Music Education in Ghana." In *Music Education in a Multicultural Society,* ed. by Jan Ole Traasdahl, 50–59. Copenhagen: Danish Music Council.

———. "Exploring Intercultural Dimensions of Music in Education." *International Music Education: ISME Yearbook* 15 (1988): 96–106.

———. *The Music of Africa.* New York: Norton, 1974.

Nzewi, Meki. "Acquiring Knowledge of the Musical Arts in Traditional Society." In *Musical Arts in Africa: Theory, Practice and Education,* ed. by Anri Herbst, Meki Nzewi, and Kofi Agawu, 13–37. Pretoria: University of South Africa, 2003.

———. "Strategies for Music Education in Africa: Towards a Meaningful Progression from Traditional to Modern." In *Conference Proceedings 23rd International Society for Music Education World Conference,* ed. by Caroline van Niekerk, 456–486. Pretoria: ISME, 1998.

O'Bryan, Ponda. "Most of It Is Playing." Interview with Huib Schippers, Melody Line Studios, Amsterdam, July 3, 2003.

Palmer, Anthony J. "Multicultural Music Education: Pathways and Byways, Purpose and Serendipity." In *World Musics and Music Education: Facing the Issues*, ed. by Bennett Reimer, 31–53. Reston, Va.: Music Educators National Conference, 2002.

Pantser of Ruggengraat (Armor or Spine)*: Cultuurnota 1997–2000*. The Hague: Ministerie van OCW, 1996.

Paynter, John. *Sound and Structure*. Cambridge, U.K.: Cambridge University Press, 1992.

Perlman, Marc. "Indonesia: Sumatra." *Grove Music Online*, edited by Laura Macy (2008). http://www.grovemusic.com (accessed September 27, 2008).

Persson, Roland S. "Brilliant Performers As Teachers: A Case Study of Commonsense Teaching in a Conservatoire Setting." *International Journal of Music Education* 28 (1996): 25–36.

Plummeridge, Charles. "Schools." III. From the Nineteenth Century. 1. National Systems of Education. *Grove Music Online*, edited by Laura Macy (2008). http://www.grovemusic.com (accessed September 1, 2008).

Polak, Rainer. "A Musical Instrument Travels around the World: Jenbe Playing in Bamako, West Africa, and Beyond." *World of Music* 42, no. 3, (2000): 7–46.

Pot, Leendert. *Saudade: World Music at the Rotterdam Conservatory*. Documentary film. Amsterdam, 1998.

Prchal, Martin, and Richard Shrewsbury, eds. *Music Education in a Multicultural European Society: First Project Report*. Utrecht, Netherlands: AEC, 2000.

Pressley, Michael. *Reading Instruction That Works: The Case for Balanced Teaching*, 3rd ed. New York: Guilford Press, 2005.

Pruett, James, and Thomas P. Slavens. *Research Guide to Musicology*. Chicago: American Library Association, 1985.

Ranade, Ashok. "Guru-Shishya Parampara: In Wider Perspective." In *Teaching of Indian Music*, ed. by Arvind Parikh. Mumbai: Sangeet Research Academy, 1999.

Ranger, Eric. "The Invention of Tradition in Colonial Africa." In *The Invention of Tradition*, ed. by Eric Hobsbawm and Terence O. Ranger, 211–262. Cambridge, U.K.: Cambridge University Press, 1983.

Reck, David. *Music of the Whole Earth*. New York: Scribners, 1977.

Reimer, Bennett. "Music Education in our Multimusical Culture." *Music Educators Journal* 79, no. 7 (1993): 22.

———. "The Need to Face the Issues." In *World Musics and Music Education: Facing the Issues*, ed. by Bennett Reimer, 3–11. Reston, Va.: Music Educators National Conference, 2002.

———. *A Philosophy of Music Education, Third Edition: Advancing the Vision*. Englewood Cliffs, N.J.: Prentice-Hall, 2003.

Rice, Timothy. "Bi-Musicality." *Grove Music Online*, edited by Laura Macy (2008). http://www.grovemusic.com (accessed February 12, 2008).

———. "Ethical Issues for Music Educators in Multicultural Societies." *Canadian Music Educator* 39, no. 2 (1998): 5–8.

———. "The Ethnomusicology of Music Learning and Teaching." *College Music Symposium* 43 (2003): 65–83.

Rice, Timothy. *May It Fill Your Soul: Experiencing Bulgarian Music*. Chicago: University of Chicago Press, 1994.

Rice, Timothy. "Transmission." *Grove Music Online*, edited by Laura Macy (2008). http://www.grovemusic.com (accessed February 12, 2008).

Ross, Alex. "The Sonata Seminar." *The New Yorker*, April 19, 2004.

Rouget, Gilbert. *Music and Trance*. Chicago: University of Chicago Press, 1985.

Ruckert, George. *The Music of Ali Akbar Khan*. Doctoral dissertation. Berkeley: University of California, 1994.

Ruim Baan voor Culturele Diversiteit (Making Way for Cultural Diversity). The Hague: Ministerie van OCW, 1999.

Rutherford, Jonathan. "The Third Space: Interview with Homi Bhabha." In *Identity: Community, Culture, Difference*, ed. by Jonathon Rutherford, 207–221. London: Lawrence and Wishart, 1990.

Saether, Eva. "The Oral University: Attitudes to Music Teaching and Learning in the Gambia." In Studies in Music and Music Education 6. Malmö, Sweden: Malmö Academy of Music, University of Lund, 2003.

———. "Training Swedish Music Teachers in Gambia: In Search of a Model for Multicultural Music Education." In *Teaching Musics of the World*, ed. by Margot Lieth-Philipp and Andreas Gutzwiller, 103–108. Affalterbach, Germany: Philipp Verlag, 1995.

Said, Edward W. *Culture and Imperialism*. New York: Knopf, 1993.

———. *Orientalism*. New York: Pantheon, 1978.

Sangeet Research Academy. *Indian Music & the West*, ed. by Arvind Parikh. Mumbai: Sangeet Research Academy, 1996.

———. *Teaching of Indian Music*, ed. by Arvind Parikh. Mumbai: Sangeet Research Academy, 1998.

Saraber, Laurien. *De Smaak van Meer: Succesfactoren in Multiculturele Kunsteducatie*. Utrecht, Netherlands: LOKV, 1998.

Schippers, Huib. "L'Art de l'Imitation et l'Imitation d'Art." In *De Bouche à l'Oreille: Cahiers de Musiques Traditionelles*, ed. by Laurent Aubert, 125–131. Geneva: GEORG Editeur, 1988.

———. "'As If a Little Bird Is Sitting on Your Finger . . .': Metaphor As a Key Instrument in Teaching and Learning Music." *International Journal for Music Education* 24, no. 3 (2006): 209–218.

———. "Blame It on the Germans! A Cross-Cultural Invitation to Revisit the Foundations of Training Professional Musicians." In *Preparing Musicians Making New Sound Worlds*, ed. by Musumeci Orlando, 199–208. Barcelona: ISME/ESMUC, 2004.

———. "Goodbye to GSP? An Invitation to Re-evaluate the Role of the Guru in Contemporary Transmission of Hindustani Music." In *Indian Music and the West*, ed. by Arvind Parikh. Mumbai: Sangeet Research Academy, 1996.

———. "The Guru Recontextualised? Perspectives on Learning North Indian Classical Music in Shifting Environments for Professional Training." *Asian Music* 38, no. 1 (2007): 123–138.

———. *Harde Noten: Muziekeducatie in Wereldperspectief*. Utrecht, Netherlands: Cultuurnetwerk.nl, 2004.

————. "Musical Chairs, or the Twelve-Step Disintegration of Preconceptions about Music Making and Learning." *International Journal of Community Music*, 1 (2004).

————. *One Monkey, No Show: Culturele Diversiteit in de Nederlandse Muziekeducatie.* Book (with accompanying video). Utrecht, Netherlands: LOKV, 1997.

————. "Sustainable Futures for Musical Traditions." *Second World Forum on Music.* Paris: International Music Council, 2007.

————. "Swara Samrat, Emperor of Melody: The Life and Music of Ali Akbar Khan." Unpublished manuscript.

————. "A Synergy of Contradictions: The Genesis of a World Music and Dance Centre." *Musiké* 3 (2007): 11–24.

————. "Taking Distance and Getting Up Close: The Seven Continuum Transmission Model." In *Cultural Diversity in Music Education: Directions and Challenges for the 21st Century*, ed. by Patricia Shehan Campbell, John Drummond, Peter Dunbar-Hall, Keith Howard, Huib Schippers, and Trevor Wiggins, 29–34. Brisbane: Australian Academic Press, 2005.

————. "Towards a Model for Cultural Diversity in Music Education." *International Journal for Music Education* 27 (1996): 16–23.

————. "Tradition, Authenticity, and Context: The Case for a Dynamic Approach." *British Journal of Music Education* 23, no. 3 (2006): 333–349.

Schneider, Marius. "Primitive Music." In *The New Oxford History of Music: Ancient and Oriental Music*, ed. by Egon Wellesz. London: Oxford University Press, 1957.

Schreuder, Adri. *Multiculturele Variaties in Muziekeducatie.* Amsterdam: Amsterdamse Hogeschool voor de Kunsten, 2008.

Schuon, Frithjof. "Principles and Criteria of Art." In *Castes and Races*, 61–88. Bedfont: Perennial Books, 1959 (English trans. 1982).

Seeger, Anthony. "Catching up with the Rest of the World: Music Education and Musical Experience." In *World Musics and Music Education: Facing the Issues*, ed. by Bennett Reimer, 103–116. Reston, Va.: Music Educators National Conference, 2002.

————. *Why Suyá Sing: A Musical Anthropology of an Amazonian People.* Cambridge, U.K.: Cambridge University Press, 1987.

Shankar, Ravi. *My Music, My Life.* New Delhi: Vikas, 1969.

Sharma, Premlata. *Inaugural Address Seminar on Tradition and Change.* Mumbai: Sangeet Research Academy, 1995.

Skyllstad, Kjell. "The Resonant Community: A School Project to Promote Interracial Understanding." In *Music of the World's Cultures: A Source Book for Music Educators*, ed. by Barbara. R. Lundquist and C. Kati Szego, 94–101. Nedlands, Australia: Callaway International Resource Center for Music Education, 1998.

Slawek, Stephen. "The Classical Master-Disciple Tradition." In *The Garland Encyclopaedia of World Music*, vol. 5, ed. by Alison Arnold. Garland Online Encyclopaedia (accessed September 20, 2008).

————. *Sitar Technique in Nibaddh Forms.* New Delhi; Motilal Banarsidas, 1987.

Slobin, Mark. *Subcultural Sounds: Micromusics of the West.* Hanover, N.H.: Wesleyan University Press, 1993.

————. "The Wesleyan Way: World Music in an American Academic System." *Musiké* 3 (2007): 45–54.

Sloboda, John A. "The Acquisition of Musical Performance Expertise: Deconstructing the 'Talent' Account of Individual Differences in Musical Expressivity." In *The Road to Excellence: The Acquisition of Expert Performance in the Arts and Sciences, Sports, and Games,* ed. by Karl Anders Ericsson, 107–126. Mahwah, N.J.: Lawrence Erlbaum, 1996.

Small, Christopher. *Music, Education and Society.* Hanover, N.H.: University Press of New England, 1996.

———. *Musicking: The Meaning of Performing and Listening.* Hanover, N.H.: University Press of New England, 1998.

Solis, Ted, ed. *Performing Ethnomusicology: Teaching and Representation in World Music Ensembles.* Berkeley: University of California Press, 2004.

Sorrell, Neil. *Indian Music in Performance: A Practical Introduction.* Manchester, U.K.: Manchester University Press, 1980.

Stock, Jonathan P. J. "Learning Huju in Shanghai, 1900–1950: Apprenticeship and the Acquisition of Expertise in a Local Opera Tradition." *Asian Music,* 33, no. 2 (2002): 1–42.

———. "Music Education: Perspectives from Current Ethnomusicology." *British Journal of Music Education* 20, no. 2 (2003): 135–145.

Stockhausen, Karlheinz. "World Music." *The World of Music* 21, no. 1 (1979): 3–16.

Stone, Ruth M., ed. *The Garland Encyclopedia of World Music.* New York: Routledge, 2002.

Sutton, R. Anderson. "Individuality and 'Writing' in Javanese Music Learning." *Asian Music,* 33, no. 1 (2002): 75–104.

Swanwick, Keith. "Authenticity and the Reality of Musical Experience." In *Musical Connections: Tradition and Change,* ed. by Heath Lees, 215–226. Auckland: International Society for Music Education, 1994.

———. *Music, Mind and Education.* London: Routledge, 1998.

———. *Teaching Music Musically.* London: Routledge, 1999.

Sweeney, Philip. *Directory of World Music.* London: Virgin Books, 1991.

Szego, C. Kati. "A Conspectus of Ethnographic Research in Ethnomusicology and Music Education." In *The New Handbook of Research on Music Teaching and Learning,* ed. by Richard Colwell and Carol Richardson, 707–729. New York: Oxford University Press, 2002.

Taylor, Timothy D. *Beyond Exoticism: Western Music and the World.* Durham, N.C.: Duke University Press, 2007.

———. *Global Pop: World Music, World Markets.* New York: Routledge, 1997.

Tenzer, Michael. *Balinese Music.* Singapore: Periplus Editions, 1991.

Thieme, Darius L. "Cantometrics." *Grove Music Online,* edited by Laura Macy (2008). http://www.grovemusic.com (accessed February 12, 2008).

Tomlinson, Gary. "The Historian, the Performer, and Authentic Meaning in Music." In *Authenticity and Early Music,* ed. by Nicholas Kenyon, 115–126. Oxford, U.K.: Oxford University Press, 1988.

Touma, Habib, H. "The Education of Musicians and Their Public in Arab Countries." *International Music Education: ISME Yearbook,* 2 (1977): 33–37.

———. *Die Musik der Araber.* Wilhelmshaven, Germany: Heinrichshofen's Verlag, 1975.

Traasdahl, Jan Ole, ed. *Music Education in a Multicultural Society.* Copenhagen: Danish Music Council, 1999.

Tracey, Hugh T. *Ngoma: An Introduction to Music for Southern Africans.* Cape Town: Galvin & Sales, 1948.

Trimillos, Ricardo D. "The Formalized Transmission of Culture: Selectivity in Traditional Teaching/Learning Systems in Four High Skill Music Traditions." *East-West Culture Learning Institute Report* (1983): 1–9.

————. "Subject, Object and the Ethnomusicology Ensemble: The Ethnomusicological 'We' and 'Them.'" In *Performing Ethnomusicology: Teaching and Representation in World Music Ensembles,* ed. by Ted Solis, 23–52. Berkeley: University of California Press, 2004.

Turkenburg, Wouter. "Classical and Jazz Music Compared to World and Pop Music in Music Education." In *Music Education in a Multicultural Society,* ed. by Jan Ole Traasdahl, 166–173. Copenhagen: Danish Music Council, 1999.

Valcke, Martin. *Onderwijskunde als Ontwerpwetenschap.* Ghent, Belgium: Academia Press, 2000.

van Amstel, Peter. *World Music Teaching Material: An Initial Survey.* Utrecht, Netherlands: Repertoire Informatiecentrum Muziek, 1993, updated 1995.

van den Bos, Paul. "Differences between Western and Non-Western Teaching Methods in Music Education: How Can Both Methods Supplement Each Other?" In *Teaching Musics of the World,* ed. by Margot Lieth-Philipp and Andreas Gutzwiller, 169–179. Affalterbach, Germany: Philipp Verlag, 1995.

————. *Saz-Onderwijs in Nederland: Een Onderzoek naar de Methodische Diversiteit van het Saz-Onderwijs aan Nederlandse Muziekscholen.* Alkmaar: Alkmaar Conservatorium, 1998.

van der Meer, Wim. *Hindustani Music in the 20th Century.* The Hague: Martinus Nijhoff, 1980.

van der Meer, Wim, and Joep Bor. *De Roep van de Kokila: Historische en Hedendaagse Aspecten van de Indiase Muziek.* The Hague: Martinus Nijhoff, 1982.

van Zanten, Wim. "Ethnomusicology in the Netherlands 1960–1995: Some General Trends." In *Oideion 2: The Performing Arts World Wide.* Leiden: CNWS, 1995.

Vansina, Jan. *Oral Tradition As History.* Madison: University of Wisconsin Press, 1985.

Veblen, Kari K. "Apples and Oranges, Solar Systems and Galaxies: Comparing Systems of Community Music." Paper presented at the ISME Community Music Activities Seminar, Bergen, Norway, 2002.

————. "Community Music and Praxialism." In *Praxial Music Education: Reflections and Dialogues,* ed. by David J. Elliott, 308–328. New York: Oxford University Press, 2005.

Veblen, Kari, and Bengt Olsson. "Community Music: Toward an International Overview." In *The New Handbook of Research on Music Teaching and Learning,* ed. by Richard Colwell and Carol Richardson, 730–753. New York: Oxford University Press, 2002.

Vereniging voor Kunstzinnige Vorming. *A Survey of Teaching World Music Initiatives in the Netherlands.* Utrecht, Netherlands: VKV, 1992.

Vernon, Paul. "Strange World." *Folk Roots,* ed. by Simon Broughton, 23–25, 194–195. London: Southern Rag, 1999.

Volk, Teresa M. "Multiculturalism: Dynamic Creativity for Music Education." In *World Musics and Music Education: Facing the Issues,* ed. by Bennett Reimer, 15–29. Reston, Va.: Music Educators National Conference, 2002.

Volk, Teresa M. *Music, Education and Multiculturalism: Foundations and Principles.* New York: Oxford University Press, 1998.

Vonck, Henrice M. "*Bali, Muziek en Dans in Theorie en Praktijk: Inhoudelijk Verslag van het Onderwijsprojekt.*" Unpublished report, 1999.

———. "In Bali, People Do Not Learn Music; They Just Sit Down and Play." Interview with Huib Schippers, May 20, 2003.

Wade, Bonnie C. *Thinking Musically: Experiencing Music, Experiencing Culture.* Oxford, U.K.: Oxford University Press, 2004.

Wachsmann, Klaus P. "Music." *Journal of the Folklore Institute,* no. 6 (1969): 164–191.

Walker, R. "Multiculturalism and Music Re-Attached to Music Education." *Philosophy of Music Education Review* 8, no. 1 (2000): 31–39.

Weber, William. "The Role of the Conservatory." *Grove Music Online,* edited by Laura Macy (2008). http://www.grovemusic.com (accessed September 1, 2008).

Wellesz, Egon. "Introduction." In *The New Oxford History of Music I—Ancient and Oriental Music,* ed. by Egon Wellesz. Oxford, U.K.: Oxford University Press, 1957.

Westerlund, Heidi. *Bridging Experience, Action, and Culture in Music Education.* Helsinki: Sibelius Academy, 2002.

———. "Universalism against Contextual Thinking in Multicultural Music Education: Western Colonialism or Pluralism? *International Journal of Music Education* 33 (1999): 94–103.

Whyton, Tony. "Birth of the School: Discursive Methodologies in Jazz Education." *Music Education Research* 8, no. 1 (2006): 65–81.

Wiggins, Trevor. "Cultivating Shadows in the Field: Challenges for Traditions in Institutional Contexts." In *Cultural Diversity in Music Education: Directions and Challenges for the 21st Century,* ed. by Patricia Shehan Campbell, John Drummond, Peter Dunbar-Hall, Keith Howard, Huib Schippers, and Trevor Wiggins, 13–21. Brisbane: Australian Academic Press, 2005.

———. "The World of Music in Education." *British Journal of Music Education* 13 (1996): 21–29.

———. "Words about Music: A Response to Some of the Points Raised by Other Speakers." In *Teaching Musics of the World,* ed. by Margot Lieth-Philipp and Andreas Gutzwiller, 82–83. Affalterbach, Germany: Philipp Verlag, 1995.

Willemsen, Harry, ed. *Woordenboek Filosofie.* Assen, Netherlands: Van Gorcum, 1992.

Wong, Deborah. *Sounding the Center: History and Aesthetics of Thai Buddhist Performance.* Chicago: University of Chicago Press, 2001.

Yung, Bell. "Teachers: East Asia & North America." In *The Garland Encyclopedia of World Music,* ed. by Ruth M. Stone, vol. 10: 17–19. New York: Routledge, 2002.

Zeserson, Katherine. "A Passionate Exchange: Participation, Power, Progress and Great Music." Paper presented at ISME Community Music Activities Seminar, Bergen, Norway, 2002.

⇥ INDEX ⇤